# Sexual Democracy

# SEXUAL
# DEMOCRACY

*Women, Oppression,
and Revolution*

## ANN FERGUSON

University of Massachusetts–Amherst

**Westview Press**

BOULDER • SAN FRANCISCO • OXFORD

*TO ANNETTE KUHN*
*for friendship*
*as well as theoretical and logistical support*
*when I needed it most*

*Feminist Theory and Politics*

Copyright © 1991 by Westview Press, Inc.

Published in 1991 in the United States of America by Westview Press, Inc., 5500 Central Avenue, Boulder, Colorado 80301, and in the United Kingdom by Westview Press, 36 Lonsdale Road, Summertown, Oxford OX2 7EW

Library of Congress Cataloging-in-Publication Data
Ferguson, Ann.
    Sexual democracy : women, oppression, and revolution / Ann Ferguson.
        p.   cm. — (Feminist theory and politics)
    Includes bibliographical references (p.   ) and index.
    ISBN 0-8133-0746-5 (hc.) — ISBN 0-8133-0747-3 (pbk.)
    1. Sex role—United States.   2. Feminism—United States.
I. Title.   II. Series.
HQ1075.5.U6F47   1991
305.42′0973—dc20                                                          90-21084
                                                                              CIP

Printed and bound in the United States of America

The paper used in this publication meets the requirements of the American National Standard for Permanence of Paper for Printed Library Materials Z39.48-1984.

10     9     8     7     6     5     4     3     2     1

# Contents

# Acknowledgments

I thank those who gave me extensive comments on the new essays in this book: Leonard Harris, John Brentlinger, Nancy Folbre, Sam Bowles, Cindy Patton, Batya Weinbaum, Jeffner Allen, Paula Rothenberg, Tom Wartenberg, Iris Young, and Sarah Begus. Those who helped with the previously published essays are thanked in endnotes to those chapters. Thanks also to the Socialist Feminist Philosophers Association (SOFPHIA) and the Radical Philosophers' Association (RPA) for their continued feedback. My colleagues at the University of Massachusetts and in Five College Women's Studies have been important for a grounded feminist intellectual community as have my supportive colleagues in the Philosophy Department. I also thank my political activist friends in feminist and solidarity work; my music band, The Diggers; and my extended family of kin and sex/affective friendships. Finally, thanks very much to Spencer Carr, Marykay Scott, and Alice Colwell of Westview Press for their patience and aid in the various revisions of the manuscript. Finally, thanks to Carol Shea for intellectual, political, and sex/affective care throughout the book process.

*Ann Ferguson*

# ONE

# *Introduction:*
# *A Personal and Political*
# *Feminist Odyssey*

For the last fifteen years I have been engaged in developing a theory of male dominance that creates a feminist-materialist methodology and categories for understanding systems of patriarchy. Feminist-materialism[1] assumes that male power (a) is based on social practices rather than simply in biological sex differences; (b) connects to systematic inequalities in the exchange of work between men and women in meeting material needs; and (c) involves historically specific rather than universal systems of male dominance. Though my work borrows some ideas from Marxism, it is quite different in its political and theoretical conclusions. For one, I reappropriate the Freudian Marxist theory of Herbert Marcuse and Wilhelm Reich, arguing that male dominance is based on the social organization of sexuality and parenting, which involves material needs. For another, I reinterpret the radical feminist view (Firestone, 1970; Small, 1975; Delphy, 1984) that the gender division of labor at home and work makes women a social class exploited by men. Though I accept the relevance of this insight to contemporary North America, I maintain that the political implications of sexual divisions are not universal human truths but are historically specific to the advanced capitalist system of the United States. In Chapter 2 of this book, then, I argue that the contemporary women's movement in the United States can be explained by the development of women as a radical social class here, much like Marx's conception of the working class in advanced capitalist societies. But this argument does not imply that women are a radical social class in all countries at the moment, and, indeed, Chapter 6, which discusses racial and class differences among women, discusses the limitations that these place on the radical potential of the women's movement.

This book is a collection of essays from the last fifteen years that together document the development of my feminist-materialism. It includes papers from both before and after the publication of my book *Blood at the Root: Motherhood, Sexuality and Male Dominance*. In the time span represented here, my ideas changed in emphasis and meaning, depending both on my political practice and on developments in the feminist theoretical debates of the times. Thus my focus shifts from a critique and expansion of Marxism (Chapter 2) to a critique of the lesbian separatist implications of Adrienne Rich's paper on compulsory heterosexuality (Chapter 3). In Chapter 4, on motherhood and sexuality, I argue for a multisystems approach to social domination. Though I use the same category of sex/affective production as in the earlier chapter on "Sex and Work,"[2] in my multisystems approach it is no longer obvious that women are a revolutionary class by themselves. Rather, radical changes can only occur on the strength of coalitions that approach the three main social domination systems in the United States today, those of gender, race, and class, as equal and independent. In subsequent chapters I develop some of the implications for a theory of self of a multisystems approach and expand a theory of racism adapted from a recent book by Michael Omi and Howard Winant (1986). In Chapter 6 I study variations across lesbian cultures to explore the political implications of differences between women for feminist theory. In the last three chapters, I evaluate the future of U.S. socialist-feminist visions and politics in the light of the successes, failures, and radical changes in state socialist countries such as the USSR and those of Eastern Europe.

Why call the book *Sexual Democracy?* In a way this title anchors the intellectual and personal odyssey that I and many other left-wing feminists have made since the beginning of the second-wave women's movement of the 1960s and 1970s. Not only did I begin to see personally and theoretically that heterosexual sex is a site for male dominance that Marxism had ignored, I also had to come to terms with the absence of a sufficient theory of the importance of political democracy in all its forms, either in mainstream or in leftist political theory. In the process of coming out as a lesbian, I had to develop a theory that justified supporting a pluralist coalitionist politics for feminism rather than a lesbian separatist position. Finally, because my life as the mother of an adopted black child is always on the margins of the white and the African-American communities, I had to understand how the visions of sexual democracy of peoples of color differ from those of white, middle-class feminists and need to be respected and understood if any effective progressive coalitions to fight sexism, racism, and capitalism are to be built.

Because stages of my theoretical development mirror the historical changes in U.S. feminist theory in the 1970s and 1980s, this book may be seen as a personal odyssey through the major feminist disputes of the period. The theoretical is the personal in the sense that the creation of a social theory is a creation of a self-meaning for the author and her intended audience.[3] Thus I decided to write this introduction on two levels: first giving a history of my personal and political experiences as background to my theoretical development, and then outlining how the theoretical and political positions I take in these essays connect to a history of the major feminist disputes during the period.

## Stage 1: 1961-1977

PERSONAL: EXPERIENCES WITH THE CIVIL RIGHTS
AND NEW LEFT MOVEMENTS

I spent the period from 1961 to 1973 involved with the New Left, supporting the civil rights, student, and anti–Vietnam War movements. In order to make sense out of the Vietnam War and of imperialism in general, I studied Marxism and became convinced that U.S. and international capitalism had structural tendencies that not only created class exploitation at home but also made it impossible for the United States to support full democratic rights to self-determination for peoples in the underdeveloped world who resisted U.S. imperialist exploitation. From the Marxist perspective, racism and sexism are secondary effects of the capitalist system used to divide and conquer the population in order to maintain ruling-class hegemony. I was a rebel who needed a simple, unitary system of thought with a tidy "unite and fight" politics. To think of capitalism as the basic enemy allowed me a comforting political strategy, overwhelmed as I was with the magnitude of the problems of social domination I was discovering. I could keep my family and male and female friends located in one undivided counterculture from which I did not have to separate in order to fight social domination in all of its forms.

Through the early 1960s I was involved primarily with the civil rights movement. I worked on fair housing issues when I was a graduate student in Providence, Rhode Island, went to the 1963 Martin Luther King, Jr., "I have a dream" rally in Washington, D.C., and when I got my first teaching job at the University of Massachusetts in 1964, I spent a summer working with the Congress of Racial Equality (CORE) in Springfield. That was not easy for a white woman, especially a young academic in a working-class neighborhood; black men who wanted to go out with me were constantly testing me to see if I was racist. Because I had a (white) boyfriend at the time, I had what I thought was a good excuse, but it didn't prevent sexual advances by my black male acquaintances, which I found alternately annoying, frightening, and exciting. From my own experience, there is no denying the special attraction between white women and black men that caused frictions in civil rights organizations (cf. Evans, 1980) and problems for sisterhood between white and black women because of sexual jealousies and rivalries. I found myself a subject of jealousy because married black men were flirting with me, and unattached black men also paid more attention to me than to the black women in the organization. At the same time, all of us, as women, were expected to defer to black male leadership. (There were very few white men in the organization in Springfield.)

As an antiracist and feminist, I have been faced with two sorts of moral dilemmas in my erotic interactions with black men. First was being able to separate what I wanted—was I really attracted to a particular man who was putting the make on me or was my motive simply white liberal guilt? The second problem was dealing with black women in relation to black men. Though I avoided involvement with black men in CORE, in my later role in New Left politics I did have an affair with a married black man who believed he had the right not to be bound by his wife's foolish insistence on monogamy. My not really knowing his wife didn't alleviate the moral dilemma I faced. Did my responsibility as a feminist, my commitment to sisterhood, mean I should end my affair with him? At the time, I didn't believe in monogamy either but decided I couldn't support what amounted to a double standard, especially given my white-skin privilege.

As I was making these hard personal decisions, I was troubled that even my sexual feelings were immersed in racist assumptions. Black men were more attractive to me than white men. At the same time they were also scary: I felt a strong taboo against interracial sex because of my upbringing in the very racist 1950s. I lived in a racially divided atmosphere in Maryland: Neighborhoods, schools, and my summer girls' camp were segregated. There was no way to get to know black people—aside from the domestic maid who came once every two weeks and was treated as a servant—on a personal level. Black men seemed erotic not because of their individual personalities but because they symbolized the forbidden sexual Other (Stember, 1976). They represented sexuality itself, as did black culture, which reached me in the form of blues music (the only sexual music I had access to because it was part of the folk tradition that was popular when I went to college).

The sexual racism of our contemporary situation is still based on fundamental asymmetries. The sexual double standard of monogamy for women and nonmonogamy for men still prevails across the race line. Furthermore, sexual desires are coded in racial gender terms. That is (speaking in generalities), there is not an equally powerful attraction between white men and black women as there is between black men and white women. We can speculate about the reasons, which are many. For one, white standards of beauty put down black women, whereas looks are not so important in male sex appeal to women. For another, black women are not perceived as a sexual challenge because the legacy of slavery suggested they were there for the taking; thus they are at the bottom of the race and gender status heap (Stember, 1976; Aptheker, 1983). Though the Black Power movement, with the attendant "Black is beautiful" ideology, has changed the situation somewhat and the number of interracial couples has increased in the last twenty years, there is still a racist and sexist asymmetry in sexuality to the disadvantage of black women. This makes it difficult for heterosexual black and white women to work together in interracial coalitions without the emergence of the sexual dynamics discussed above.

From 1965 on I became heavily involved in the anti–Vietnam War movement. I was one of the faculty advisers for the Young Socialist Alliance (YSA), which on our campus was allied with Students for a Democratic Society (SDS). We organized rallies and sit-ins on campuses, marches on Washington, and, in 1970 and 1972, took part in major campus strikes. Informal networks of New Left faculty participated in these activities, and after the shutdown of the campus in the 1970 strike, ten of us who were on the faculties at the University of Massachusetts and Amherst College organized a group pretentiously called The Collective.

It was here that I experienced early bouts with New Left sexism. Some of the men in the group were clearly sexist and fancied themselves leaders of a faculty-student movement. Their narcissism and put-downs of women were not easy to combat. After all, there were only three women in the group, each different and all either married to or lovers of men in the group. We were thus treated as wives, and our input was not taken as seriously as that of the men in the group. It was the combination of this experience and that of the sexism of the men in my department when I came up for tenure in 1971 that turned me toward feminism. Before that, I had considered myself one of the boys and had rather looked down on women who did "women's work," particularly housewives. Now I found that being a philosophy professor did not exempt me from sexist treatment, even by fellow Marxist radicals.

Many other women had had similar experiences with the New Left in the civil rights and antiwar movement, and in the early 1970s the socialist-feminist wing of the autonomous women's movement was born. Very influential in the development of this tendency was the model theorized and practiced by the Chicago Women's Liberation Union (CWLU, 1973) and replicated by women's groups in Berkeley-Oakland, Columbus, Dayton, Boston, and Chapel Hill, among other places. Patriarchy and capitalism were described as two separate but intertwined systems to be fought simultaneously. CWLU organized autonomous women's work groups around particular local issues in order to empower women through radical reforms in such areas as childcare, unionization, and women's presses. These local groups were to send a spokesperson to a steering committee but to make their own political decisions and do their own organizing. The goal was nonhierarchical consensus decisionmaking, with the whole membership of the union meeting once a month to do internal education and to discuss projects of its associated work groups that required support by the entire union. In 1973 the Valley Women's Union (VWU), fashioned after this model, came into existence; I was a member of the organizing collective of this group, which lasted four years and was one of the formative experiences of my feminist theory and politics.

In our political discussions at the VWU, we debated the view that compulsory heterosexuality was the political base of patriarchy (Myron and Bunch, 1975). Though this theory was compelling to me in some ways, it didn't easily fit into my Marxist world view. I became determined to find a way to expand Marxist political and economic categories so as to understand both how women as a social group did not correspond to the traditional Marxist concept of class and how to expand Marxist categories of exploitation to deal with the organization of sexuality and parenting—a topic not undertaken in any systematic fashion by Marx and Engels.

I was then, as now, juggling autonomous women's movement politics with mixed left politics. As I mentioned above, my own experiences in a mixed left faculty and staff collective forced me to acknowledge the sexism of the men I worked with and their refusal to prioritize parenting and sexuality as political issues. On the other hand, I was uncomfortable with the mostly white, middle-class bias of the women in the Valley Women's Union and wanted some theoretical approach that would make classism and racism live forces in our thinking and organizing.

Racism in particular had become quite a personal issue for me, as I struggled to raise an adopted mixed-race child while co-parenting with a white (later ex-) husband. I rejected liberal feminism but wanted to incorporate some of the insights of radical feminism (e.g., Firestone, 1970; Dworkin, 1974; Small, 1975) into Marxism so as to create a distinctive socialist-feminist position. Chapter 2 shows the result of that effort.

THEORETICAL AND POLITICAL:
WOMEN AS A RADICAL CLASS

Chapter 2, "Sex and Work: Women as a New Revolutionary Class in the United States," represents a feminist critique of Marxism, still within the Marxist paradigm of social explanation. It argues that Marxist categories must be expanded to deal with women as a sex class, that is, as a social group with an oppressed status cutting across racial, ethnic, and economic-class lines. This socialist-feminist position is an attempt to reconcile the insights of early 1970s radical feminism that women's oppression by men was analogous to the oppression of the working class by the capitalist class—that is, that there is a material conflict of interest between the sexes ignored by male Marxist theorists of historical materialism (cf. Firestone, 1970; Small, 1975; Flax, 1976).

Though this chapter appears to critique Marxism from a feminist perspective, it does not so much distance itself from Marxism as it does attempt to expand the application of Marxist concepts so as to incorporate an analysis of male domination. The basic claim, that U.S. women are historically coming to form a revolutionary sex class, still assumes two Marxist ideas: (1) that certain classes are revolutionary vanguards of radical social change and (2) that changing material conditions can develop a revolutionary consciousness in these groups. I now think that the idea that sexuality, social bonding, and parenting are involved in what I call "modes of sex/affective production" should be taken independently of the Marxist model, without assuming any analogy between a traditional Marxist and a feminist model of revolutionary change.

My theoretical voice of the mid-1970s was part of a dialogue importantly based on New Left politics. Feminist theory at the time had two separate political traditions, the reformist politics of liberal feminism—Betty Friedan, Gloria Steinem, and their political organizations, the National Organization of Women (NOW) and *Ms.*—and radical feminism. Radical feminism developed among women activists initially involved in the student, civil rights, and anti–Vietnam War movements of the 1960s who were disillusioned with the male chauvinism of these movements (Willis, 1984).

The New Left had proposed an anarchist conception of democracy, participatory democracy, that critiqued hierarchical political decision-making. It was a short step from that critique of leaders who form political elites to the perception that the men in the movements were a privileged sex class. The feminist slogan "The personal is the political" was born out of the understanding that the sexual interactions between men and women created gender power for men in the political sphere. Hence, just as Marxism proposed to shatter the appearance of fairness of a capitalist system based on market exchanges in the sphere of circulation by exposing the power relations in the supposedly non-political sphere of production, so radical feminists argued that gender exploitation in the private, supposedly apolitical world of sex and love supported male dominance in the public world of politics.

## Stage 2: 1974–1981

### PERSONAL: THE LESBIAN-STRAIGHT SPLIT IN THE WOMEN'S MOVEMENT

The lesbian-straight split in the women's movement initially occurred in the Northampton-Amherst area from around 1974 to 1976. This was profoundly upsetting to me. Though I believed in the necessity of an autonomous women's movement, I was disturbed by the separatist conclusion that men and straight women alike were feminism's enemies. Not only did this split between straight and lesbian feminists finally destroy the Northampton Valley Women's Union as a political organization, it also made for constant wrangling about whether we would work in coalition with mixed left groups, for example, by working with antiracist groups protesting segregation in Boston schools.

It wasn't only my theories that were affected by this split. My first lover had been a woman, and though I was married at this time, I had had an intense affair with a woman in the early 1970s. So I was on a personal guilt trip because of the implication that I should give up my husband and choose to be with women. I was certainly capable of such a choice, but should I do it for political reasons? Somehow I felt that the personal as the political shouldn't be pushed so far, yet I had to admit that all my relations with men, even with the best of them—and I included my husband among these—had been fraught with gender roles and inequalities.

In 1975 my husband and I split up for reasons not immediately related to my personal dilemma of sexual preference. But this gave me an opportunity to decide to try women again after being deferred by homophobia in my youth. Probably I would not have made that choice without the support of the lesbian feminist women's movement. On the other hand, separatist feelings in those days ran strong and extended to many members of the Northampton Valley Women's Union who refused to rotate childcare work for our meetings because of the so-called heterosexual privilege of the mothers in the group. As a single mother, I felt that this application of the concept was outrageous. By this point, it was clear that many mothers, particularly single mothers, simply had neither the time nor material support they needed to come to our socialist-feminist meetings, which were supposed to empower all women, regardless of race and class! Thus I ended up in the ironic situation of helping to form a "unity caucus" for those women, straight and lesbian, who felt their interests were excluded from the lesbian caucus of the VWU.

The lesbian caucus eventually became so separatist that it refused to share with straight women the upstairs floor it used for meetings. This was the beginning of the end of the trust necessary to continue the union, though the autonomous work-group format allowed us to struggle on for several years, as the nonseparatists were working in unionization and antinuclear power groups while the separatists were working in the women's press group.

THEORETICAL AND POLITICAL:
POLITICAL LESBIANISM

The development of women's consciousness-raising groups and an autonomous women's movement was the outcome of the politicizing of personal politics. Soon, however, it led to two further splits within the women's movement that importantly changed the center of feminist theorizing. No longer was the goal simply to come to terms with left-wing theory and force it to acknowledge feminist issues. Rather, the goal became to develop an independent and more sophisticated feminist theory of social domination. The women's movement thus divided along the lines of sexual preference (the lesbian-straight split of the early to middle 1970s) and class and race (the tension between white, middle-class women and women of color and between working-class and middle-class women). Both splits concern the politics of identity and thus can be said to have arisen as a result of applying the slogan "The personal is the political." Because the personal experience of oppression was highlighted, ways in which women felt marginalized and controlled by other women became legitimate topics of political concern.

Homophobia in women's support groups and the initial reluctance of NOW to accept lesbian rights as a feminist issue had made lesbians feel marginalized in the early women's movement. The development of a politics focusing on the gender power dynamics of sexuality, however, suggested that heterosexual desire itself may be a part of the way that male dominance works to divide women. The group Radicalesbians wrote a position paper called "The Woman-identified Woman" (Radicalesbians, 1970), which suggested that the lesbian personified the rage of all women against male dominance. It was a short step from this defense of the rights of lesbians as a feminist issue to the idea, set forth by Charlotte Bunch and the lesbian journal collective, the Furies, that male dominance is embedded in a socially constructed, compulsory heterosexuality and thus that lesbians represent a sexual vanguard of the women's movement against male dominance (Myron and Bunch, 1975).

Unfortunately, the sexual vanguardism of this lesbian feminist theoretical move led lesbians to distrust straight women and made straight women feel guilty about their supposed "choice" of heterosexuality: "Any woman can be a lesbian," stated the popular Lavender Jane song of the time. Locally based socialist-feminist women's unions split on this issue.

Feminist theory has gone in two directions in response to the splits between lesbians and heterosexuals and the challenges concerning classism and racism within the movement. One branch has emphasized the universal continuity of forms of male dominance by the social imposition of a male dominant heterosexuality. The other branch, which includes most socialist-feminists and many postmodern feminist theorists, emphasizes historical discontinuities and the importance of understanding differences in gender issues connected to various race, ethnic, and class contexts.

In the universalist camp, radical lesbian feminism has preserved and expanded the claim that compulsory heterosexuality is at the base of male dominance, thus tending to validate a lesbian separatist politics. Adrienne Rich's essay "Compulsory Heterosexuality and Lesbian Existence" (1980) has been read by lesbian separatists in this way, that is, as a defense of a view that a lesbian continuum includes all feminist women whether they are explicitly involved in sexual relations with women or not, with sexual lesbians at the apex of the continuum. It is this reading of Rich's essay that I critique in "Patriarchy, Sexual Identity, and the Sexual Revolution," Chapter 3 of this book (cf. Ferguson, 1981b)—for one reason because it is not the reading Rich prefers. Rich does not accept the separatist move and wrote the essay to try to emphasize commonalities, not vanguard differences, among women. A further problem, however, is that the theory of compulsory heterosexuality she presents is too universalist and too static: It implies that the historical differences in the social construction of heterosexuality are irrelevant for feminist purposes. On the contrary, I maintain that they are key to understanding not only women's resistances to male dominance but also the uniqueness of contemporary lesbian subcultures in Western industrial societies. Conceiving male dominant systems of sexuality as historically various, as more discontinuous than continuous, also allows us to see that sexuality is socially constructed through forms of class, race, and ethnic domination, specific forms that radical feminists overlook in their search for universality.

What went wrong with radical feminist theory? In my view, radical feminists were correct to target the social construction of sexuality as part of the material base of male dominance in any social order. Their mistake was to *essentialize* the concept of "compulsory heterosexuality"— that is, to generalize it in such an ahistorical way that there seemed to be no space for women to resist male sexual control other than to become lesbians.

## Stage 3: 1977–1984

### PERSONAL: HOMOPHOBIA, RACISM, AND CLASS PRIVILEGE IN ACTION

I came out as a lesbian after two marriages. One of these had lasted for eight years and involved me with two stepsons, a foster son, and an adopted black interracial daughter. Consequently, I found myself with a political dilemma. As the single mother of a black daughter, I wanted to maintain ties with a progressive interracial community. So I joined a parents' cooperative alternative school, composed mostly of black and Latino families, that was committed to teaching our children about racism, sexism, classism, and imperialism (cf. Ferguson, 1981b). In that school, in subsequent left-wing politics and in a black studies/ women's studies faculty seminar, I found myself under pressure as a lesbian feminist, particularly from a number of black men who suspected white lesbian feminists of wanting to divide the black community by pointing out its sexist aspects.

As a politically correct lesbian feminist, I had resolved to give up the heterosexual privilege of using the "flirting game" to mollify male egos. Of course, this decision made me even more suspect in the eyes of some of the blacks in the school, and, looking back, I think they may have been right in perceiving some racism in my actions. At any rate, the members were heterosexist—no one wanted to challenge homophobia in the group, and this made membership difficult for me, though I felt I had to remain in the school collective for my daughter's sake. I made a similar decision to stay in the faculty seminar because

I needed the intellectual contacts to think about racism. Both experiences taught me some of the costs of U.S. identity politics, where there is a strong tendency for oppressed groups to stress common identity rather than validating differences.

The theory presented in this book about the connection of racism to sexuality makes sense out of my experiences of the changing nature of racism in our society and the ways it continues to be a factor in all aspects of social life, from state policy, on the one hand, to social movements like the women's movement, on the other.[4]

In the school collective I also went through the dilemma of trying to do political work with those for whom my class privilege as a white professor was oppressive. A number of the parents in the group were poor, single mothers of color. Even the couples in the group were poorer than I, as they were either students or low-income residents of the community. There was thus often no easy way I could avoid coming off as arrogant "Miss Ann," insisting on feminist issues with ease because of my class and race privilege and because I did not have to bond materially with a man of my class and race in order to maintain my status. I learned that feminism, to broaden its base beyond white, middle-class women, has to connect itself with demands that will also benefit poor and working-class men and people of color, both men and women. If not, even radical feminism will be perceived as a species of white, liberal cop-out (cf. Hooks, 1984) brought on by class and race privilege. Thus I came to the conclusion that some type of democratic socialist vision is an absolute necessity for a successful feminist movement.

My daughter, Kathy, has had a hard time with her political parents. As a mixed-race child of divorced left-wing white parents, one of whom is a lesbian, she has felt like an outsider in relation to her peers in just about every possible way. When she was young, she couldn't understand why she was called black because her skin was nearly as white as mine. (How do you explain to a four-year-old that color terms in a racist society don't refer to the actual color of your skin?) Now that she is older she has found that black men find her more attractive than do white men, so she is finally participating in African-American culture.

Kathy had conflicts with my life-style choices. She didn't want me to be a lesbian, of course, and still challenges what she defines as my "hippie" disregard of conventional beauty standards and dress codes. As a young woman who is not an intellectual, she does not have access to the class privileges I have in my job. For her and many other young women, the feminism of the 1960s is neither desirable nor easily available (Stacey, 1987). Only a major social upheaval could politicize her, and it would have to be a multi-issue progressive movement or coalition of movements that dealt with racism and elitism as well as sexism. She remains a touchstone for me of why a socialist-feminist vision and radical coalitionist strategy is necessary to politicize the majority of women and men in our society in a way that could lead to a serious challenge to social domination.

## THEORETICAL AND POLITICAL: DIFFERENCE, RACISM, AND THE WOMEN'S MOVEMENT

At about the time of the lesbian-straight split, working-class women and women of color were arguing that feminist theory and practice didn't take sufficient account of the material privileges that racism and classism gave to white, middle-class women. The theory that women could overcome race and economic-class divisions to unite around their sex class oppression was too facile an assumption. It was supposed that sexism operated independently of race and class privilege and thus that oppressions were additive rather than contextually interdependent (Spelman, 1988; Lorde, 1984; Moraga and Anzaldua, 1981).

At this stage the women's movement tended to define feminist issues too simply and in too reformist a way. So, for example, the demand for reproductive rights for women was originally understood as the demand for the legal right to abortion. This ignores class and race issues—forced sterilization of black and Latino women, the inability to pay for abortions, the privilege to have children that economic status brings to middle-class women, and so on. Similarly, the movement by women against violence against women demanded stiffer penalties for rapists but initially ignored the problem of sexual racism: that black men have suffered racial discrimination before the law based on framed rape charges (Davis, 1977, 1981; Aptheker, 1983). Thus it was the voices of black and other women of color, Jewish and Latino women, that led me to a "multisystems" theory of social domination. Chapters 4 and 6 of the present collection develop this theme further than does Chapter 2.

Though "Sex and Work" offers a plausible internal critique of Marxism—it points out that Marxists do not take seriously enough the ambiguity of the key concept of economic class when applied to women and other oppressed groups such as racial and ethnic minorities—it does not really eliminate the Marxist notion of how radical social change occurs. As a result, it downplays the radical contingency of coalitions dealing with sexism across race and economic-class lines, implying instead that the march of history, having reduced social differences between women, now assures sex class bonding for a women's movement.

Multisystems theory as I develop it in Chapter 4 argues that racism, sexism, and class-divided economic systems like capitalism are irreducible and semiautonomous systems of social domination. Thus none of them can be said to act as the social base of the others, nor will eliminating one automatically eliminate the others. I argue that modes of sex/affective production—historically specific forms of sexuality, social bonding, and parenting—interact with particular economic systems to organize forms of racism and patriarchy in a society.

Multisystems theory shares an aspect of postmodernism in that it rejects universalist humanist assumptions. It is an antihumanist theory in the sense that it does not presuppose a common yet alienated human nature that at base desires social equality if only social relations were different. Chapter 5, "A Feminist Aspect Theory of Self" (Ferguson, 1987) presents an antihumanist theory of the self. There I attack the notion of a unified self, whether it is conceived of as the conscious selfsame observer of all one's experiences or as a rational, self-interested agent (as in mainstream, Marxist, and radical feminist economic theory). I also critique the idea that selves are permanently divided into two opposing genders based on unconscious selves formed differently in childhood, as neo-Freudian feminism would have it.

In the aspect theory of self, a person is not composed of one univocal self whose self-interests or desires can be said to be alienated by social structures of domination and exploitation. Rather, the notion of self must be deconstructed into a relational view that sees personal identity as emerging out of relations to others in distinctive social practices. Where the expectations for a person's behavior clash in different social practices, as, for example, for a woman in a male-identified career who is also a wife and mother in a heterosexual marriage, conflicting personal aspects will be developed and activated. Liberation for a person involved in such practices should not be posed as shedding an inauthentic self for an authentic one hidden underneath. A better model might be one of networking with others in similar structural positions in such practices to challenge the "rules of the game" that set up socially defined inequalities (cf. Weedon, 1987; Laclau and Mouffe, 1985).[5]

Because racism, sexism, and capitalism are different systems of social domination, the optimistic idea that women are ineluctably coming to prioritize their gender identity over their racial and economic class identities becomes questionable. Rather, as I suggest in Chapter 6, "Racial Formation, Gender, and Class in U.S. Welfare State Capitalism," and Chapter 11, "Socialist-Feminist and Antiracist Politics," we must accept the idea that different racial formations in the United States have created racial divisions as deep as gender divisions. Thus we would do better to think of personal identities as being race gendered in such a way that instead of merely two genders, there are many racial genders: white men, white women, Afro-American men, Afro-American women, Latino men, Latino women, Asian men, Asian women, native American men, and native American women.

There are two ways to bridge this troubling political gap between the progressive sectors of white communities and communities of color: interracial friendships on the one hand (Lugones, 1986) and interracial sexual liaisons on the other. But only a vast network of socialist-feminist and antiracist coalitions could create the mass movement for social change and social revolution that must occur to eliminate patriarchy, racism, and capitalism as we know them.

There are still confusing aspects to making coalitions across racial and ethnic lines. There are the obvious conflicts that must be dealt with, such as that between blacks and Jews. But newer conflicts have been set up in the United States between Latinos and blacks (consider Miami) and between Asians and blacks (consider New York City). The ambiguity about the connection between race and ethnicity, including country of origin, in this land of immigrants creates a problem for racial identity politics. For example, is a black Latino considered an Afro-American as well as a Latin American, or are Afro-Americans only those whose ancestors have been here since slavery? Jesse Jackson's recent suggestion that black Americans should be described as African-Americans is an attempt to translate a racial concept into an ethnic one and hence to make black Americans more like other immigrant groups. The theory of racialization developed in Chapter 6 holds that there is no right answer to the question whether black Americans should be referred to by their color or their ancestors' place of origin.[6] Instead, it is a political question of self-naming, of how best to counter the dominant racist structures in place today.

If race and gender identities are inextricably intertwined, sisterhood as a political concept involves something much more complicated than building an autonomous women's movement that recognizes various commonalities across economic-class and race lines. To be sure, we can organize around common issues like reproductive rights and violence against women, such as sexual harassment, domestic battering, rape, and incest. We can also formulate state policies to deal with single motherhood and asymmetrical parenting work, and can educate about gender inequalities in sexual practices, such as the objectification of women in the mass media and pornography. But white, middle-class women need to understand the ways that the deep structures of racism will keep the mass of black and other racial minority women from accepting the prioritizing of any feminist connection that implies that

alliances with those of their own race should be secondary. I discuss the
political implications of this type of coalition-building in Chapter 11.

## Stage 4: 1984–Present

PERSONAL: DEALING WITH AGEING, REAGAN,
AND THE NEW RIGHT

The 1980s was a depressing decade in many ways. The civil rights
movement, the New Left, and the women's movement all lost steam
in the face of the rise of the New Right and the successes of the
Reagan administration in dismantling social services and the legal gains
of reproductive rights, Affirmative Action, and gay and lesbian rights.
As I became part of the older generation for my students, I began
to change my views about lesbian separatism. Rather than a wrong-
headed and elitist strategy for the women's movement, I now see it as
a necessary stage that many young lesbians need to empower themselves,
particularly in the context of New Right attacks on feminists, people
of color, and lesbians and gays. Ironically, the upsurge of AIDS created
a medical and political crisis that tended to bring back many former
lesbian separatists to work with gay men against the cultural homophobia
that began to connect gay sex with death. Still, there is the ongoing
danger that the gay rights health movement will continue to be sexist
in its concentration on AIDS to the exclusion of demands for more
research on women's health issues, such as breast and ovarian cancer.

The rise of the antipornography movement and the Dworkin-
MacKinnon ordinance,[7] which would have allowed women harmed by
porn to bring legal charges against traffickers, split the women's movement between those radical feminists who wanted to take action against
the patriarchal sexual objectification of women in male-dominated pornography and those libertarian or pluralist feminists who accused the
other camp of being sexual prudes and of wishing to act as the moral
censors and moral police of the women's movement.

I found myself again in the middle, as I had been in the lesbian-
straight split of the 1970s: on the one hand understanding the importance of feminist moral critiques of pornography and on the other
seeing the limits to identity politics that would define anyone who
enjoyed pornography or engaged in "kinky" sex of any sort (e.g.,
consensual sadomasochist, or S/M, sex) as not a true feminist. Out of
this I began to see the importance of a mediative feminist stance, that
is, one that can find a middle ground between polar disagreements
within the women's movement. We must insist that the personal be

political and at the same time find a way to agree to disagree on some personal preferences and life-style choices that involve moral differences of opinion. From this perspective came a series of papers attempting to stake out a middle position in the sex wars concerning pornography, roled sex, and consensual S/M sex.

My personal life in the Northampton-Amherst lesbian community continues to be problematic because of my refusal to accept either pole of these strongly held sexual politics views. I have friends in both camps but find it difficult to take concrete action with lesbians against pornography because of our political disagreements. I continue to juggle memberships in communities that are deeply suspicious of one another: university intellectuals versus town activists, the lesbian community versus the mixed left. Happily, at least the leftists in my area have become more profeminist as a result of past battles. My daughter still lives with me, and I get along famously with her boyfriend, though their friends find it difficult to mix with my lesbian friends. Kathy and I have agreed to have no overt lesbian signs on the downstairs bulletin board or gay and lesbian magazines in the bathroom.

It is hard to empower my various self-aspects, in part because of the fragmented nature of feminist and leftist organizing these days. Ad hoc leftist and feminist single-issue groups are many but short-lived and don't often work in coalition with others. How, then, can I combine my leftist, feminist, and lesbian-identified aspects, not to mention my intellectual and activist proclivities, in such a way as to be an effective agent of social change?

Leftist political activism in response to Reaganomics was muted at best. I tried membership in the Democratic Socialists of America (DSA) and, briefly, Jesse Jackson's Rainbow Coalition. Neither was satisfactory, in part because of the nature of the local groups, so I put more energy into anti-imperialist solidarity work. I had been to Cuba in 1976 and 1980, had organized against U.S. military aid to El Salvador in the late 1970s, and became involved with a local Five College network of Faculty and Staff for Peace in Central America (FSPCA) in 1985. This led me to take several trips to Nicaragua in 1987 and 1990 to do solidarity work. Out of this came an interest in doing international feminist and lesbian-gay support work as well as generally supporting struggles for national liberation, such as the Frente Sandinista Liberación Nacionale (FSLN) in Nicaragua. At the present I and several other women in western Massachusetts have formed a group called Feminist Aid to Central America to raise material aid for feminist, grassroots self-help and political projects in Central America.

THEORETICAL AND POLITICAL:
LESBIAN IDENTITY, SOCIALIST-FEMINISM FOR THE FUTURE

The radical changes in Eastern Europe and the defeat of the Sandinistas in the February 1990 national elections in Nicaragua require that we forge a new understanding, both of our socialist and feminist visions and of a practical politics in this country, that can give us a plausible scenario of where and how we can go from here in challenging multisystems social domination.

In Chapter 3 I imply that an identity politics based on sexual preference is a progressive development for feminism and for women's sexual liberation. There is something correct and something incorrect about this view. If it is accepted that the contents of gender and sexual identities, like the contents of racial identities, are historically various and are both imposed by the dominant sexual and racial formation and at the same time resisted by counterhegemonic characterizations, then it is correct to suppose that lesbianism, as a contested sexual category, could be given a different meaning by the lesbian subculture than it has in the dominant culture. The incorrect idea is to suppose that this can be done in a purely voluntaristic way: that individuals and political tendencies have total leeway to redefine a term in a Humpty Dumpty fashion, so that "it means exactly what I say it does, neither more nor less." Furthermore, the meaning of lesbianism is always being co-opted in dominant cultural meanings as a titillating alternative to, but not destruction of, heteropatriarchal gender roles.

Countercultural values have restrictions placed on them by the historical and material conditions in which they arise. For example, the integrationist idea, associated with Martin Luther King, Jr., that the color of a person's skin is not an essential part of personhood implies that we ought to adopt a color-blind discourse in which race would not be considered relevant to a person's identity. But as subsequent events in the civil rights movement suggested, black nationalism, with its attendant color-charged discourse that re-appropriates and revalues blackness as a beautiful and essential part of a person's identity, was a necessary phase in dismantling the racial privilege of whiteness in U.S. society. Thus identity politics, at times a requisite stage in the development of oppositional cultural networks, is often co-optive and a hindrance to furthering those networks. This dialectic must be understood if we are to build a stronger cultural politics of resistance.

Implications of this historicist methodology of researching lesbian identity are drawn out in Chapter 7, "Is There a Lesbian Culture?"[8] With respect to understanding international lesbian feminist politics, we need to reject universal, discontinuous, and deconstructive approaches for a dialectical interest in historical specificity.[9] We should create a history of those lesbianisms that have been and can be political resistances to any male dominant order. We need to supplement the "history of the present" vantage point endemic to discontinuity approaches that borrow from Michel Foucault. One reading of Foucault, one with which he would probably not agree, valorizes our present lesbian and feminist countercultures and sees all other sexualities, whether historical or in other contemporary social formations, as basically discontinuous or different from this. This position leaves us with an unsatisfactory sexual identity politics, as it has no other base than what presently exists (no historical tendencies, deep structures of domination, and so on) on which to build a politics (Weeks, 1986). In particular, it can give us no clue whatsoever about how to go about building an international gay and lesbian movement with those engaged in homosexual practices in societies that lack a gay and lesbian identity in the sense that has developed in Western industrial societies.

My dialectical approach assumes that oppositional lesbian subcultures tend to arise in complicated societies with more than one mode of organizing sexuality, parenting, and kinship relationships (what I define as "modes of sex/affective production"). Because they involve different sexual mores based on class and race, as well as cultural and historical contexts, we cannot generalize what a universally correct "lesbian feminist politics" would be, for example, whether it would eschew butch/femme roles or find common cause with heterosexual feminists or gay men.

Such a history of lesbian subcultures suggests that we adopt a coalitionist and radical pluralist (cf. Weeks, 1986) rather than a vanguardist strategy for building international feminist, lesbian, and gay movements. We should avoid the notion that developed industrial countries and, within those countries, white, middle-class lesbian subcultures are vanguards for an international lesbian and feminist culture. Rather than mourning for the impossible goal of a unified lesbian or women's counterculture, we should be encouraging political networking of those who can accept the minimal symbolic demands of each other's oppositional subculture identities.[10] Our vision, that is, of historical advance for women and lesbians, should not require that lesbians and women in all countries, and all classes and races within one country, adopt a similar set of sexual practices and identities. Of course, this will mean that there will always be moral disagreements on the acceptable "minimal symbolic demand" for groups engaging in coalition politics to ask and receive of one another.[11]

In the present historical context in the United States, it seems clear that the New Left visions of a socialism based on participatory democracy, and the associated feminist vision of an androgynous society where gender is eliminated, were both flawed and hopelessly utopian. Events in Eastern Europe and China have cast doubt on whether socialism of any sort is a viable project. Feminist revisions of Freudianism have challenged the idea that gender, even if it is socially constructed, is eliminable. Radical feminists have argued that the concept of androgyny is itself fatally inconsistent—the attempt, as Mary Daly suggests, to create a pastiche of the human ideal consisting of Brigitte Bardot and John Wayne in the end still ends up as male-identified! Does this mean that socialist-feminism is bankrupt?

My answer to this question is a resounding no! If anything, events in Eastern Europe and China only confirm my view that socialism and feminism require each other and cannot succeed without each other, as I discuss in Chapter 8. Furthermore, there are ways to understand the elimination of gender dualism and the ideal of androgyny—I now call it gynandry—that avoid the pastiche problem. Included in this collection is my original essay on androgyny (Chapter 9) and an appendix that redefines the goal as gynandry and replies to radical feminist and Freudian critics of the concept. Though gynandry is a vision, it does not follow that our contemporary politics should ignore the persistence of gender as a division in our lives, nor that we can do without an autonomous women's movement. Our existing identities cannot just be thrown out the window with the intellectual discovery that they have been socially created. Thus we will need a coalition of autonomous caucuses—women's movement, men's movement, lesbians, gay men, and other more specific groups (for example, single parents), who need to organize both autonomously and yet collectively around issues of self-interest and solidarity in challenging gender dualism.

With respect to socialism, as a longtime political activist in the North American Left, I have read much about the socialist revolutions and the current socialist states in the world, including the Soviet Union, China, Vietnam, Yugoslavia, and Cuba. In visits to revolutionary Cuba and Nicaragua I spent time working and talking with as many people as I could, including workers, women, gays, intellectuals, and artists. I became convinced that Cuba and Nicaragua, until the recent Sandinista defeat, have been much less exploitative societies than they were previously when controlled by imperialist relations with the United States. Yet I came to doubt that the Marxist-Leninist idea of socialist revolution and a socialist society was an adequate conception of participatory democracy or effective in developing workers' control of the economy. Instead, we need a model of democratic socialism that takes as much from the anarchist tradition as it does from traditional Marxism, that uses a pluralist coalition approach rather than a vanguard party model to understand how to include racism and sexism as equal evils to be fought in the transition to democratic socialism (cf. Albert and Hahnel, 1981).

It will be interesting to see what will develop in the next few years in Eastern Europe and China. Though most of the movements in Eastern Europe seem to have assumed that the totalitarian nature of their Stalinist governments is an automatic consequence of socialism, they have also grown used to socialist controls on the economy that minimize unemployment, provide low-cost health care and housing, and subsidize public education, transportation, and childcare. Will these countries be the first to develop forms of market socialism that are more effective and more democratic than those until recently in place in Yugoslavia when it was reigned by an old-style Communist party? The Western press usually obscures that the student unrest in China and the subsequent workers' support of that movement were not merely for more formal democratic rights but also protested the wide-scale corruption and class privileges that had come into place with the recent Chinese experimentation with some market economy measures. No wonder President Bush insists on most-favored-nation status for the capitalist China he hopes will develop and refuses to support a student movement that could come to resemble the movement of the 1960s in this country!

Will developments in China, then, involve a replay of New Left developments in the United States and in France, with a challenge to old-style Communist party politics and an insistence on a participatory democracy connected to a council socialist model? Only time will tell. But it seems likely that socialism is far from dead and will revive in a transformed fashion, linked to movements that insist on the connection, rather than the separation, between the goals of democracy and the goals of socialism.

In this country, too, the slide into a New Right fascism is not at all inevitable. The women's movement has recovered from a slump in the early 1980s to reorganize a more vital reproductive rights movement that is class and race conscious. The Jackson Rainbow Coalition, though it has serious problems as a grassroots movement because of its emphasis on presidential electoral politics, indicates that there is a movable base of people waiting to be organized if only a new vision of radical democracy, that is, a feminist, lesbian/gay, antiracist, and populist socialist model, can be developed by the Left, and appropriate coalition politics can be forged.

What would such a reconstructed radical democratic vision look like? Although in *Blood at the Root* I argued that this would involve a decentralized council socialist model, I would now include a market socialist model as well. This is not out of preference to the second, but simply to acknowledge that our visions must be historically viable, and it may well be that a democratic market socialism is the only type of socialism (cf. Nove, 1983) we can expect to achieve in the near future. I explore both these possibilities in Chapter 10.

Why must we assume that feminism requires socialism, as historically the existing socialist countries have not succeeded in eliminating patriarchy? In part the answer is pragmatic: To be successful feminism requires coalitionist politics that challenges racism, classism, and heterosexism. That is, without a socialist-feminist emphasis on socialist measures such as national health care, sufficient research on AIDS, antiracism coalitions, homes for the homeless, reproductive rights in all forms—including federally funded abortions, childcare centers, lesbian and gay parenting rights, and anti–sterilization abuse—we will never have a women's movement strong enough to be successful in challenging patriarchy.

But there is also a theoretical reason. The achievement of a feminist vision of an egalitarian, gender-equal society requires the establishment of a democratic socialist society. Given that socialism is a necessary condition for feminism, why has it not been sufficient? Indeed, are there ways that existing socialist state priorities have actually retarded the development of gender equality?

In Chapter 8 I explore the historical connection between feminism and historical socialist revolutions. I argue that although such revolutions have importantly furthered the goals of de-institutionalizing forms of patriarchy, they have failed to equalize women and men. This is not only because of the persistent problem of the scarcity of material resources but also because of the lack of a completely satisfactory feminist theory and strategy for ongoing challenge to patriarchal structures. Modes of organizing parenthood, sexuality, and biological reproduction are not seriously theorized as semiautonomous domination structures that persist after the transition to socialism. Thus the need for truly autonomous women's organizations and movements, and not just those supporting the line of the vanguard party, are not acknowledged.

Marxist-Leninist-led revolutions have failed to recognize the material conflict between the goals of rapid industrialization and preserving women's self-determination in the sphere of biological reproduction. Furthermore, there are reasons to believe that challenging the patriarchal nuclear family household is actually a problem for socialist accumulation (Weinbaum, 1976). Finally, none of the existing socialist countries has sufficiently acknowledged the importance of consciousness-raising techniques that valorize the idea that the personal is the political. Nonetheless, the attempts to socialize housework, with state-supported childcare and paid maternity leaves and the social supports for children (health care, free public education) that are the hallmark of most socialist programs, are necessary features of a feminist structure that the United States lacks.

We need, then, to merge the strengths of our women's movement with the strengths of the Marxist-based women's organizations in previous state socialist countries to develop a better amalgam of material and personal strategies for women's liberation. Such an amalgam requires international solidarity among women who understand the connections among imperialism, capitalism, and patriarchy. Such linkages are already happening on a grassroots level, for example, as U.S. feminists interact with Central American feminists through structures such as women's peace convoys to Central America and Witness for Peace activities in Nicaragua. In this process, there is an exchange of North American and Central American views on what is necessary to empower women, and we influence one another.

In this book I argue that complex societies like our own perpetuate racial and gender dominance through interconnected economic, social, and symbolic systems I call "sex/affective production systems." Challenging this domination requires altering individuals' sex/affective relations with one another. Because sex/affective production systems involve structures that are partly economic, partly bodily, and partly social, such a change would mean a major social reorganization— indeed a true gender and sexual revolution.

A satisfactory sexual revolution will involve altering family structures, racial and gendered divisions of labor, community living patterns, schooling, and mass media images. This will require New Left, feminist, and antiracist sexual morality and politics that further the positive developments yet correct the mistakes of the so-called sexual revolution of the 1960s.

In Chapter 10 I sketch a vision that could serve as a minimum common goal for radical coalitions that could coalesce around some tendencies persisting here since the 1960s and developing anew in grassroots progressive networks such as the Rainbow Coalition, the Coalition of Labor Union Women (CLUW), the Reproductive Rights National Network (R2N2), the Democratic Socialists of America, and college campus movements for a peaceful conversion of the military budget, anti-CIA and anti-apartheid organizing, and anti-imperialist solidarity work.

. In Chapter 11 I outline a contemporary politics for promoting sexual democracy. The general values we must foster to create a cross-class, cross-race, cross-gender, and cross-sexual coalition should include the goals of democratic socialism and the process values of self-determination, respect, and pluralism. I consider some issues that divide and some that unite feminists and social egalitarians across race and class lines, and I suggest a common agenda for such a coalition. I also discuss some of the countercultural practices that, if prevalent, could set the stage for developing the counterhegemonic culture that will be necessary to the process of gender and sexual revolution. We will need both intra- and intergender, racial, class, and sexual identity networks of friends engaged in consciousness-raising groups on issues of racism, sexism, classism, and heterosexism. A radical movement for social and sexual democracy will require both its separatist and co-alitionist wings. Group solidarity could be built on some common interracial, cross-class, and gender-mixed social life that would value minority racial and ethnic cultures in spiritual, music, dance, and food rituals. At the same time, autonomous networks of minority peoples, women, lesbians and gays, and working-class-based organizations would be accepted as necessary to undo the oppressive relations between members of the coalition that would otherwise undermine the search for a social egalitarian and self-determining process of social change.

The type of radical social change we require to create a true social and sexual democracy in the United States will not come easily. Indeed, it may not occur in my lifetime. But the twenty-first century will also not be a static period. The economic recessions and even depressions that are inevitable here and elsewhere in the world capitalist system are sure to create a crisis of faith in business as usual, as we face the consequences of years of overspending on the military, the nuclear arms race, and the costly financial insanity of corporate mergers, leveraged buyouts, and the savings and loan scandal in the United States. The civil rights and women's movements in the United States have raised expectations for social justice that will not be satisfied with the old solution of throwing the major costs of such economic crises of capitalism on the shoulders of the poor, racial minorities, and women.

The end of the nuclear arms race between East and West and the revolutions in Eastern Europe give us a new chance to learn from history. The shortcomings of existing patriarchal and racist capitalist systems and downfalls of Stalinist state socialist systems show that neither of these is the solution. We must forge ahead with the attempt to synthesize a democratic socialism and feminism that avoids the pitfalls of either pole of the present alternatives.

Each of us committed to the struggle for a new world needs three tools: personal insights gleaned from applying the idea that the personal is the political, experience gained from ongoing political activism, and the theory and strategy of understanding and challenging social domination that an engaged philosophical outlook can provide. In this book I hope to combine the personal, the political, and the theoretical in a way that provides these tools for all those concerned with progressive social change. We cannot afford to divide our forces among those who feel, those who do, and those who think. To make accomplishments in each of these areas calls for as many of us as possible who desire social justice to learn how to use all three kinds of knowledge. Only practice can make this possible, a practice that is no longer a luxury or an onus but an absolute necessity for bringing about social and sexual democracy in our time.

## Notes

1. I use the convention of a hyphen between "feminist" and "materialism" to indicate that neither of these terms is primary. One cannot, for example, understand my theory as simply an addition to a base of another materialist theory of human nature and society such as Marxian historical materialism.

2. Although the version of this essay that appears here as Chapter 2 was actually published later (in Gottlieb, 1989) than the motherhood and sexuality paper (Trebilcot, 1984), Chapter 4, it is actually a revision of the essay "Women as a Revolutionary Class in the United States" that was written in 1977 and appeared in Walker, 1979.

3. I owe this idea to my former graduate student, Tamsin Lorraine, who develops it in her psychoanalytic treatment of philosophical theories of the self (cf. Lorraine, 1990). Of course the personal, political, and theoretical are distinct even though they interconnect. Though theory is a creation of self-meaning, it is also a form that can be adopted by others as well. Thus it is always subject to critique from its intended audience in the way the personal is not. The political, like the theoretical, makes claims to a more general audience. The difference is that the political concerns implications for action whereas the theoretical gives a way of understanding the world. Both, however, as they involve generalizations from personal meanings, are always relevant sites for disagreement.

4. I developed the multisystems perspective on social domination with the aid of several race, class, and gender conferences sponsored by the Radical Philosophy Association, the Black Philosophers' Association, and the Society for Women in Philosophy. In particular I learned much from the comments on my papers made by Leonard Harris, Oma Narayan, and Lou Outlaw.

5. In rejecting an essentialist and unitary theory of self, my theory is similar to postmodernist feminisms, such as Weedon, 1987, and Butler, 1987. My theory, however, is not exactly a postmodernist theory in the full sense of that term, as it still presumes to develop analytic categories (e.g., "modes of sex/affective production") with which to understand the historical variations in patriarchy and racism. In this limited sense, even though the multisystems aspect of my theory mitigates against ahistorical universalism, it is still a totalist

project in ways that many postmodernist approaches would reject (cf. Nicholson, 1986).

6. The question of origin is itself complicated. Ethnic differences between West Indian black Americans and "native" black Americans are ignored by lumping all blacks into the category "African-American."

7. This ordinance was initially approved by the cities of Minneapolis and Indianapolis but was struck down as unconstitutional by the Supreme Court, which claimed it violated the right to free speech.

8. For a shorter version of this paper, see the essay by the same title in Jeffner Allen, 1990.

9. It should be noted that my critique of Frye and Wittig does not imply that all deconstructive methods should be abandoned: Indeed, my dialectical approach is a type of deconstructive method. Rather, I am showing the limitations of an ahistorical use of the deconstructive method stemming from Martin Heidegger and Jacques Derrida. In this method, a dominant discourse is critiqued for a dualist set of categories that fail to deal with what Derrida calls the "supplement," those objects, practices, and so on that cannot be subsumed under these categories and thus are rendered invisible. So, the patriarchal discourse of "man" and "woman" that supposes that each is a heterosexual complement of the other makes lesbians invisible.

The problem with this method as Frye and Wittig use it is that their criticisms of the dominant discourse of gender assumes it is a "block" discourse, that is, one that is so hegemonic that it allows no exceptions. But this is certainly not true with the categories of man/woman or gay/lesbian as they are used in ordinary communication. Thus, ironically, Frye and Wittig's critique hides more than it reveals of the gaps and contradictions in the power of the prevailing discourse as well as the failure of the discourse in question to be translatable into other cultural contexts and periods. This is ironic because a more revealing use of deconstruction would highlight just these contradictions in contemporary discourse.

10. Since I wrote this paper on lesbian culture several years ago, there has been a new development in sexual identity politics in the United States— bisexuality as a radical sexual identity has come of age. In various places, and certainly in the Northampton-Amherst area, bisexuals are insisting on being included in the annual lesbian and gay pride march no longer merely as allies but as a named identity, making it the "Lesbian/Gay/Bisexual Pride March." Although lesbian separatists have been resisting the change, other lesbians are coming out as bisexual lesbians or as lesbians whose lovers are bisexual and who are tired of separatist politics that exclude them from the lesbian counterculture. As a bisexual lesbian myself, I applaud the development in the hope that the struggle against heterosexism can be strengthened by the inclusion of more who consider themselves hurt by it. A lesbian/gay/bisexual liberation march that demands the elimination of homophobia and heterosexism meets a minimum symbolic demand that bisexuals acknowledge the importance of challenging heterosexism. But it is far from clear whether those in the existing bisexual countercultural community in the Northampton-Amherst area today

can be trusted to be serious allies of lesbians and gays (cf. issues of *Gay Community News,* spring 1990). Nonetheless, the controversy itself shows the transitoriness of sexual identity categories and the importance of a radical coalitionist politics that relies on more than merely the fashionable identities of the day to establish its alliances.

11. One example of a conflict about symbols is that over public displays of S/M regalia among feminists. Some S/M lesbian feminists insist on the right to wear S/M insignia in public, which alienates many radical lesbian feminists who feel this symbolizes violence against women. Thus some lesbian feminists refused to take part in the 1987 National Lesbian and Gay Pride March in Washington, D.C., which permitted S/M groups to march in full regalia. For more discussion on this and other disagreements between feminists on sexual morality, see my discussion in *Blood at the Root,* ch. 10 (Ferguson, 1989a).

# Part One

## THE THEORY OF SEX/AFFECTIVE PRODUCTION

TWO

# Sex and Work:
# Women as a New Revolutionary
# Class in the United States

Love, sex, and work—these are areas in which different camps of
radical social theorists (radical feminists, neo-Freudians and Marxists,
respectively) have sought the creation and perpetuation of male dominance. The Freudian view is that the Oedipal love of children for
their mother, repressed because of the power of the father, creates
gender identities and sexual desires that perpetuate male dominance
through the masculine desire to possess and dominate women and a
feminine desire to be possessed and dominated by men. The standard
Marxist position faults Freudianism for its ahistoricism, and argues
that sexism is a by-product of class societies that will lose its material
base under communism. Radical feminism critiques both Freudianism
and Marxism, on the grounds that male power precedes both classism
and repressed Oedipal love. Thus, for radical feminists, the primary
social contradiction, one that ultimately explains all systems of social
domination, is that between men and women.

Contemporary socialist-feminists have been uneasy with the three
options offered above, and most have argued that there are two
interlocking but semiautonomous systems, capitalism and patriarchy,
which together reinforce the continued existence of economic classes
and male dominance. But there are many different views within the
socialist-feminist camp of just what patriarchy is, why it continues, and
just how it connects with capitalism. What I shall do in this essay is
to present one type of socialist-feminist analysis that clarifies the base
of male dominance, explains its persistence, and draws the conclusion
that the changing position of men and women in the family and in
the economy creates the possibility of women as a new revolutionary
class in the contemporary United States.[1]

## Sexuality and History

A basic omission in the classical Marxist texts is the lack of a historical theory of the social production of sexuality. My perspective on sexuality is a dialectical materialist development of scattered remarks in *The German Ideology*. Marx and Engels waffle on the question of whether sex is a material need that should be considered a part of the material base of social organization. In one place they suggest "the reproduction of daily life" (which could include meeting sexual needs, producing children, and so forth) is co-equal in importance to "the production of daily life," while in another they suggest that the family, originally part of the economic base of society (i.e., a primary form of organization to meet material needs) has become part of the superstructure of capitalist society, i.e., no longer a necessary form of organization to meet material needs. In other places, Marx suggests that sex and procreation, as "natural" needs, do not need to be socially produced.

In short, classical Marxism is ambiguous as to whether or not sex is an instinct that requires no social organization, a basic material need whose objects may be plastic but whose fulfillment requires social organization, or a social need created instrumentally to achieve other more basic needs (e.g., to provide for the procreation of the future labor force). Thus, it has no way of posing the question as to whether the different historical organizations of sexuality, the production of children, and social bonding (what I call *modes of sex/affective production*) create systems in which men have a material interest in dominating and exploiting women that does not derive merely from the mechanisms that reproduce class domination (cf. also Rubin, 1975; Flax, 1976; Eisenstein, 1979).

I maintain that the standard Marxist idea of an exclusive class position for each individual no longer captures the complicated and contradictory reality of productive relations in racist capitalist public patriarchy. Rather, there are at least *four* different historically developed class relationships that can characterize a person at the same time: *race class, sex class, family class,* and *individual economic class.* Given the appropriate historical conditions, an individual's subordinate class role in any one of these aspects can serve as the material base for their development of revolutionary agency.

## A Socialist-Feminist Trisystems Theory

The significance of using the concept of *class* to refer to the social opposition of races, genders, families, and individuals (e.g., race class, sex class, family class, and economic class) in U.S. society today is to insist that referring to an *individual's* relation to production with narrow Marxist characterizations of *class* in capitalist society obscures a number of other social oppositions that turn on one's relation to production in other ways than simply whether one is a wage laborer or an owner. Thus, other ways that the material interests of groups may be socially structured in opposition to each other are ignored.

Consider the puzzle of defining an individual's economic class solely by relation to his or her individual relation to capitalist production. By this criterion, someone is a member of the working class if she or he works for wages and a member of the capitalist class if his or her income is gained primarily from returns on private ownership of the means of production. But not all members of society have an individual economic class: For example, full-time housewives are defined by their husband's relation to production, and minors are defined by their parent's relation to production.

Whether or not a person has an individual economic class, they do at least (and in addition) have a family class, that is, a position in a family whose individual "breadwinner(s)" bear(s) (a) certain relation(s) to production. One of the confusions about class identity comes from the situation in which an individual whose family class as defined by the father's work is different than the individual's economic class as an adult, or new family class, if she or he marries a man with an economic class position different from her or his father's. This puzzle can be resolved by defining two relations—individual economic and family economic class—and realizing that the historical and cultural self-identity relevant for political organizing will depend as much on the latter as on the former. That is, since one's self-identified class depends to a large degree on education, life-style, social identification, and social bonds, we cannot see family class as simply an additive function of the individual economic relations of husband and wife. Thus a man may own a small grocery store and his wife may work part time in a factory, or she may be a full-time housewife. In either case, because of the cultural implications of the man's position and money, the family class of the couple would likely be petit bourgeois.

Analogously, we can see the sexual and racial divisions of labor in wage labor, family households, and community living situations as aspects of the productive organization of our society that create an opposition of material interests between men and women, whites and nonwhites. The structural likelihood that women and minorities, no matter what individual or family class they come from, will be in less-rewarded types of work than males and whites and that minorities will be in less-privileged neighborhoods suggests that racial and gender identities should be seen as economic oppositions in a racist and sexist society that creates gender and race as oppositional classes. Gender- and race-segregated labor and the lower relative income available to minorities and women benefit the white, male working class, thus challenging Marx's idea that capitalism homogenizes labor. By conceptualizing racism, sexism, and capitalism as semiautonomous systems of social domination, we see that it is not just the capitalist class who exploits the working class; the white, male working class can also be said to exploit women and minorities (Bowles and Gintis, 1977).[2]

Three key overlapping systems of social domination (capitalism, racism, and sexism) define an individual's material interests in our society. Developing contradictions between these class positions that define individuals (due to changes in the family and the economy) create the potential for women to become a new revolutionary class in the United States. My analysis provides a methodological framework for socialist-feminist intuitions that male control in the family and in wage labor is just as important to understand the persistence of male domination as is capitalist control of economic production. The historically developing contradictions among race, sex, family, and economic class are instabilities on which it is important to focus our political organizing as feminists.

## The Marxist Concept of Class

But are, or can, women be a class? To answer this question we must first define and clarify the concept of class. One of the strengths of the Marxist approach to understanding society and revolutionary change is its ability to explain revolutionary change. Marx and Engels justify their theory that class struggle is the moving force of history by using a class analysis to explain the transition from feudalism to capitalism, the French Revolution, the Paris Commune, and so forth. The concept of economic class they develop is not simply an intellectual starting point that must be assumed to accept the rest of their theory; rather, they apply their concept in a way that helps us make sense out of a period of revolutionary change. And their concept not only seems to explain past historical change, it also helps identify those groups who may be key political agents for revolutionary change in present society.

A problem with applying the Marxist concept of class to analyze new developments in advanced capitalism is that the cluster of criteria associated with the applications Marx and Engels made of the concept to understand feudalism and early capitalism may no longer identify one unambiguous group in the social relations of production. We need, therefore, to unpack the Marxist concept of *economic class* to see which of the traditional criteria still apply.

The common core of the Marxist concept of economic class is a group defined in both political and economic terms; that is a *class* is a group of people who, because of the kind of work they do and the power relations involved in that work in relation to other groups, have a common interest in either maintaining the system or overthrowing it. Class, then, has to be specified in terms of certain relations to production that individuals bear to each other in a given mode of production.

We need to specify more clearly what the relevant relation to production is, and what sort of power relations are involved, in order to make the concept of class concrete. We can isolate at least five criteria of class that have been given or assumed by Marxists in their discussions of class differences. The first three criteria are clearly part of the basic conceptual apparatus of the classical Marxist theorists: Marx and Engels, Lenin, and Stalin.

## CRITERION 1: EXPLOITATION RELATIONS

According to this criterion, an exploiting class in a society is one that owns and/or controls the means of production in that society in a way that allows it to expropriate the social surplus of a society. Whether that is defined in terms of surplus labor time or of surplus value depends on what specific mode of production (e.g., feudalism, capitalism) is involved. The other classes of society are then defined in contrast to the exploiting class: that is, producers who are not owners but who have rights to appropriate part of their product (e.g., peasants), or producers who sell their labor as a commodity (proletariat). I call this criterion the *economic criterion of class.*

## CRITERION 2: POLITICAL RELATIONS

Central to the classical Marxist conception of history is the idea that class conflict is the moving force for social revolution. Classes thought of as political entities are defined in terms of their potential as a cohesive reactionary or revolutionary force—that is, groups that, because of their economic relation to production as defined in criterion 1, are expected to develop cohesive interests and a common self-consciousness. The four thinkers mentioned earlier all seem to have held an inevitability thesis with respect to the relations between criteria 1 and 2 for certain key classes. That is, certain groups of individuals with objectively similar exploited positions in production, a "class in itself," would come to be a class "for itself," a group that is conscious of its common situation and comes to identify itself as a political group fighting for a common interest.[3] Not all economic classes would become political classes. As we will see, for example, Marx did not think peasants could become a political class. Hence peasants by themselves could not become a revolutionary class. The key to whether or not an economic group will become a political group seems to be the existence of historical and social conditions that give the group *historical cohesiveness*. This is our third criterion of class.

CRITERION 3: HISTORICAL COHESIVENESS

This criterion stresses the point that classes are not simply abstract collections of individuals who fit under certain labels because social scientists find it helpful to so describe them. Rather, they are groups of people who share a common historical background, a common culture, common values, and, therefore, in one way or another, some collective self-consciousness of themselves as members of a group with a common identity and common interests.[4] The way I see it, there may be both structural and accidental reasons for an economic class not developing the historical cohesiveness that is a necessary condition for further development into a political class "for itself." Marx appears to be giving some structural arguments why peasants do not form a class, according to criteria 2 and 3, in *The Eighteenth Brumaire:*

> The small-holding peasants form a vast mass, the members of which live in similar conditions but without entering into manifold relations with one another. Their mode of production isolates them from one another instead of bringing them into mutual intercourse. The isolation is increased by France's bad means of communication and by the poverty of the peasants. In so far as there is merely local interconnection among these small-holding peasants, and the identity of their interests begets no community, no national bond and no political organization among them, they do not form a class. They are consequently incapable of enforcing their class interests in their own name, whether through parliament or through a convention. They cannot represent themselves, they must be represented. (Marx, 1972, pp. 123–124)

There are plausible historical reasons why the U.S. working class has not developed the class unity necessary to meet criteria 2 and 3, such as ethnic differences resulting from successive waves of immigration from different cultures; racism caused by the historical presence of slavery in the United States; work patterns of noise and isolation, which make it difficult for workers to communicate on the job; suburbanization, which fragments workers' sense of common social community with each other; and elitist trade unions, which, by dividing skilled from unskilled workers, have defused the trade union movement to the point where fewer than 15 percent of American workers are represented by trade unions.

An implicit appeal to the criterion of historical cohesiveness as a means of categorizing individuals who otherwise have disparate relations to production (hence do not meet criterion 1) seems to underlie Poulantzas's categorization of salaried teachers, entertainers, middle managers, and others as the "new petty bourgeoisie" (Poulantzas, 1975). Though they are not self-employed, as are the traditional petty bourgeoisie, they share the values and ideological outlook of this group, that is, they are individualistic, educated defenders of the values of free enterprise.

The second set of criteria for class has been developed by neo-Marxists out of the criteria that may have been implicit in some of the works of the classical writers but were never spelled out. It seems fair to summarize the historical function of these criteria for Marxist theory by saying that they all attempt to account for the failure of the working classes in the advanced capitalist countries to become a unified revolutionary class. Either they stress the relations of political *domination and submission* between capitalist and working classes because of the growth of the state and ideological institutions like the mass media, or they isolate some new class that has a privileged position in the new social relations of production by virtue of its control and *autonomy* and whose ideological and *social function* perpetuates the status quo (Poulantzas, 1975; Gorz, 1967; Wright, 1978; Ehrenreich and Ehrenreich, 1979).

## CRITERION 4: DOMINATION RELATIONS

This criterion for making distinctions between classes is based on relations of domination and submission, primarily tied to authority and control of the process of work. Those who control the labor power of others are in one class, whereas those who do not are in another. People who are supervisors, managers, or foremen are obvious examples of those who control other workers. Less obvious examples are doctors' control of nurses, teachers' control over their students (who can be seen as "workers in training"), welfare officials' control of recipients' "work" in child-raising, men's control of women's work in the home, and parents' control of children (future workers). Some of these examples would be disputed by those Marxists who still hold that exploitation relations are the only means of distinguishing classes. They would deny that work in the home or work in the learning at school fits into the category of "productive work," that is, work that produces surplus value. They would conclude that such domination relations cannot be seen to be "exploitative" in the important sense that constitutes a class distinction. Others would call them classes but relegate them to a secondary status in any revolutionary process (e.g., Resnick and Wolff distinguish between "fundamental" and "subsumed" classes: Only the former can be dynamic movers and changers of a society, whereas the latter serve to reproduce status quo domination relations; see Wolff and Resnick, 1987).

Another aspect of work relations closely related to domination/submission is autonomy, that is, how much autonomy a worker has in producing his or her product and shaping the work process relative to other workers. This suggests a fifth criterion.

CRITERION 5: AUTONOMY

We might want to maintain that those who control their own labor and the product of their labor are in one class, whereas those who are controlled are in another class.[5]

This group overlaps but is not quite coextensive with the dominating, as opposed to the dominated, class covered by criterion 4. Individuals might control their own labor (e.g., a free-lance photographer) yet not control the labor power of others. Conversely, a person might be a dominator (e.g., a foreman or police officer) yet not be autonomous if he or she is, in turn, controlled by bosses.

## Sex/Affective Production

If women and men belong to oppositional sex classes, in addition to having different relations to capitalist production as individuals and as members of their specific races and families, what system of production so divides them? My theory holds that sexism is based in a semiautonomous system of social domination that persists throughout different modes of economic production. There are historically various ways of organizing, shaping, and molding the human desires connected to sexuality and love, and, consequently, parenting and social bonding. These systems, which I call modes of "sex/affective production," have also been called "desiring production" by Deleuze and Guattari (1977) and "sex/gender systems" by Gayle Rubin (1975). It is in part through these systems, which socially construct and produce the specific forms of the more general human material need for social union and physical sexual satisfaction I call "sex/affective energy," that different forms of male dominance as well as other types of social domination (e.g., racism, ethnicism, capitalism, and other class-divided systems of social domination) are reproduced.

My approach to understanding sexuality, social bonding, and nurturance is that these are all material needs that, since they have no specific biologically given objects, must be socially organized and produced. In this respect sex/affective energy is like the material need for hunger and shelter: Though they have a biological base, their specific objects (e.g., particular food and shelter preferences) must be culturally produced. Furthermore, the by-product of heterosexual sexuality, children, not only is functionally connected to the reproduction of the economy of any society but also generates new sex/affective needs for, and objects of, nurturant energy.

Thus sex/affective productive systems are both *like* economic modes of production and *functionally part* of such systems in that they are human modes of organizing that both create the social objects of the material needs connected to sex/affective energy and then organize human labor to achieve them. Like economic modes of production, they can also contain dialectical aspects: That is, there may be opposing tendencies in the system that undermine its ability to reproduce itself. Just as Marx thought that the dialectical instabilities in the capitalist system were bound to create a revolutionary movement for social change in the hitherto oppressed working class, the instabilities in our present form of patriarchal sex/affective production present the possibilities for a radical movement for social change in the oppressed sex class of women.

Every society must have one or more historically developed modes of sex/affective production to meet key human needs whose satisfaction is just as basic to the functioning of human society as is the satisfaction of the material needs of hunger and physical security. The satisfaction of these other key human needs—sexuality, nurturance, and children— has been based in the family household in the earlier phases of capitalism. And though our contemporary mode of sex/affective production, racist public patriarchal capitalism, has involved a shift in the *material base* of patriarchy (it is now jointly reproduced by sex/affective relations in the public spheres of wage labor and the welfare state, as well as those in the family), a complete understanding of the power and class relations in capitalism still must include an analysis of the sex/class relations of *family production*.

One way to characterize the interdependence between relations of sex/affective production and the economic system as a whole is to use the concept of a *social formation*. A social formation is a system of production in use in a particular society at a specific time that may contain within it several different historically developed modes of production. A historical example of a social formation is the combined U.S. capitalist/slave modes of production before the Civil War. Our present U.S. economic system can be thought of as a social formation consisting in part of capitalist and patriarchal modes of production. It has a codominant set of relations: (1) those between capital and wage labor and (2) those between men and women in patriarchal sex/affective production. It also has a subordinate set of class relations characteristic of welfare state capitalism—the existence of a class of institutionalized poor, that is, those subsidized by the state on welfare or unemployment. Its radical divisions of wage labor and its general separation of races into different living communities create a set of economic and sex/affective domination relations between the white dominant race and subordinate nonwhite races. Finally, the dominant mode of capitalist production is that controlled by multinational corporations, while a small subordinate sector of capitalist production involves small family businesses (the traditional petite bourgeoisie).

"Patriarchy" I define as a system of social relations in a society such that those who perform what is regarded as the "male" role (e.g., do "male" work) have more social power than, *exploit*, and *control* those who perform what is regarded as the "female" role (i.e., do women's work).[6] This use of the concept of patriarchy is somewhat broader than its original use, to mean "control by the father." I use the term *patriarchy* rather than the vaguer concept of *male dominance* as my technical term because in my view the origin, persistence, and potential undermining of male power and domination of women in all the institutions of society stems from the relative strength or weakness of male dominance and exploitation of women in the family and/or associated kin networks.

An argument for the claim that male/female social relations are codominant with other social relations of production is the universal presence in all societies of what Gayle Rubin calls "sex/gender" systems (Rubin, 1975), that is, culturally defined male and female roles children learn as part of their social identity.[7] The sex/gender system organizes material work and services, by defining what is culturally acceptable as man's and woman's work. It also organizes nurturance, sexuality, and procreation by directing sexual urges (in most societies toward heterosexual relations and nonincestuous ties), by indicating possible friendships, and by defining parenthood roles and/or kinship ties and responsibilities.[8]

Patriarchal relations have persisted through many different modes of economic production, including socialist modes of production such as those in the Soviet Union, China, and Cuba. The articulation of different modes of patriarchal sex/affective production with different economic modes of production has meant that the *content* of the sexual division of labor varies (e.g., in some modes of sex/affective production and some social formations men work for wage labor and women do not; in others, e.g., feudal production, neither men nor women work for wages). Other relations of exploitation vary as well (e.g., whether it is a feudal lord, the male head of the family, or a capitalist who benefits from the reproduction of labor power in a family).

Patriarchal family production involves unequal and exploitative relations between men and women in domestic maintenance and sex/affective work. However, the *amount* of power the man has in relation to the woman in the family varies with their relation to the dominant mode of production. So if the woman has an individual economic class (e.g., if she is working for wage labor or has an independent income) and if she is making equal wages, it will be harder for the man to appropriate the surplus in wages after basic family needs are met. In general the typical nuclear family in the United States is less patriarchal than those in earlier periods, and a substantial minority of households are woman-headed. Nonetheless, the historical prevalence of the patriarchal family and a sexual division of labor has created a male-dominated sexual division of wage labor in which women's work is paid less, is usually part time, and has less job security than men's (Davies, 1979; Hartmann, 1981b). Those women-headed households cannot be said to be matriarchal: That the majority live below the poverty line and that more than a third must depend on the federal government for welfare payments (whose size and availability depend on the changing largesse of a male-dominated government) suggests that the *fact* of male domination has not changed as much as the mechanisms by which it is reinforced.

## Women as Sex Class
## in the Patriarchal Nuclear Family

Men and women are in *sex classes* in capitalist society today, classes defined by the sexual division of labor in the family (in both the male-headed nuclear family and the mother-headed family) and reinforced by the sexual division of wage labor. In this section I present my arguments to show that women are exploited relative to men in most contemporary forms of the family, that they are dominated and have little autonomy. They thus meet criteria 1, 4, and 5 for class identity discussed earlier. In the following section I discuss the historical cohesiveness of the class (criterion 3) and the implications of whether women can become a "class for itself" (criterion 2).

By the capitalist patriarchal nuclear family (CPNF) I mean an economic unit of man, woman, and possibly children, in which the man works full time in wage labor (is thus the main breadwinner), while the woman works as the primary domestic and childcare worker in the home.[9] If she is employed in wage labor, she is not employed more than part time.

How then do men exploit women in the CPNF? Four goods are produced in sex/affective production in the family: domestic maintenance, children, nurturance, and sexuality. Since a sex/affective productive system is a system of exchange of goods and labor, we can classify it in terms of the power relations involved; that is, is there an equal exchange between producers? If not, who controls the exchange? Patriarchal sex/affective production is characterized by unequal exchange between men and women: Women receive less of the goods produced than men, and typically work harder, that is, spend more time producing them. The relations between men and women can be considered *exploitative* because the man is able to appropriate more of the woman's labor time for his own use than she is of his, and he also gets more of the goods produced (see also Delphy, 1984; Folbre, 1982, 1983).[10] It is *oppressive* because the sex/gender roles taught to boys and girls to perpetuate the sexual division of labor develop a female personality structure that internalizes the goal to produce more for men and to accept less for herself (see also Barrett, 1980).

The points made here about the exploitation and control by men of women in the CPNF apply as well to most other types of family household in the United States today. Although many families are not of the CPNF structure (e.g., female-headed households, or families in which both husband and wife work full time), most other families with children involve exploitation of the mother's work by the father. This result is partly structural and partly due to social pressure on the mother to accept an unequal sexual division of labor. After all, the CPNF is the legitimized arrangement to which schools, wage-labor jobs, and many social services (e.g., welfare, social security) are coordinated (Barrett and McIntosh, 1982). Those who do not live in a patriarchal nuclear family are not only inconvenienced but suffer a loss of status. Schools and older kin make full-time wage-earning mothers feel guilty for time not spent with their children. The absence of affordable childcare and the relatively better pay of husbands make it reasonable for mothers rather than fathers to work low-pay jobs whose flexible hours allow mothers to do childcare. Thus mothers, not fathers, tend to suffer the second-shift problem of a full shift of wage work added to another shift of childcare and housework at home.

Many female-headed households suffer a loss of family class: Their new individual economic class is lower than their family class was (when this is defined by their father or former husband's relations to production) (Sidel, 1986). As Delphy (1984) has pointed out, women in such families continue to be exploited by the absent fathers, for women now must perform two full-time jobs without much help: being the breadwinner and doing the housework and childcare.

Let me sum up the points presented about the inequalities between men and women in patriarchal capitalism in relation to the criteria for class identity to show why I maintain that women and men form sex classes.

Use of the first criterion, exploitation relations, usually assumes that exploitation involves ownership and/or control of production. I have argued here that men in capitalist patriarchies (whether or not they are actually present in the family household) own the wage and thus control sex/affective production in such a way as to be able to expropriate the surplus: surplus wages, surplus nurturance, and sexuality. Though the CPNF is no longer the dominant site of domestic maintenance and sex/affective production, its historical impact on the sexual division of wage labor, welfare state provisions, and the legal structures of child support continues to create a situation of exploitative sex/affective exchange between men and women, whether in other family households, in wage labor, in politics, or in the courts.

The fourth and fifth criteria, domination and autonomy relations, can be shown to apply to men and women as sex classes, both in the family and in other spheres of social life. If we remember that we are comparing power relations not only in the spheres of housework versus wage work but also the sex/affective work of sexuality and nurturance, it becomes clearer how the analogy holds. After all, the type of work women do in wage labor is primarily gendered sex/affective labor, that is, it involves women doing physical maintenance (nursing, health care), providing nurturance and sexuality (waitressing and other service work with sexual overtones) in which men as clients, bosses, and customers control the exchange.

Men dominate and control women in sexual activity and in nurturance (see Deming, 1973; Tax, 1970). It can be argued further that men are more autonomous in their sexual activities because they do them as consumers and not as part of their gender-defined work in the family. Here is a quote from a worker at Fisher Body Plant about the connections between his sexuality and his wife's:

> Because my need to be sexually re-vitalized each day is so great, it becomes the first and most basic part of a contract I need to make in order to ensure it.

The goal of this contract is stability, and it includes whatever I
need to consume: sex, food, clothes, a house, perhaps children. My
partner in this contract is in most cases a woman; by now she is as
much a slave to my need to consume as I am a slave to Fisher Body's
need to consume me. What does she produce? Again, sex, food,
clothes, a house, babies. What does she consume for all this effort?—
all the material wealth I can offer plus a life outside of a brutal and
uncompromising labor market. Within this picture, it's easy to see
why many women get bored with sex. They get bored for the same
reason I get bored with stacking bucket seats in cars. (Lippert, 1977)

If sex is work for women and play for men, nurturance is as well.
This is why those men who have picked up some nurturance skills
tend to be more autonomous in their use. That is, since men's sense
of gender success is not bound up with being a good nurturer, they
are freer not to use nurturance skills in ways that may be self-destructive
of their other needs (as in the self-sacrifice in which women often
engage).

In this section I have argued that three out of the five criteria
Marxists have put forward to pick out class identity apply to men and
women as sex classes. In the next section we consider whether women
as a group have the sort of political potential Marx and Engels originally
foresaw for the working class in capitalism. Are women a revolutionary
class? Do we have historical cohesiveness (criterion 3)? And can we
become a "class for itself" (criterion 2)?

## Women as a Revolutionary Class

The theoretical framework I have advanced here allows individuals
to be members of overlapping classes: family class, sex class, race
class,[11] and individual economic class. We need to know what class an
individual will be likely to identify with if she or he is a member of
several classes whose interests contradict each other. Are there laws
of motion of advanced capitalist patriarchal social formations that can
indicate where key contradictions will develop that allow the political
importance of membership in one class to supersede that of membership
in another class?

The task is to show that women are unlike Marx's characterization
of peasants and like his characterization of the working class. Women
have to be able to identify with sex class over family class, to be aware
of ourselves as a historically cohesive group, with a common culture
and common interests by virtue of our position in the sexual division
of labor in the family and in society. We need evidence of the existence

of different men's and women's cultures, as well as some understanding of how growing contradictions between sex class and family class identification for women tend to push women to identify with the first.

There is certainly evidence of separate men's and women's cultures that are more distinctive the more patriarchal the society.[12] Historically, however, there are few occasions in which sex class bonding has taken precedence to family class bonding, and these exceptions have often occurred, as in the first wave women's movement in the nineteenth-century United States, when family class positions as well as gender roles were in a state of transition because of changes in the mode of material economic production (Rossi, 1974b). That movement failed to sustain the connection between middle-class and working-class women, or between northern white and southern black women because the family class identification of the middle-class women (primarily petit bourgeois and wealthy farmers) prevented them from challenging either the economic or the racial class structure of American racist capitalism (Davis, 1981; Kraditor, 1965).

The situation is changing, however, in advanced capitalist societies. There are increasing contradictions between the social relations of capitalist production and the social relations of patriarchal sex/affective production in the family. The economic material conditions for these developments include: (1) the existence of wage-labor jobs for women that pay a subsistence wage, (2) the existence of state welfare that will support women and children without a husband, coupled with (3) the availability of mass-produced contraceptives that allow women more control over their fertility, and (4) inflationary pressures on family income, which cause women to seek part- or full-time wage work to supplement their husband's income.

What results from these conditions is an increasingly high rate of instability in patriarchal nuclear families: more divorce, fewer communal moral sanctions about "keeping the family together for the children," and more of an emphasis on the individual happiness of each partner. U.S. individualism, which always encouraged men to "do their own thing," is now increasingly an acceptable value system for women unhappy in marriage. This shift in morality parallels the change in material conditions that allow for the possibility that women can support themselves outside of the patriarchal family. Inequalities in capitalist patriarchal sex/affective production have historically been maintained because most women have not had many viable alternatives outside the nuclear family except prostitution. But the increasing number of state sector, clerical, and service jobs defined as "women's work" has now provided women with such options. Even those women who are not seeking to stay single or to break out of unhappy marriages can become caught up in the contradiction between the wage-labor job they take to increase their family's income and the strain that subsequently occurs in family relations because of the increase in the unequal sexual division of labor this causes. (Is the husband now going to shoulder more housework? Are the kids? How will all of them deal with less attention from wife and mom?)

It is not only the new available options for work outside the family that are relevant to women's changing position. The fact is that with the increased instability of nuclear families, women can no longer count on being maintained in families as non-wage-earning housewives and thus achieve the old "wife-mother" gender ideal.[13] This makes it more likely that women will relate to sex class rather than family class as their prime source of identity. As wageworkers women are thrown into proximity with other women not in their family. Because of sexual segregation of the work force into men's and women's jobs, women can identify with other women and make sex class identification primary.

Another reason that women are forced to rely more on their sex class identity than on their family class identity these days is that many women have to face the likelihood that they will lose their family class. Most wage-labor possibilities for women are working-class jobs. If a woman remains single, she must either take a working-class job or be "poor" (e.g., go on welfare, an option open primarily to single mothers). If a woman marries, she will likely be divorced at least once in her lifetime, in which case she faces the same possibilities. Many single and divorced women whose family class was professional-managerial are now members of the working class, as defined by their individual economic class (Sidel, 1986); and increasing numbers of women whose original family class was working class have moved downward to the poor (on welfare).[14]

Alimony and child support do not cushion women from these hazards of being a woman in U.S. society today. Only 14 percent of divorced women in the United States in 1976 were even awarded alimony by the courts, and only half that number collected it regularly. As for child support, a full half of the men ordered to pay child support are paying "practically nothing," and 90 percent of women receiving child support do not receive it regularly (Women's Agenda, 1976b). "No-fault" divorce legislation has not improved matters, either. A recent study of the effects of the California no-fault legislation discovered that women's incomes dropped 45 percent, while men's increased 73 percent as the result of divorce (Weitzman, 1985). Furthermore, a homemaker is not entitled to social security benefits if her marriage lasted less than twenty years when divorced, so she has no prospects of a pension to support her in old age. A middle-aged divorcee is often thrown on the streets after years of homemaking with no marketable skills and not the energy or sense of self to start from the beginning to make a new life for herself.

Not only can women not count on wife and motherhood as a life concentration that will allow for a secure economic future, but they cannot count on an easy way to care for their children. There is a contradiction between capitalist production demands and the existing patriarchal sex/affective production system for handling childcare. Inflation requires many women to supplement the husband's income by wage labor, yet there is no available childcare for children under six. In 1976 wage-working mothers had 27.6 million children under six (public school age), yet there were only 1 million licensed daycare slots for these children (Women's Agenda, 1976a). Sadly, after eleven years the situation had not improved by 1987. Both single and married working mothers thus can identify around the sex class issue of childcare.

I have given reasons to support the belief that women constitute a sex class that is developing historical cohesiveness that cuts across family and race class lines because of contradictions in the social relations of material and sex/affective production. But is this enough to make women a revolutionary class?

Yes! Because women are a pivotal class in terms of the work we perform in reproducing both capitalist and patriarchal relations of production. Women are the "culture-bearers" of family class *and* sex class values. We teach children expectations and goals, train them in rules of obedience to authority (acting as their first and most important role models in this area), and, in general, as the major childrearers, do essential work in child socialization necessary to continuing capitalist and patriarchal culture. Second, men depend on women for the reproduction of their labor power by continued women's work in domestic maintenance, nurturance, and sexuality.

Women as a sex class, then, do have potential disruptive power in the interconnected systems of capitalist and patriarchal sex/affective production. If women refuse to do their work as presently organized, neither capitalism nor patriarchy could continue to function.

Though women are a sex class that cuts across family, individual economic, and race classes, most women (all but those in the capitalist class) are a potentially revolutionary class because we have no objective interests as a sex class in maintaining the present system. Thus when women organize with other women in sex class identification, we can use the pivotal power gained by the importance of our social function in reproducing capitalist patriarchy to challenge the continuance of the patriarchal family and to raise the progressive aspects involved in family class identification for members of the professional-managerial class, working class, or poor. The fact that women as a sex class cut across the divisions of professional-managerial, working class, and poor, as well as across race class, can be a key to organizing progressive class alliances between these groups. There are some indications that the increasing consciousness of economic class and race issues[15] has allowed the women's movement to correct some of its earlier middle-class approach, for example, broadening such demands as the right to abortion and birth control to include opposition to forced sterilization and demands for state and federal funds for abortion. Developing working women's unions is another way to connect feminism with working-class women (Nine to Five in Boston, CLUW, WAGE in California).

## Conclusion

I have argued that women are a potentially revolutionary class. But we are not the only one. The working class is potentially revolutionary, as are minority races and elements of the professional-managerial class. Indeed, because of the complicated objective contradictions between the professional-managerial and working classes, and among sex class, family class, race class, and individual economic class, a socialist and feminist revolution is not possible in this country without class alliances of progressive people who identify the trisystem social formation of capitalism, patriarchy, *and* racism as the enemy. It stands to reason that different people will take different issues as their primary focus for organizing, some identifying working class, some women's issues, some racism, and some joint professional-managerial and working-class issues. It is unclear at this point what kind of structure—coalitions, a party, grassroots organizations, caucuses—is needed to produce the ideal alliance. The practical implication of this essay is that only an analysis that takes into account objective contradictions between classes in the United States today and the diverse class positions occupied by women and men can provide us with the understanding necessary to engage in the kind of practice that will teach us how and who to organize in the fight against racism, capitalism, and patriarchy.

## Notes

This chapter was previously published in Roger Gottlieb, ed., *An Anthology of Western Marxism*. New York: Oxford University Press, 1989. Copyright © 1989 by Ann Ferguson. Published by permission of the copyright holder and publisher.

1. My theory has developed with the aid of numerous discussions with members of the former Marxist Activist Philosophers group (MAP), now the Socialist-Feminist Philosophers Association (SOFPHIA), as well as Sam Bowles and Nancy Folbre. I wish to thank them for all their substantial help, even when they did not agree with me! For more development of my theory, see Ferguson, 1984a, 1986b, 1987, and 1989.

2. According to Bowles and Gintis (1977), different rates of exploitation can be assigned to different types of labor within the wage-labor force. Once we can say some workers *exploit* others, we can argue either that these sectors of the working class occupy class-contradictory positions (Wright, 1978), different classes (Ehrenreich and Ehrenreich, 1979; Poulantzas, 1975), or more than one class at a time including sex class and race class. The latter is my position.

3. The failure of working classes in Western capitalist countries to become revolutionary classes seems to undermine this prediction, leading Lukács to develop the concept of "false consciousness" (Lukács, 1968) and Gramsci the notion of the cultural "hegemony" (i.e., pervasiveness and power) of values and ideas defending the status quo and hence the interest of the capitalist class (Gramsci, 1971).

4. The classic emphasis on the importance of class culture in the formation of a class is E. P. Thompson's *The Making of the English Working Class* (1966).

5. Gorz (1967) argues that technicians and professionals are a key strata of the new working class precisely because their autonomous work conditions create an expectation that they should make all decisions controlling their work process. This expectation is increasingly in conflict with the interests of the capitalist class to control production arbitrarily for profit considerations.

6. This definition has an important caveat: Technically it should include the restriction that those who perform the male role have more power than those who perform the female role *only if* all other social factors are equal, viz., provided the "male" actors involved are not from individual economic or family classes (or oppressed race or ethnic groups) that are subordinate to those of the "female" actors.

7. One of the important aspects of gender roles is the fact that they are *socially,* not biologically, defined. Although it is almost always men who occupy the male role and women the female role, this is not always so: There are societies like the Mohave Indians in which homosexuals are accepted as male or female regardless of biological sex, depending only on the gender role they decide to play.

8. The universal sexual division of labor, and societies with communal modes of production in which the sexual division of labor nonetheless gives men more power than women, suggests that Engels's historical theory of the origins of patriarchy (that the oppression of women occurs because of the need of men to control heirs and amass private property) is mistaken (Engels, 1972). A counterhypothesis is offered by Lévi-Strauss, who argues that women are the first property, traded to cement bonds between tribes before the development of other types of private property and economic classes (Lévi-

Strauss, 1969). Gerda Lerner (1986) adds to this hypothesis the view that women are the first slaves, more valuable than male slaves because of their reproductive capacity (see also Meillassoux, 1981) and their closer bonds to their offspring, which make them easier to discipline and retain.

Another origin thesis compatible with Lévi-Strauss, Lerner, and Meillassoux is that societies developed matriarchal, egalitarian, or patriarchal kinship arrangements fairly haphazardly through the period of human prehistory when tribes were isolated from each other. When societies began to overlap, however, and to compete for hunting areas and land, those that were organized patriarchally were able to overcome matriarchal and egalitarian societies, and to impose their form of male-female patterns on those conquered.

Patriarchal forms of organizing society have two advantages, in survival terms, when they compete with nonpatriarchal societies: (1) They can create very efficient armies; (2) They can generate a high population rate to replace fallen soldiers and/or to provide laborers for production. We can find a direct correlation between high birthrate and high degree of male control over women in historical societies, which suggests that when women have the power to determine their own pregnancies, they tend to keep the birthrate low. If we extrapolate this information to prehistoric societies, we can surmise that many egalitarian or matriarchal societies were not able to compete with militaristic, high-population-producing patriarchal societies. (I owe this line of thought to Nancy Folbre.)

9. It should be noted that this characterization excludes most capitalist-class families, for the male breadwinner is usually not working full time because of his unearned income from capital investments. Indeed, male-female relations are sufficiently different that they have no material base for patriarchy. Neither men nor women have to work: They can hire nannies for the children and maintain separate houses for their lovers, so it seems false that women in the capitalist class should be thought of as part of an exploited sex class. Divorced women from this class never lose their family class status because of alimony and child support, income from trust funds, and so on. The men, on the other hand, are still members of the exploiter sex class, for their relation to the material means of reproduction allows them the power to exploit women from subordinate family and economic class positions.

10. What evidence is there for the view that men exploit women in sex/affective production? There is clear evidence that women spend more time on housework than men do on wage labor. The figure given by the Chase Manhattan Bank survey is that a full-time housewife puts in an average 99.6 hours of housework a week (Girard, 1968). We also know that the inequality in relation to hours of work a week put in by husband and wife persists even when the wife is working in wage labor as well, for in that situation, studies have shown that the wife still puts in roughly forty-four hours of housework a week in addition to her wage work, while the husband only puts in eleven hours of work in addition to his wage work (Ryan, 1975).

Because family production is not commodity production, there is no exact quantitative way to measure and compare the values of goods produced for use. Nor does it make sense to speak of the man "building up capital" with his human goods. Nonetheless, we can approximate quantitative measurements of the inequalities involved in the exchange by comparing the market commodity costs of the equivalent amounts of sexuality, childcare, maintenance, and nurturance done by men and women. For an economic model of this, see Nancy Folbre (1982).

11. The concept of race class needs to be further developed. Though the sexual division of labor in the family tends to ensure that women's sex class identity exists across family and economic class lines, the corresponding social divisions of race are not quite as hard and fast. Though there is a racial division of wage labor, the black and other minority petit bourgeois and professionals have escaped that division. And though the neighborhood segregation of many minority middle-class individuals tends to be similar to that of black and minority working class ghettos, integrated neighborhoods also break down that cultural identification. Some have taken this diffusion of the racial distinctions in productive relations to indicate the declining significance of race in the United States today (Wilson, 1978). Others have strongly disputed this (Marable, 1981). My own view is that race class is still a meaningful concept, in part because the family class of most middle- and even upper-class black and minority people was working class. Hence racial identity resulting from racial labor and community segregation was a part of their childhood identity.

12. By "culture," I mean a very broad concept that includes accepted patterns of acting, ways of treating each other, values, aesthetic and expressive forms, preferences for friendships, and so forth. The evidence presented by conservative writers such as Tiger (1969) about male bonding supports the idea that men act as a sex class, and there is also evidence that women bond (Leis, 1974), although in strongly patriarchal societies this tends to be restricted to female kin and bound up with the family.

The recent discussion in the U.S. women's movement on the problem of differences between women related to racism, classism, heterosexual orientation, and cultural ethnicity has raised a serious theoretical question about the early radical feminist claims of a universal women's culture, which cuts across race, class, and cultural differences (see Burris, 1973; Leghorn and Parker, 1981). Although the universal claims of some feminist theorists should indeed be reined in (e.g., Young, 1984; Joseph and Lewis, 1981; Hooks, 1984), I would defend the view that women's sex/affective labor in the family in nurturing young children *does* create a minimal common cultural base for women from different cultures (e.g., see Justus, 1981, for an application of Chodorow's hypothesis to West Indian society).

13. For some U.S. subcultures, e.g., black Americans, this has long been true (see Degler, 1980).

14. Kollias (1975) has good distinctions between working class and poor.

15. See Myron and Bunch, 1975; Moraga and Anzaldua, 1981; Bulkin, Pratt, and Smith, 1984.

THREE

# Patriarchy, Sexual Identity, and the Sexual Revolution

Adrienne Rich's paper "Compulsory Heterosexuality and Lesbian Existence"[1] (Rich, 1980) suggests two important theses for further development by feminist thinkers. First, she maintains that compulsory heterosexuality is the central social structure perpetuating male domination. Second, she suggests a reconstruction of the concept *lesbian* in terms of a cross-cultural, transhistorical lesbian continuum which can capture women's ongoing resistance to patriarchal domination. Rich's paper is an insightful and significant contribution to the development of a radical feminist approach to patriarchy, human nature, and sexual identity. Her synthetic and creative approach is a necessary first step to further work on the concept of compulsory heterosexuality. Nonetheless, her position contains serious flaws from a socialist-feminist perspective. In this chapter I shall argue against her main theses while presenting a different, historically linked concept of lesbian identity.

Rich develops her insight on the concept *lesbian* from de Beauvoir's classic treatment of lesbianism in *The Second Sex,* where lesbianism is seen as a deliberate refusal to submit to the coercive force of heterosexual ideology, a refusal which acts as an underground feminist resistance to patriarchy. From this base Rich constructs a lesbian feminist approach to lesbian history. As she writes elsewhere: "I feel that the search for lesbian history needs to be understood *politically,* not simply as the search for exceptional women who were lesbians, but as the search for power, for nascent undefined feminism, for the ways that women-loving women have been nay-sayers to male possession and control of women" (Schwartz, 1979, p. 6).

To use such an approach as an aid to discover "nascent undefined feminism" in any historical period, the feminist historian has to know what she is looking for. We need, in other words, a clear understanding of what is involved in the concept *lesbian* so as to be able to identify such women. Rich introduces the concepts *lesbian identity* and *lesbian continuum* as substitutes for the limited and clinical sense of "lesbian" commonly used. Her new concepts imply that genital sexual relations or sexual attractions between women are neither necessary nor sufficient conditions for someone to be thought a lesbian in the full sense of the term. If we were to present Rich's definition of lesbian identity it would therefore be somewhat as follows:

1. *Lesbian identity* (Rich) is the sense of self of a woman bonded primarily to women who is sexually and emotionally independent of men.

Her concept of lesbian continuum describes a wide range of "woman-identified experience; not simply the fact that a woman has had or consciously desired genital sexual experience with another woman." Instead we should "expand it to embrace many more forms of primary intensity between and among women, including the sharing of a rich inner life, the bonding against male tyranny, the giving and receiving of practical and political support; if we can also hear in it such associations as *marriage resistance* . . . we begin to grasp breadths of female history and psychology which have lain out of reach as a consequence of limited, mostly clinical definitions of 'lesbianism' " (Rich, 1980, pp. 648–649).

Rich, in short, conceives of lesbian identity as a transhistorical phenomenon, while I maintain, to the contrary, that the development of a distinctive homosexual (and specifically lesbian) identity is a historical phenomenon, not applicable to all societies and all periods of history. Her idea that the degree to which a woman is sexually and emotionally independent of men while bonding with women measures resistance to patriarchy oversimplifies and romanticizes the notion of such resistance without really defining the conditions that make for successful resistance rather than mere victimization. Her model does not allow us to understand the collective and social nature of a lesbian identity as opposed to lesbian practices or behaviors. Although I agree with Rich's insight (p. 650) that some of the clinical definitions of lesbian tend to create ways of viewing women's lives in which "female friendships and comradeship have been set apart from the erotic: thus limiting the erotic itself," I think her view undervalues the important historical development of an explicit lesbian identity connected to genital sexuality. My own view is that the development of such an identity, and with it the development of a sexuality valued and accepted in a community of peers, extended women's life options and degree of independence from men. I argue that the concept of lesbian identity as distinct from lesbian practices arose in advanced capitalist countries in Western Europe and the United States in the late nineteenth and early twentieth centuries from the conjunction of two forces. In part it was an ideological concept created by the sexologists who framed a changing patriarchal ideology of sexuality and the family; in part it was chosen by independent women and feminists who formed their own urban subcultures as an escape from the new, mystified form of patriarchal dominance that developed in the late 1920s: the companionate nuclear family (cf. Foucault, 1978; Weeks, 1979; McIntosh, 1968; and Simons, 1979).

## Defining "Lesbian"

Radicalesbians were the first lesbian-feminist theorists to suggest a reconstruction of the concept *lesbian* (Radicalesbians, 1970). Their goal was not merely to locate some central characteristic of lesbianism but also to find a way to eliminate the standard, pejorative connotation of the term. They wanted, that is, to rid the term of the heterosexist implications that lesbians are deviant, sick, unhealthy beings—a task important not merely as a defense of the lesbian community but of the feminist community and, indeed, of all women. The problem is that Radicalesbians as well as Rich do not clearly distinguish between three different goals of definitional strategy: first, valorizing the concept *lesbian;* second, giving a sociopolitical definition of the contemporary lesbian community; and finally, reconceptualizing history from a lesbian and feminist perspective. These goals are conceptually distinct and may not be achievable by one concept, namely, the lesbian continuum.

In the remainder of this section I will criticize the definitions of lesbian that have been offered in the literature and in common usage; I will argue that none succeeds completely in achieving any one of these tasks. (In fact, the truth may be that the first task cannot be accomplished at all in the opinion of those espousing values of the dominant culture.) In subsequent sections I will give my own suggestion for a sociopolitical definition of the contemporary lesbian community and some thoughts about transhistorical feminist concepts.

What then are some proposed definitions of the concept *lesbian?* First, let us consider the meaning the concept might have in 1981 for an average lay person not deeply engaged in gay, lesbian, or feminist politics:

2. *Lesbian* (ordinary definition) is a woman who has sexual
   attractions toward and relationships with other women.

One problem with the use of definition 2 as the instrument for delineating members of the contemporary lesbian community (the second goal) is that its meaning does not exclude practicing bisexual women. In fact, many commonsense usages of the term *lesbian* do not make the lesbian/bisexual distinction. Many women who have loved men and had sexual relationships with them come later to have sexual relationships with women and to think of themselves as lesbians without bothering to consider the metaphysical significance of the distinction between being a bisexual who loves a woman and a lesbian who loves a woman. What does this ambiguity in the application of the concept *lesbian* suggest about the usefulness of definition 2?

One thing it suggests is that homosexual practices by themselves are not sufficient or definitive constituents of a homosexual identity. A certain kind of political context is required. Therefore, when considering sexual identity, we should be wary of attempts to make oversimplified cross-cultural parallels. Most known societies have had some form of legitimate, or at least expected, homosexual practices in spite of the widespread persistence of culturally enforced heterosexuality; but from this we cannot conclude that individuals within those societies had homosexual identities in our modern understanding of the concept. Thus, among the Mohave Indians, those of either sex who so wished could choose to become socially a member of the opposite sex. The "woman" male might simulate pregnancy and menstruation, and the "man" female play the father role to her chosen partner's child by a biological male. Nonetheless the society distinguished between the two partners in such a homosexual pair. The social but nonbiological male or female was deviant, while the social and biological males and females were unfortunate but normal members of society. This distinction is not present today in society's concept of homosexual identity that would equally stigmatize as deviant both partners in a sexual relationship between two people of the same sex.

We could try to correct definition 2 while still seeking some ahistorical descriptive component of lesbian and say that:

3. *Lesbian* is a woman who is sexual exclusively in relation to women.

This definition certainly captures one important use of the concept *lesbian* in contemporary lesbian politics, in that it describes identified members of the lesbian subculture in such a way as to exclude women who engage in bisexual practices. But it also cuts from lesbian history many women like Sappho, Vita Sackville-West, and Eleanor Roosevelt, whom most lesbian feminists would like to include. Yet should a woman be accepted as a lesbian if she engaged in bisexual practices only if she is a historical personage and is not presently demanding to be included in the lesbian community? Surely, this is rather ad hoc!

The problem is that a strict distinction between lesbian/homosexual and bisexual rules out many commonly accepted historical situations involving homosexual practices, for example, those of Greece and Lesbos, because the aristocratic men and women involved (including Sappho) had same-sex love relations but also formed economic and procreative marriages with the opposite sex.

One further definitional strategy would eliminate genital sexual practices as relevant to the concept *lesbian*, thus at once avoiding the standard, pejorative connotations of the term and extending its meaning to include celibate women who are otherwise excluded by definition 3 from the lesbian sisterhood (cf. Yarborough, 1979). It is the trivializing of lesbian relations through emphasis on genital practice, many feel, that continues to stigmatize lesbianism. Instead, we should substitute traits valued highly, at least by the intended audience of feminists, and thus cleanse the concept of its negative implications.

This is the definitional strategy suggested by Blanche Weisen Cook from which Rich, Nancy Sahli (1979), and other recent writers take their cues. The resulting definition is based on Cook's quoted words but with a clause added on the possibility of sexual love between women as a challenge to people's negative feelings about such love:

4. *Lesbian* (Cook) is ". . . a woman who loves women, who chooses women to nurture and support and to create a living environment in which to work creatively and independently" (Cook, 1977), whether or not her relations with these women are sexual.

My main criticism of definition 4 is a political one. This extension and reconstruction of the term *lesbian* would seem to eliminate women like Virginia Woolf, Gertrude Stein, and so on—in fact, all women who were sexually attracted to women but who worked with men or in a circle of mixed male and female friends such as the Bloomsbury group. When juxtaposed to Rich's idea of a lesbian continuum as an indicator of resistance to patriarchy, this definition suggests that female couples like Jane Addams and Mary Rozet Smith or women like Lilian Wald whose community of friends were almost entirely feminist are more important role models for lesbian feminists than women like Gertrude Stein or Bessie Smith.

This approach also leaves out the historical context in which women live. At certain historical periods, when there is no large or visible oppositional women's culture, women who show that they can challenge the sexual division of labor—that is, who work with and perform as well as men—are just as important for questioning the patriarchal ideology of inevitable sex roles, including compulsory heterosexuality, as are the woman-identified women described by Cook. At certain periods even women who pass for men—such as those adventurers Dona Catalina De Erauso, Anny Bonny, and Mary Read (cf. Myron and Bunch, 1974b)—are just as important as models of resistance to patriarchy as the celibate Emily Dickinson may have been in her time.

For these reasons I reject the political implication of radical feminist theory that there is some universal way to understand "true" as opposed to "false" acts of resistance to patriarchy. Consider that implication as expressed in this quote from Rich's interview in *Frontiers:* "We need also to research and analyze the lives of women who have been lesbians in the most limited sense of genital sexual activity while otherwise bonding with men. Because lesbianism in that limited sense has confused and blocked resistance and survival" (quoted in Schwartz, 1979, p. 6). I wonder, for instance, whether it is not racist or classist to urge Third World women to bond with white women in "Take Back the Night" marches, rather than with Third World men in protest against repressive racial violence toward minority men suspected of violence against white women. On the other hand, Emily Dickinson may have bonded with other women, but it is not clear to me that her life is not the sad case of a victim, rather than a successful resister, of patriarchy. Feminists mindful of the different forms of patriarchal hierarchy, including discrimination based on class and race, ought to be very wary of positing universal formulas and strategies for ending it. Hence, I reject the notion of a lesbian continuum because it is too linear and ahistorical.

My final objection to the reconstruction of the concept *lesbian* suggested in definition 4 is that the definition ignores the important sense in which the sexual revolution of the late nineteenth and twentieth centuries was a positive advance for women. The ability to take one's own genital sexual needs seriously is a necessary component of an egalitarian love relation, whether it be with a man or a woman. Furthermore, I would argue that the possibility of a sexual relationship between women is an important challenge to patriarchy because it acts as an alternative to the patriarchal heterosexual couple, thus challenging the heterosexual ideology that women are dependent on men for romantic/sexual love and satisfaction. Therefore, any definitional strategy which seeks to drop the sexual component of "lesbian" in favor of an emotional commitment to, or preference for, women[2] tends to lead feminists to downplay the historical importance of the movement for sexual liberation. The negative results of that movement—by which sexual objectification replaces material objectification, the nineteenth-century concept of woman as a "womb on legs" becoming the twentieth-century one of a "vagina on legs"—do not justify dismissal of the real advances that were made for women, not the least being the possibility of a lesbian identity in the sexual sense of the term.[3]

I conclude that none of the definitions given above succeeds in accomplishing the tasks which those interested in lesbian history have put forward: first, freeing the concept *lesbian* from narrow clinical uses and negative emotive connotations; second, aiding the development of feminist categories for drawing clear lines among contemporary sexual identities; and finally, illuminating women's history by developing trans-historical categories that give us a better understanding of women's historical resistance to patriarchal domination.

## An Alternative Approach: The New Lesbian Identity

### SOME METHODOLOGICAL CONSIDERATIONS

The major problem with definitions 1 through 4 is that they are ahistorical; that is, they all implicitly assume some universal way to define lesbianism across cultures, classes, and races. But this approach, as I hope I have shown, is bankrupt. Nonetheless, I think we can offer a historically specific definition of lesbian for advanced industrial societies that will meet the second goal listed above. But first we need to consider the prior social conditions necessary for one to be conscious of sexual orientation as part of one's personal identity.

Our contemporary sexual identities are predicated upon two conditions. First, and tautologically, a person cannot be said to have a sexual identity that is not self-conscious, that is, it is not meaningful to conjecture that someone is a lesbian who refuses to acknowledge herself as such. Taking on a lesbian identity is a self-conscious commitment or decision. Identity concepts are, thus, to be distinguished from social and biological categories which apply to persons simply because of their position in the social structure, for example, their economic class, their sex, or their racial classification. For this reason, labeling theorists make a distinction between primary and secondary deviance: One can engage in deviant acts (primary deviance) without labeling oneself a deviant, but acquiring a personal identity as a deviant (secondary deviance) requires a self-conscious acceptance of the label as applying to oneself.

A second condition for a self-conscious lesbian identity is that one live in a culture where the concept has relevance. For example, a person cannot have a black identity unless the concept of blackness exists in the person's cultural environment. (Various shades of brown all get termed "black" in North American culture but not in Caribbean cultures, partly because of the greater racism in our culture.) Connected to this is the idea, borrowed from Sartre, that a person cannot be anything unless others can identify her or him as such. So, just as a person cannot be self-conscious about being black unless there is a potentially self-conscious community of others prepared to accept the label for themselves, so a person cannot be said to have a sexual identity unless there is in his or her historical period and cultural environment a community of others who think of themselves as having the sexual identity in question. Thus, in a period of human history where the distinctions between heterosexual, bisexual, and homosexual identity are not present as cultural categories (namely, until the twentieth century), people cannot correctly be said to have been lesbian or bisexual, although they may be described as having been sexually deviant. This point is emphasized by Carroll Smith-Rosenberg in her classic treatment of the particularly passionate and emotionally consuming friendships of nineteenth-century middle-class women for other women (Smith-Rosenberg, 1975; Weeks, 1977).

The definition of lesbian that I suggest, one that conforms to the two methodological considerations above, is the following:

5. *Lesbian* is a woman who has sexual and erotic-emotional ties primarily with women or who sees herself as centrally involved with a community of self-identified lesbians whose sexual and erotic-emotional ties are primarily with women; and who is herself a self-identified lesbian.

My definition is a sociopolitical one; that is, it attempts to include in the term *lesbian* the contemporary sense of lesbianism as connected with a subcultural community, many members of which are opposed to defining themselves as dependent on or subordinate to men. It defines both bisexual and celibate women as lesbians as long as they identify themselves as such and have their primary emotional identification with a community of self-defined lesbians. Furthermore, for reasons I will outline shortly, there was no lesbian community in which to ground a sense of self before the twentieth century, a fact which distinguishes the male homosexual community from the lesbian community. Finally, it is arguable that not until this particular stage in the second wave of the women's movement and in the lesbian feminist movement has it been politically feasible to include self-defined lesbian bisexual women into the lesbian community.[4]

Many lesbian feminists may not agree with this inclusion. But it may be argued that to exclude lesbian bisexuals from the community on the grounds that "they give energy to men" is overly defensive at this point. After all, a strong women's community does not have to operate on a scarcity theory of nurturant energy! On feminist principles the criterion for membership in the community should be a woman's commitment to giving positive erotic-emotional energy to women. Whether women who give such energy to women can also give energy to individual men (friends, fathers, sons, lovers) is not the community's concern.

## THE HISTORICAL DEVELOPMENT OF
## THE SEXUAL IDENTITY *LESBIAN*

In considering some reasons why the cultural concept *lesbian* came to exist in the United States and Western Europe only in the early twentieth century, we must ask what particular preconditions underlay the development in the later nineteenth century of the concept of a homosexual type or personality. If we take a socialist-feminist perspective on preconditions for radical social change—the general assumption is (to paraphrase Marx) that people can change their personal/social identities but not under conditions of their own choosing—we can focus on three factors: material (economic), ideological, and motivational.

In other places I have developed the argument that the "material base" of patriarchy lies in male dominance in the family and extended kin networks (Ferguson, 1979, 1989a, and Chapter 2 of this book; Ferguson and Folbre, 1981). However brutal its economic exploitation, nineteenth-century industrial capitalism did have one positive aspect for women in that it eventually weakened the patriarchal power of fathers and sons and, thus, the life choices of women increased. This relative gain in freedom was not an instant effect of capitalism, of course; early wage labor for women gave most women too little money to survive on their own. Nonetheless, acquisition of an income gave women new options, for example, sharing boardinghouse rooms with other women; and eventually some work done by women drew a sufficient wage to allow for economic independence. Then, too, commercial capital's growth spurred the growth of urban areas, which in turn gave feminist and deviant women the possibility of escaping the confines of rigidly traditional, patriarchal farm communities for an independent, if often impoverished, life in the cities.

Yet as the patriarchal family's direct, personal control over women weakened, the less personal control of a growing class of male professionals (physicians, therapists, and social workers) over the physical and mental health of women grew in strength. At the same time, a growing percentage of women were being incorporated into sex-segregated wage labor for longer and longer periods. Ehrenreich and English argue that the shift from a patriarchal ideology based in the male-dominated family to a more diffuse masculinist ideology was in no sense a weakening of patriarchy, or male dominance, but simply represented a shift in power from fathers and husbands to male professionals and bosses.[5]

It is my view, on the contrary, that the weakening of the patriarchal family during this period created the material conditions needed for the growth of lesbianism as a self-conscious cultural choice for women— a choice that in turn helped to free them from an ideology that stressed their emotional and sexual dependence upon men. Accelerating the process were the studies in human sexuality made around the turn of the century by Freud, Ellis, Krafft-Ebing, and Hirschfield. The ideological shift in the understanding of human nature that their findings involved set the stage for a new permissiveness in sexual mores and the realization that both men and women have sexual drives. This change legitimated the demand of women to be equal sexual partners with men. It also suggested that women could add another dimension of joy to their already emotionally intense friendships with women. As it developed, the concept of a lesbian identity challenged the connection between women's sexuality and motherhood that had kept women's erotic energy either sublimated in love for children or frustrated because heterosexual privilege often kept women from giving priority to their relations with other women.

Noting the ideological changes that made possible the development of a lesbian identity leaves the deeper motivational questions unanswered. First, what lies behind the creation of a new dominant ideology, creating, in turn, a new way of viewing legitimate and illegitimate sexual behavior and changing the previous distinction between "natural" and "unnatural" sexuality to that between "normal" as opposed to "deviant" sexuality and sexual identity? Second, what motivation leads women to accept a deviant label and adopt a lesbian identity?

The answer to the first question is suggested by Michel Foucault's introduction to *The History of Sexuality*, vol. 1 (1978). The rising bourgeois class gradually creates a new ideology for itself that shifts the emphasis from control of social process through marriage alliance to the control of sexuality as a way of maintaining class hegemony. Jacques Donzelot (1979) documents how the developing category of sexual health and its obverse, sexual sickness (e.g., the hysterical woman, the psychotic child, the homosexual invert), allow for growing intervention in the family by therapists, social workers, and male professionals as mediators for the capitalist patriarchal welfare state. By providing a clear-cut, publicized line between permissible and illegitimate behavior, these categories enforce the social segregation of "deviants" from "normals," thus keeping the normals pure (and under control) (McIntosh, 1968).

One thing that Foucault and Donzelot as male leftists fail to emphasize is the way that the ideological reorganization they speak of serves not only the bourgeois class but also men reorganizing patriarchy. Christina Simons's important article (1979) documents the fact that self-styled progressive thinkers and humanists of the 1920s and 1930s who developed the ideal of the sexually equal "companionate marriage" did so in order to project their newly mystified form of the patriarchal family (in which the male is instrumental breadwinner and the female is the expressive, nurturant, but sexy mom-housewife) in order to protect young people from the lesbian/homosexual threat.

Foucault also fails to emphasize popular resistance to the ideas and forces of social domination. As Rich points out, women have always resisted patriarchy, but why did women choose the particular avenue of lesbianism in the face of intense social stigma attached to it? A general answer is found in the sociology of normal/deviant categories. Once a particular deviation is identified in popular discourse, those dissatisfied with the conventional options have the conscious possibility of pursuing the deviant alternative. We could then expect that among participants in the first-wave women's movements a growing resentment of male domination in the family and the economy may have led some women to turn from sexual relations with men to sexual relations with women.

There is some evidence that in both the United States and Western Europe the growth of lesbianism among middle- and upper-class women was as closely connected with the first wave of the women's movement as the growth of lesbian feminism is with the second wave of the movement. Marcus Hirschfield claimed that in Germany 10 percent of feminists were lesbian. In England, Stella Browne, the British pioneer in birth control and abortion rights, defended lesbianism publicly (Weeks, 1979). Upper-class women like Vita Sackville-West, Virginia Woolf, and Natalie Barney involved themselves in lesbian relationships. The fact that the lesbian subculture did not develop extensively until the 1930s in most countries, however, indicates how difficult it still was for most single women to be economically independent of men. With the rise of somewhat better wage-labor positions for women in the 1920s, 1930s, and onward, the gradual rise of an independent subculture of self-defined lesbians can be seen as a pocket of resistance to marriage. The second-wave women's movement in the 1960s and

1970s made possible a further extension of that subculture and a clearer definition of its counterpatriarchal, strongly feminist nature.

## HETEROSEXUAL IDEOLOGY AS A COERCIVE FORCE

Rich makes two basic assumptions in her defense of the lesbian continuum as a construct for understanding female resistance to patriarchy. First, she assumes that the institution of compulsory heterosexuality is the key mechanism underlying and perpetuating male dominance. Second, she implies that all heterosexual relations are coercive or compulsory relations. No arguments are given to support these crucial assumptions, an omission which I take as a fundamental flaw. While I agree that lesbian and male-male attractions are indeed suppressed cross-culturally and that the resulting institution of heterosexuality is coercive, I do not think it plausible to assume such suppression is sufficient by itself to perpetuate male dominance. It may be one of the mechanisms, but it surely is not the single or sufficient one. Others, such as the control of female biological reproduction, male control of state and political power, and economic systems involving discrimination based on class and race, seem analytically distinct from coercive heterosexuality, yet are causes which support and perpetuate male dominance.

Targeting heterosexuality as the key mechanism of male dominance romanticizes lesbianism and ignores the actual quality of individual lesbian or heterosexual women's lives. Calling women who resist patriarchy the lesbian continuum assumes not only that all lesbians have resisted patriarchy but that all true patriarchal resisters are lesbians or approach lesbianism. This ignores, on the one hand, the "old lesbian" subculture that contains many nonpolitical, co-opted, and economically comfortable lesbians. It also ignores the existence of some heterosexual couples in which women who are feminists maintain an equal relationship with men. Such women would deny that their involvements are coercive, or even that they are forced to put second their own needs, their self-respect, or their relationships with women.

Part of the problem is the concept of "compulsory heterosexuality." Sometimes Rich seems to imply that women who are essentially or naturally lesbians are coerced by the social mechanisms of the patriarchal family to "turn to the father," hence to men. But if a girl's original love for her mother is itself due to the social fact that women, and not men, mother, then neither lesbianism nor heterosexuality can be said to be women's natural (uncoerced) sexual preference. If humans are basically bisexual or transsexual at birth, it will not do to suggest that lesbianism is the more authentic sexual preference for feminists, and that heterosexual feminists who do not change their sexual preference are simply lying to themselves about their true sexuality.

The notion that heterosexuality is central to women's oppression is plausible only if one assumes that it is women's emotional dependence on men as lovers in conjunction with other mechanisms of male dominance (e.g., marriage, motherhood, women's economic dependence on men) which allows men to control women's bodies as instruments for their own purposes. But single mothers, black women, and economically independent women, for example, may in their heterosexual relations with men escape or avoid these other mechanisms.

Rich's emphasis on compulsory heterosexuality as the key mechanism of male domination implies that the quality of straight women's resistance must be questioned. But this ignores other equally important practices of resistance to male domination, for example, women's work networks and trade unions, and welfare mothers organizing against social service cutbacks. The (perhaps unintended) lesbian-separatist implications of her analysis are disturbing. If compulsory heterosexuality is the problem, why bother to make alliances with straight women from minority and working-class communities around issues relating to sex and race discrimination at the workplace, cutbacks in Medicaid abortions, the lack of daycare centers, cutbacks in food stamps, and questions about nuclear power and the arms race? Just stop sleeping with men, withdraw from heterosexual practices, and the whole system of male dominance will collapse on its own!

A socialist-feminist analysis of male dominance sees the systems that oppress women as more complex and difficult to dislodge than does the utopian and idealist simplicity of lesbian separatism. They are at least *dual* systems (Young, 1980), and more likely multiple systems, of dominance which at times support and at times contradict each other: capitalism, patriarchy, heterosexism, racism, imperialism. We need autonomous groups of resisters opposing each of these forms of dominance; but we also need alliances among ourselves. If feminism as a movement is truly revolutionary, it cannot give priority to one form of male domination (heterosexism) to the exclusion of others. One's sexual preference may indeed be a political act, but it is not necessarily the best, nor the paradigmatic, feminist political act. Naming the continuum of resistance to patriarchy the lesbian continuum has the political implication that it is.

To conclude, let me agree with Rich that some transhistorical concepts may be needed to stress the continuity of women's resistance to patriarchy. Nonetheless, the concepts we pick should not ignore either the political complexity of our present tasks as feminists nor our historically specific political consciousness as lesbians. Rich's argument, on the one hand that compulsory heterosexuality is the key mechanism of patriarchy, and on the other hand that the lesbian continuum is the key resistance to it, has both of these unfortunate consequences.

## Notes

This chapter is reprinted from *Signs* 7, vol. 7, no. 1 (Autumn 1981) by permission of the University of Chicago Press. Copyright © 1981 by The University of Chicago. All rights reserved.

1. An earlier version of this paper was read at a philosophy and feminism colloquium at the University of Cincinnati, November 15, 1980. I would like to acknowledge the formative aid of Francine Rainone in the ideas and revision of this paper, as well as the helpful comments made by Kim Christensen, Annette Kuhn, Jacquelyn Zita, and Kathy Pyne Addelson on earlier drafts.

2. Cf. Joyce Trebilcot's (1979) discussion of the related development of the concept of "woman-identified woman."

3. Historical and political reasons lead me to reject Annabel Faraday's suggestion that we should get beyond the theoretical task of defining lesbian to the more important task of researching male methods of theorizing and controlling women's sexuality. We do indeed need to do this, but understanding the historical development of a lesbian identity and of a lesbian community as a potential resistance to male control is one part of this broader task. See Annabel Faraday (1981).

4. Some responses to the recent vanguardism of political lesbianism in the women's movement have suggested that we avoid such labels as "heterosexual," "bisexual," and "lesbian feminist" and begin to frame a bisexual or pansexual politics. See Beatrix Campbell (1980). I agree that we need new ideas to get beyond existing labels, but it would be utopian to ignore the ongoing strength of heterosexism, which continues to stigmatize and deprive lesbians more than heterosexual women. We need, then, a clearly defined lesbian oppositional culture, a culture of resistance, but as feminists we need also to find ways to strengthen our women's community with other feminists as well as to recruit new members into the feminist community. One way to accomplish both these tasks in part is to accept the inclusive definition of lesbian I offer above.

5. See Ehrenreich and English (1979), Daly (1978), ch. 7. Other work that supports this perspective is Ewen (1976) and Hartmann (1981b).

FOUR

# On Conceiving Motherhood
# and Sexuality:
# A Feminist-Materialist Approach

## Analytic Categories

The cathexis between mother and daughter—essential, distorted,
misused—is the great unwritten story. Probably there is nothing in
human nature more resonant with charges than the flow of energy
between two biologically alike bodies, one of which has lain in
amniotic bliss inside the other, one of which has labored to give birth
to the other.
  The "childless woman" and the "mother" are a false polarity which
has served the institutions of both motherhood and heterosexuality.
. . . We are, none of us, "either" mothers or daughters; to our
amazement, confusion, and greater complexity, we are both.
                                    Adrienne Rich, *Of Woman Born*[1]


Every woman has had at least one mother, and the overwhelming
majority of women have had the experience of being mothered. Many
women, like me, are also mothers. Having been mothered and being
a mother give one some insights into the mothering relationship. But
by itself, the experience of mothering can tell us little about the
*conception* of motherhood prevalent in a society at a certain time, or
differences in the conception of motherhood that are prevalent in
different economic classes or different racial and ethnic groups.

To understand conceptions of motherhood and sexuality, their connections and interactions, the changes they undergo in different historical periods in a society, and the differences between conceptions
of motherhood and sexuality in different cultures, we require an
analytic framework of categories. As a feminist social theorist, I focus
on the connections between motherhood and sexuality because I wish

to develop a general paradigm of the cross-cultural persistence of male domination based on the two cross-cultural constants common to all or most women: (a) that we are or can become biological mothers and (b) that the vast majority of us were primarily "mothered" rather than "fathered," i.e., socially cared for in infancy and early childhood by mothers/women. These cross-cultural constants ensure that women's experience of parenting and sexuality will be different from men's. Does the sexual division of labor in parenting and the different consequences of sexuality for men and women also suggest a base for the persistence of male dominance cross-culturally?

To answer this question, which is actually a question of power, i.e., the relative power that the relations of parenting and sexuality give to men versus women, we must introduce an analytic framework of categories that does not attribute a falsely universalist and static quality to male dominance. The relations of motherhood and sexuality, and the relative power of men and women in these relations, vary not only in different societies but in different societies at different historical periods, and in the same society across class, ethnic, and race lines.

## A MULTISYSTEMS APPROACH TO DOMINATION RELATIONS

My approach to understanding motherhood and sexuality is a multisystems feminist-materialist (or socialist-feminist) approach. By "multisystem," I mean an approach that is not reductive, that is, one that does not attempt to reduce male domination to a function of capitalist or commodity production economic systems (classic Marxism), nor to reduce race and class domination to a function of patriarchy (classic radical feminism). Rather, I assume that much of human history can be understood only by conceiving societies in terms of interacting but semiautonomous systems of human domination, three important ones having been class, race/ethnic, and sex/gender. These domination systems may not always support each other, particularly in periods of rapid change or social crisis. One way to understand the social movements of a particular historical period, such as the black civil rights movement of the 1960s or the women's movement of the 1970s in the United States, is to conjecture that a dialectical undermining of one domination system by the historical development of another, e.g., race and sex domination undermined by capitalist development, has provoked a social crisis. A multisystems theory, unlike a reductivist approach, does not posit that social crises are automatically resolved by the development of a new social "equilibrium" that guarantees the same level of class, race, or male domination.

What distinguishes my particular multisystems socialist-feminist theory of male domination from others is the concept of "sex/affective production." The concept of sex/affective production develops Gayle Rubin's point (Rubin, 1975) that every society has a "sex/gender system" that arranges a sexual division of labor, organizes sexuality and kinship interactions, and teaches sex/gender. It also is connected to Habermas's insight (Habermas, 1979) that what is distinctive about humans as a species is the way human societies construct human nature through different types of family and kinship networks. My theory, unlike one tendency within classic Marxist theory, does not privilege the economic realm (the production of *things* to meet human material needs and the manner in which the social surplus gets appropriated) as the material base for all human domination relations. Rather, I conceptualize the production and reproduction of *people* in family and kinship networks as a production process that may take different *forms* or *modes*, depending on the historical relations among parenting, kinship, and sexual structures and economic modes of production. Just as Marxism postulates distinctive "logics" (structural rules) that are characteristic of different modes of class production, so I suggest that each mode of sex/affective production will have its own distinctive logic of exchange of the human services of sexuality, nurturance, and affection, and will therefore differently constitute the human nature of its special product: human children. Because I think that infancy and early childhood form a crucial period in the formation of gender identity and attendant masculine and feminine personality structure, I privilege family and kin networks as an important material base for sex/affective production. It does not follow, however, that sex/affective production is limited to family and kin networks. On the contrary, I argue that modes of sex/affective production specific to capitalist economic development create problematic and contradictory gender identities in both boys and girls in childhood, identities which then make subsequent experiences in peer interaction in schools and communities, and later in workplaces, very important in determining sexual preference, sexual practices, and the ultimate content of one's gender identity.

The separation between the public and the private, the realm of economic production and the realm of domestic life specific to capitalist society, should not lead us to the error of conceptualizing sex/affective production, or the production of people, as a process occurring in a place or realm different from that where the production of things takes place. The sexual division of wage labor, sexual harassment in the workplace, male decisionmaking and female obedience roles, and high-status male work versus low-status female work are all specific aspects of the capitalist production process which are its sex/affective production component. In the same way the power of the male wage earner versus the nonpaid housewife and class differences in women's ability to pay for childcare and thus obtain leisure time for themselves as mothers are specific examples of the capitalist aspect of sex/affective production. The production of things and the production of people thus interpenetrate. The point of conceptualizing them as separate production systems is that they have different logics, logics which must be understood historically and specifically if we are to understand possibilities for change and strategies of resistance to domination relations embedded in both sorts of production.

Before the specific types of sex/affective production are analyzed, the concepts involved and the underlying assumptions about affection, parenting, and sexuality need to be examined.

## THE CONCEPT OF SEX/AFFECTIVE PRODUCTION

The conceptual category of *sex/affective production* is a way of understanding the social organization of labor and the exchange of services that occurs between men and women in the production of children, affection, and sexuality. Every human society has its particular mode or modes of organizing and controlling sexuality, affectionate interactions (e.g., friendships, social bonding, alliances), and parenting relationships. Complex class and race/ethnic-divided societies like our own may have a number of different modes centered in different organizations of family households and kin networks.

Central to all previous modes of organization of this work and service has been a sexual division of labor in the performance of the tasks and the distribution of the services involved. The sexual division of labor in the production and exchange of these sex/affective services (sexuality, affection, parenting) is a central key to the social production of people as gendered, i.e., as having the consciousness of self as male or female. This consciousness is always relational (i.e., what is male is not-female, and what is female is not-male), thus connecting one to a social sex class which is expected to have certain ideal masculine or feminine characteristics. One of these ideal characteristics is, usually, a sexual attraction for the opposite sex.[2] It is important to note, however, that there is no automatic (merely a strong contingent) connection between gender identity and sexual identity (i.e., sexual preference): One is a deviant male if one is sexually attracted only to men, but one is still a male ( and similarly for females who are attracted to females).

In stratified class and caste societies, different economic classes and racial/ethnic groups may hold different sex/gender ideals, although when this happens the lower classes are usually categorized as inferior male and female types "by nature." Often, split categories stereotype the good and bad woman—e.g., the Madonna (Mother)/Whore—exemplifying the hegemony of dominant classes' ideals for men and women, which allows their members (but not those of subordinate classes) to fulfill those preferred ideals.

Many different modes of sex/affective production are male dominant (or patriarchal).[3] In general, they all have in common an unequal and exploitative production and exchange of sexuality, affection, and parenting between men and women; that is, women have less control over the process of production (e.g., control of human reproductive decisions) and the exchange of services; and men characteristically get more than they give in the exchange of these services. They differ in the specific sexual division of labor and the social mechanisms by which men dominate and exploit women, as well as in the female strategies of resistance, escape, and sabotage of male power in parenting, sexuality, and affectional bonding.[4]

In order to understand the "unity" of sex/affective production, we need to explore further its philosophical underpinnings. Why, for example, is it assumed that sexuality, affection, and parenting are intertwined in a way that the production of goods to meet material survival needs are not? What underlying theories of sexuality, affection, and production are assumed? What implications are there for the concepts of human agency, domination, and exploitation that are used in the classification of different modes of sex/affective production? Why link *sexuality* and *affection* in sex/affective production? The underlying assumption is that both sexuality and affection are *bodily* as well as *social* energies, and that they are each specific manifestations of a general type of physical/social energy we can call "sex/affective" energy.[5] We tend to think of affectional bonds as emotional rather than bodily and of sexual bonds as bodily rather than emotional or social. In fact, however, I would claim that this is a distortion that comes about because of Western dualistic thought patterns. It may be more helpful to conceive of sex/affective energy as a spectrum ranging from the affectional/spiritual/not-specifically-physical interactions, at one pole, to genital sexual exchanges that are physical but not specifically affectional, at the other. A second way to conceive of sex/affective energy is as presenting two different dimensions or aspects which can admit of degree: a dimension of *physical* involvement, attraction, and interconnection of a human being with (an)other human being(s) or objects symbolizing human beings, and a *social/emotional* dimension of involvement, attraction, and interdefinition of self with (an)other human being(s).

We need now to consider some of the insights and problems of the sex/affective production paradigm.

First, a thesis about human nature: Humans do not reproduce themselves (i.e., have children) merely as a means to guarantee that their material needs for physical survival will be met (e.g., that they will have children to care for them in old age). Rather, humans are a social species whose needs to connect to one another in some form of sexual and/or affectional interaction are as basic as their material needs as an animal species to produce a material livelihood. Heterosexual mating leads, intentionally or inadvertently, to human procreation, which leads to parenting. Thus, the sexuality and affection that heterosexual mates give each other requires the social development of parenting systems in which nurturance/affection, socialization, and physical maintenance of the young are organized. Since patriarchal parenting systems also organize adult sexuality (most often by compulsory heterosexuality in marriage arrangements which impose double-standard monogamy), an interaction exists between the type of sexual exchanges engaged in by adults and the nature, amount, and control of parenting work engaged in by each sex/gender.

A second thesis is that the position of sex/affective production systems as a base for male dominance is a feminist-*materialist* approach in two specific senses. First, we know that human babies require affection and nurturance in order to survive. Thus, mothering or caretaking that involves more than simply feeding and clothing is a material requirement for the reproduction of the human species. Second, human young, unlike other animal species, have bodily energies (e.g., affectional, sexual, nutritional) that are initially without specific objects. The fact that humans are without instincts with fixed goals requires a period of care and socialization of the young that make some system of parenting, and the organization of sexuality and affection around these tasks, a material necessity for the human species.

We need thus to widen the concept of production as socially necessary labor to satisfy basic human material needs that Marx and Engels introduced in *The German Ideology* to include not merely a transformation of nature to meet human needs, but also the production and reproduction of new life, i.e., the production and transformation of *people* via various historical parenting and sexual systems embedded in family and kin networks.[6]

Let me take a moment to contrast the concept of sex/affective production with other feminist revisions of classical Marxist categories. Some Marxist-feminists attempt to revise the classical Marxist emphasis on the primacy of the economic sphere in human social organization (particularly in systems where the production of things involves the creation and distribution of a social surplus). They argue that every economic system involves both production and reproduction, and therefore that modes of reproduction of a system (including the reproduction of labor power and thus modes of procreation) are just as important to the total operation of the system as the production of things. They argue either that we should reject the concept of the social primacy of the economic (the base/superstructure distinction), or that modes of reproduction in family and kin networks are just as much a part of the economic base of a social formation as is the production of things.

The problem with the concepts of modes of reproduction (Brown, 1981) and modes of procreation (McDonough and Harrison, 1978) is that either (a) they ambiguously mean both human biological and human social reproduction, or (b) they emphasize the production of children as the goal and aim of this form of social relations. Neither approach is satisfactory. The former case allows confusion with the Marxist categories of production/reproduction (Barrett, 1980), where the mode of social reproduction of an economic system can be said to occur simultaneously at every site of social relations—e.g., in the factory, state, and schools as well as in the family. This concept of social reproduction does not give us any nonfunctionalist way to conceive of, for example, the relationship between capitalism and patriarchy.

In the second alternative (modes of procreation), human biological reproduction and the regulation of fertility rates would be seen as the goal of these systems. Such an emphasis marginalizes the human incentives to experience the pleasures of sexuality not as reproductive instruments but as intrinsic energizers. We would also miss the ways that affectional and sexual same-sex relations, which develop for their own sake in sexual divisions of labor, are used as mechanisms both to cement (if dominant male) or to resist (if subordinate or deviant male or female) patriarchal sex/affective production processes (Hartmann, 1981b).

The sex/affective production paradigm is superior to these other approaches because conceiving of a semiautonomous system of the organization of sexuality, affection, and the production of children in family and kin networks can allow us to understand how patriarchal relations can persist (since embedded and reproduced in family and kin networks) through changes in modes of production of things (feudalism, capitalism, state socialism). It can conceptualize how changes in family structure due to capitalist development might weaken certain forms of patriarchal sex/affective production while allowing for the possibility that other adaptive forms are developing.

A serious philosophical problem that the concept of sex/affective production raises is how we can distinguish between childcare and sexual or nurturant activities that are work or *labor* and those that are *leisure* activities. Using the concept of production assumes one can empirically distinguish between labor (activity socially necessary to meet human material needs) and activity which may be work (not thought of as leisure by its agent) but not labor per se, and activity which is play. Childcare is an aspect of housework that mothers perform at home while caring for infants and small children, yet we know that the very idea that childcare and housework are separate work activities is a historical development caused by the separation of the home from economic production with the development of capitalist production. Ehrenreich and English (1975 and 1978) have documented how the combined effect of the domestic science movement, the development of the medical establishment, child development experts, and consumer capitalism in the early twentieth century expanded rather than reduced the tasks thought socially necessary in parenting work.

A parallel historical argument would challenge the view of some feminists that sexual exchanges between men and women in patriarchal societies involve work on the part of women that is not repaid, since the control and sexual satisfaction involved are not equal for both male and female partners. How can we make this argument if we accept recent historical arguments (Foucault, 1978; Weeks, 1979, 1981) that our very conception of sexuality, its exchange and deployment, as at the center of bodily and mental health, is a recent social construction of discourses developed by bourgeois sexologists and therapists? And if the conception of sexual health itself is historically relative, how can we defend the claim that there is an exchange of socially necessary labor in parenting, sexuality, and affection? Or the claim that patriarchal parenting and sexual systems allow men to control and exploit the productive process of parenting and sexual exchange by contributing less (labor or services) and receiving more (leisure, services, pleasures)?

Even if one admits that there are no ahistorical universal requirements for good parenting, sexuality, or friendship, it does not follow that there is no empirical and historical way to compare male and female inputs, rewards from, and control of these production processes. Marx's concept of socially necessary labor has a "historical and moral element" which in part depends on what has come to be accepted as a decent minimal standard of living, given the available resources and expectations of a society at a particular historical period. Similarly, women's expectations of acceptable sexual satisfaction have changed since the nineteenth century, in part because of the writings of sexologists and in part because of the second-wave women's movement.

The inequality of patriarchal forms of sexual exchange lies not simply in the fact that men characteristically experience more orgasms and sexual satisfaction than women, although this is certainly relevant and can be empirically measured. It is the aspect of domination, the fact that men usually control the nature of the interaction itself as the sexual initiators, that perpetuates the image of women as the sexual objects of men, and women's bodies as the instruments of men's pleasure. In such a situation it would seem that a woman has less agency in the sexual encounter, even though she may experience more orgasms than the man she relates to.

We will not really be able to measure the relative equality or inequality of sexual exchanges until we have a physical model of sexual satisfaction and sexual agency that allows us to make connections between certain bodily states such as body blocks, orgasms, complete orgiastic release (Reich, 1970), and the experience of sexual agency versus sexual passivity. But that we have no complete theory suggests merely the need for further empirical sexual research rather than a dead end for the sex/affective production paradigm. No matter how we ultimately measure equality in sexual exchange, we do have some intuitive criteria we can use in the meantime: For example, most would agree that any sexual exchange in which one partner but not the other enjoys orgasms regularly and in which the enjoying partner also controls the sexual process is an unequal exchange.

Finally, the question of one's power or control/agency in sexual and parenting exchanges cannot be separated from the economic, political/legal, and cultural constraints that may limit women's freedom of choice more than men's. Such constraints as economic dependence, legal restrictions on reproductive control, lack of strong female bonding networks that support sexual freedom for women or parental responsibilities for men, and physical violence by one's partner are all empirical factors that make women less free in parenting and sexuality than men. This shows the way in which sex/affective production systems are not autonomous from the economic mode of production, the nature of the state, etc.

In determining which parental interactions with children are labor and which are leisure, we can agree that this is historically relative to social (and perhaps class and ethnic) expectations of parents and still find a way to compare the equality or inequality of the exchange between women and men in parenting work. No matter how the line between parenting labor and leisure is culturally drawn, it remains clear that most mothers in patriarchal modes of sex/affective production do more direct and indirect parenting work than men in terms of total labor hours spent (where "indirect parenting work" would include wage earning as well as unpaid productive work which produces, or exchanges for, goods necessary to the physical maintenance of infants and children). Folbre (1982) is developing an economic model to compare the waged and nonwaged work (parenting and housework) in the family economy so as to develop a way to measure the relative exploitation of women versus men, and parents versus children. Delphy (1984) argues that the male-dominated family economy continues after divorce, since mothers are saddled with much more direct and indirect parenting work and few fathers provide much in child support funds. Thus, in this sense male exploitation of women who are mothers increases with divorce, which suggests that the rise of single-mother families should be seen not simply as a decline in husband-patriarchy, but rather as the rise of a new patriarchal sex/affective form, which we might call "single mother patriarchy" and which is connected to the shift from family-centered patriarchal forms to more impersonal forms of state patriarchy (Hooks, 1981; and see below).

A final question concerns the relativity versus universality of the connections between affection, sexuality, and parenting. The analytic categories of sex/affective production would seem to suggest a universal mate-self-child sex/affective triangle which has historically specific forms. Nevertheless, Ariès (1962) and Shorter (1975) argue that affectionate interactions among children, kin, and spouses is characteristic neither of peasant nor of aristocratic families in the medieval period. Rather, it develops as a part of the bourgeois sentimental family, which develops a new conception of childhood and an increased emphasis on affection.

I would agree that we need to conceptualize a different form of patriarchial sex/affective production for aristocratic and peasant families than for bourgeois families. The interpersonal dynamic among parents, children, and mates will obviously be different when affectionate connections are present, or absent, or not exclusive (as when children are cared for by wet nurses, nannies, or extended kin networks). It is obvious that sexual intercourse to produce heirs has a different dynamic than when the resulting children and sexual energy are valued for their own sake.

Despite the relativity of who performs nurturant/affectionate services to children, a caretaker must provide a minimal affection quotient for the child to survive. Thus, the procuring of someone to perform these services is a necessary part of sex/affective production even in aristocratic families. Furthermore, it may be argued that courtly love ideals for extramarital relationships among the medieval aristocracy, idealized homosexual love relationships among ancient Greek male aristocracy, and close same-sex bonding among peasants are evidence that affectionate interactions will come to be institutionalized in some form in human societies where they are lacking in parenting and marriage interactions.

## DOUBLE CONSCIOUSNESS AND THE SEX/AFFECTIVE TRIANGLE

In this section I will explore a mechanism for perpetuating male dominance through motherhood in specific modes of patriarchal sex/affective production, particularly nuclear family forms as they develop with the growth of capitalism and the breakdown of feudalism. I call these forms "bourgeois patriarchal family forms," where this is understood to include families in independent rural production (as in colonial America), working-class nuclearized families, and families of the bourgeois classes. These are the dominant family forms of the period of American history that I will consider later.

The family form involves a sex/affective triangle of father-mother-child(ren) that creates a structural contradiction of sex/affective interests for mothers but not fathers. This explains a psychological mechanism through which male dominance is internalized by women: the phenomenon of women's double consciousness. On the other hand, the structural triangle also sets the conditions for mothers' internal resistance to patriarchy and the progressive development of successively less strong patriarchal family forms in American history.

The structural situation is this: The sexual division of labor in childrearing in which women mother, i.e., perform primary infant and childcare, gives the mother a greater, because longer and more intense, affectionate relationship with the offspring. This situation tends to make her identify with the sex/affective interests of the child more than does the father.[7] In addition, the situation of childbirth and breastfeeding, plus the greater physical nurturance the mother gives the young child, arouses maternal erotic and sexual feelings toward the child that are repressed due to the weight of patriarchal incest taboo. Nonetheless, the persistence of these feelings creates a much stronger mother-child than father-child sex/affective bond (Weisskopf, 1980; Person, 1980; Rich, 1980).

The greater absorption of mothers than fathers in the sex/affective interests of children may not be only because of the psychological investment of time and energy in the child. Some feminists have argued that the metaphysical and psychological indeterminacy of the boundaries of one's body versus the child's in childbirth and breastfeeding gives mothers a special "epistemological standpoint" different from men's (Hartsock, 1983).[8]

The potential contradiction of the sex/affective triangle for the mother is highlighted by her involvement as well in the other leg of the mate-self-child sex/affective triangle. As the present and/or former mate of the father, she is also identified with his sex/affective interests. Thus the woman's, but not the man's, own sex/affective interests as a rational agent are bound up with promoting both a woman-mate bond and a woman-child bond. She is forced into the position of negotiator of the sexual and emotional jealousies (conflicts of sex/affective interests) between children and father.

What this imbalance in parenting work creates for mothers is a *double consciousness:* a consciousness of the potential conflict between their own interests as sexual agents/partners in a peer-mate relationship and their interests as mothers in a nonpeer mother-child relationship. Women's sex/affective energy is consequently more bound than men's into adjudicating actual and potential conflicts of interests in the sex/affective family triangle. The relatively greater absorption of energy this involves often occurs at the expense of their other needs. Consider, for example, the routine sacrifices undergone by women for children and mates: given up are leisure time, job-training possibilities, access to greater economic productive resources, political liaisons, and sexual liaisons with other mates.

The structural double consciousness created by the imbalance in parenting work between men and women explains how women internalize the oppression of male domination as long as they are engaged in such a patriarchal parenting process. Double consciousness creates a double or split self-image for women. On the one hand, most mothers have a positive image of themselves and positive gratification from their mothering work with children. On the other hand, most women have a negative self-image when father and child jealousy is a factor. Women feel both more responsible than men for adjudicating this conflict and more to blame when they do not succeed in negotiating it.

One implication of this sex/affective triangle in bourgeois patriarchal family forms is the possibility of father-daughter incest as a response by the father to the divided loyalty of the mother (Herman, 1982). Incest is a patriarchal tool of domination by the father which disrupts the strength of the mother-daughter bond by a possessive sexual relationship that forces the daughter's sex/affective involvement away from the mother. Incest occurs when fathers, jealous of the attention that mothers give to daughters and/or angry at the lack of sex/affective attention from mothers, sexualize their relations with their daughters. This turns the daughters into substitute mothers, turns daughters against mothers, and makes mothers feel themselves to be the guilty accomplices of their daughter's sexual abuse. Mothers, on the contrary, are more sensitive than fathers to the power imbalance between adults and children, and are often powerless themselves to escape from the father. Thus, mothers are more likely to refrain from sexual relations with their children, not only for the child's good and from guilt feelings about the father's needs, but also from a powerlessness to escape the oppressive economic, political, and psychological structure of the family household engaged in patriarchal sex/affective production.

We have already alluded to the difficulty of drawing the line between parenting labor and parenting leisure activities with children. For the mother this is due in part, again, to the phenomenon of double consciousness: After all, if cooking and serving a meal to husband and children increases the sex/affective energy available to everyone— mate, self, and children—how can one see it as *work*? Thus many women do not experience unequal sexual division of labor in parenting as exploitative. It is often only when one is forced to change one's social relations of parenting (by divorce, by stepparenting, by a change to lesbian parenting, etc.) that one experiences an alternative arrangement which allows for a higher level of sex/affective energy in both mating and mothering due to a more egalitarian organization of parenting work. In hindsight, one can then see the previous organization of sex/affective production as exploitative.

If the mother's absorption in both legs of the sex/affective triangle immerses her in a self-sacrificing negotiator role vis-à-vis the sex/ affective interests of father-mate and child(ren), we could expect to see in history various forms of female resistance to this self-sacrificing role. Women may be oppressed within patriarchal structures, but they are also always partial agents within these structures and, as such, can try to alter the power relations within the structure, often in favorable historical conditions thus altering the structure themselves. Some of the forms of historical resistance we might expect to find to bourgeois patriarchal family forms include the following: (a) Women could refuse marriage altogether (in the contemporary period, this includes the possibility of choosing a lesbian relationship); (b) women could marry yet resist childbearing; (c) women could favor one leg of the triangle (e.g., relation to child or relation to mate) at the expense of the other; or (d) women could emphasize outside kin and friendship networks with peers as a way of withholding energy, either to male mates or to the mother-child bond; (e) if economically viable, women could engage in serial monogamy and several marriages, which would tend to diminish loyalty to the mate bond and expand loyalty to the mother-child bond (the one that lasts).

I have argued in this section that unequal relations of childrearing create in bourgeois family forms a double consciousness in women due to their structural inequality in the mate-child-self sex/affective parenting triangle. This analysis I find superior to Chodorow's (1978b) neo-Freudian approach to understanding the way that the reproduction of mothering perpetuates male dominance. In the next section, I will provide a brief historical sketch of changes in patriarchal sex/affective production in American history which will indicate the sex/affective production paradigm's usefulness in explaining historical change in parenting patterns and ideologies.

## Historical Applications

I have maintained that a multisystems approach to analyzing male dominance is best; i.e., one that takes account of the economic *class* structure of a given historical period (the mode of economic production), the *racial/ethnic* dominance patterns of the period (what we could call the mode of community relations—Albert and Hahnel, 1978), and the *sex/gender* dominance patterns of the period (the mode of sex/affective production). To understand the relative strengths of each domination system, we will also have to consider other aspects of a society, such as the form of the state and its relation to the economy. The relationship between the three domination systems is dialectical or conflictual rather than functional: There is no automatic fit between different systems of dominance. Nonetheless, those on top in various domination systems will attempt to maintain their positions. Historical alliances will be created by various representative elements of dominant groups, alliances that during periods of social crisis or protracted change may be undermined or superseded. Ongoing developments in one mode of social organization may undermine social dominance patterns in another, and this will create an intersystemic social crisis. It is at these historical junctures that social change of appreciable dimensions is likely to occur. The structures of sex/affective production as they are reconstituted after a period of major social change will depend in large part on the consciousness and collective power of existing social movements of subordinate groups: women, minority racial and ethnic groups, and subordinate economic classes.

### PERIODS OF SEX/AFFECTIVE PRODUCTION
### IN AMERICAN HISTORY

Since colonial times, there have been three main periods of patriarchal sex/affective production in American history.[9] Each of these periods involves a different sort of patriarchal relationship among men, women, and children, and each of them has its different basic mechanisms for maintaining male dominance. In the colonial period, father patriarchy was reproduced by father's legal/economic control of inheritance through family property vested in sons, not daughters. In the romantic/Victorian period, husband patriarchy was reproduced by the institution of the "family wage," which was vested in husbands who were the family breadwinners. And in the present period of the consumer economy, public patriarchy has been reproduced through a number of mechanisms; these include the gender division of wage labor, laws restricting birth control and abortion, state welfare support of single mothers, the growth of the advertising industry and the manipulation of women's images (Ewen, 1976), as well as market mechanisms encouraging repressive desublimation (Marcuse, 1964) such as pornography, media violence against women, and sexual advertising, which promote the sexual objectification of women.

Let us consider each period in greater detail.

*Period I: Father Patriarchy.* White European settlers, primarily English religious Puritans, established a mode of agricultural production based in family households in the New England states that lasted from about 1620 to 1799. The mode of economic production was characterized by farm households producing primarily for use and not for market and was consolidated by force against existing native American economies which were hunting/gathering, nomadic societies. Dominance relations between men and women were perpetuated by father patriarchy, a combination of economic, political/legal, and childrearing structures in which the father owned property and dispensed it at will to his children, the land to sons and a lesser dowry to daughters. The father was the religious/moral head of the household. Children needed their fathers' permission to marry and were completely dependent on his largesse in inheritance.

The father in a Puritan household was not only the supreme authority in sex/affective production relations with wife and children; he was usually also master to indentured servants and young relatives who were apprenticed from adjacent family households. Thus, class relations were internal family household relations as well. Although a small artisan class grew with the rise of commercial capitalism and urban centers, which afforded an escape for men of the subsumed servant class from the family patriarchal domination of the rural family household, it was not possible for a woman, regardless of economic class, to have any economic independence or any escape from father patriarchy, unless she was a widow and could take over her husband's business, trade, or land.

The conception of motherhood in the Puritan era was derived from Old Testament beliefs that women were weaker in reason and more emotional and therefore in need of practical moral and intellectual control by men. This, in turn, was due to the conception of motherhood as a natural, nearly automatic consequence of women's bodies. Since bodies themselves had evil lusts, women were thought to be more innately subject to sin than men. The ideal standard of parenthood was the same for both sexes, and both men and women were conceived to be innately sexual beings as well as feeling beings. But since feelings uncontrolled by reason were suspect, maternal feeling itself was dangerous and without moral authority, and thus had to be subjected to father authority for appropriate correction. Women were often chastized for showing their offspring too much natural affection. Since children were thought to be sinful, depraved creatures in Calvinist ideology, which lacked a developmental theory of the human ego, there was little distinction between appropriate punishment for a child and for an adult. The key feature of the Puritan ideology of childrearing was to break the child's will as soon as possible to create a proper fear of those in authority, i.e., the hierarchy of patriarchs who controlled sinful desires and affections—individually in their homes and collectively as church/state elders (Stewart, 1981).

Some authors (Ryan, 1975) have argued that the Puritan emphasis on women as helpmates to men, the absence of an ideology of romantic love, and a more egalitarian sexual ideology that posited sexual drives in both men and women, were indications that women were more equal as sexual partners in the Puritan period than in the subsequent romantic era. It certainly is true that there was less of a sexual double standard in the Puritan period than subsequently: Men could be punished for raping wives or for fornication outside of marriage. Nonetheless, I think some authors overplay "egalitarian" implications of sexual practices in Puritan society (Mitchell, 1973): Sexual double standards still persisted with respect to adultery, and a woman who became pregnant by rape outside of marriage could still be flogged or fined.

Three distinctive features of Puritan sex/affective production indicate that women had *less* power over mothering than in subsequent periods. First, children were regularly sent at young ages (around seven) to live on relatives' farms. This was in part to counter the excessive affection which was thought to permeate natal families (Stewart, 1981). Thus, an intense mother-child bond was not only ideologically suspect but difficult to maintain because of physical distance. This meant that mothers not only had less control over the dispensation of nurturance and discipline than in subsequent periods but also less ability to "corner the market" on the positive satisfactions of an intense affectionate relationship with children.

Second, the pervasive presence of the father and his ideological hegemony over childrearing undermined an independent authority of mothers over children. Fathers, not mothers, seem to have been the major enforcers of the "breaking of the will" practices that were used on children particularly during the separation/individuation period around the age of two. (This shows that it is not simply shared childrearing which is necessary to overcome gender-differentiated personality development in childhood.)[10]

Third, Demos (1970) presents a fascinating sketch of Puritan weaning practices which suggests that mother-child identification was rudely severed by the abrupt weaning of the eighteen-month-old child at the moment of the birth of the next child. This abrupt separation, in connection with "breaking the will" practices to stifle the child's attempts at separation/autonomy, created an authoritarian (repressed but dependent) individual particularly subject to male-domination structures.

*Period II: Husband Patriarchy.* American society went through a period of rapid social change after the American Revolution and through the Jacksonian period. The shift from rural production to commercial capitalism, the beginning of industrial capitalism, and the expansion of slavery in the South occurred in the context of the creation of a new political entity, the national state of the United States. These changes also meant changes in the family, mothering, and sexuality.

A new ideology of motherhood and sexuality came into existence at this time in American history: the moral motherhood/cult of domesticity paradigm. In this ideology which, as we shall see, did not refer to all women, women were no longer conceived as inferior helpmates to men. Rather, women were "moral mothers." The domestic world was now conceptualized as a separate sphere and motherhood as a chosen vocation, one that required specialized skills (moral perception, intuitive and emotional connection). Men could not achieve these skills, for they were constrained to act within the public sphere of the capitalist marketplace, which required that they develop the skills necessary to survive there: egoism, individualism, cunning, and immorality. Instead of *natural* (sinful) mothers who subjected themselves to the superior moral authority of men, women had become the *chosen* mothers, the moral and spiritual superiors of men in their protected sphere of the home.

My explanation of this shift in the practices and ideology of parenting differs from those theories (Zaretsky, 1976; Benston, 1969; Douglas, 1977) that suggest that moral motherhood ideology was a sentimental response that sought to hide from consciousness the actual devaluation of women's role with the developing split between home and commodity production (i.e., the public/private split). What is wrong with the sentimentalist hypothesis is the assumption that middle-class women were the *victims* of an ideology meant to hide their parasitical dependence on men. Rather, I would argue from the multisystems approach that the reformation of parenting and sexual practices as reflected by the moral motherhood ideology was the result of a dialectical struggle among middle-class men, women, and ministers/writers, i.e., social groups whose roles were in transition. The evangelical ministers involved in the Great Awakening spiritual revival movement made common cause with middle-class women, who formed the majority of their congregations, to elevate women's spiritual status in the church. Thus, middle-class women were partial agents in a reformation of bourgeois patriarchal sex/affective production in order to gain greater power as mothers than they had in the Puritan period, while they nonetheless preserved some aspects of men's power in the family as husbands.

Daniel Scott Smith argues for this perspective in an important paper in which he dubs as "domestic feminism" the underground social movement by women in the nineteenth century, in which women increased female control over reproductive sexuality and increased their autonomous control over childrearing (Smith, 1974). He dubs as "maritarchalism" the weaker form of patriarchy that developed during this period, in which men as fathers lost power but women were still controlled by men's economic and legal power as husbands.

Smith's evidence that women essentially gained rather than lost power in nineteenth-century maritarchal sex/affective production rests primarily on the declining fertility rate. From the sex/affective production paradigm, we can further develop Smith's insight that women, by reducing fertility, increased their control over mothering work. Reduced fertility not only means less risk of maternal mortality but the possibility of increased attention to each child. Thus, the emphasis on new theories of childhood as a distinctive stage of human life and the conceptualization of childhood through the notion of developmental stages suggest the need for an increased intuitive-affective understanding of each child (possible for women but not for men, since the latter are absent from the home in commodity production). The stage is set for the theory of childrearing that emphasizes the internalization of values through identification and guilt, rather than through the imposition of values by external force (shame). Each of the elements of the romantic view of childhood can be seen as legitimizing the priority of the mother-child bond *over* the father-child bond. In terms of the father-mother-child parenting triangle, sex/affective energy between mother and child is increased at the expense of sex/affective energy between father and mother, thus giving women increased bargaining power in sex/affective power relationships.[11]

The connection of moral motherhood with asexuality is important for understanding nineteenth-century sex/affective ideology. How can conceptualizing good women as asexual (versus men who are naturally lustful) and bad women as sexual (whores) have been used as a tool to increase women's power in the family?

First, the voluntary motherhood and social purity movements of the late nineteenth century used the notion of the morally pure, asexual woman to insist that sexuality needed to be controlled by women. As Linda Gordon has pointed out (Gordon, 1976, ch. 5), this was not necessarily because advocates of social purity were opposed to sexuality per se. Rather, they argued that sexuality needed to be controlled by women in order to bring men under the same standard of sexual morality as women, thus eliminating the double standard. Not only was this designed to allow women to control the timing and frequency of genital intercourse so as to give more control over reproductive sexuality, it was also used as part of the campaign to eliminate prostitution at its perceived source, i.e., male sexual promiscuity.

The reversal of the emphasis prevalent today in sex/affective relationships seems to have characterized middle-class women's lives in the nineteenth century. Given that genital sexual relationships were unsatisfactory and men's and women's work worlds so different, it is not surprising that the affectionate relations that women had with other women most often contained higher levels of erotic energy than did relations, whether genital or affectionate, with men (Sahli, 1979; Faderman, 1981). And as we have argued, the primacy of the mother-child bond over the heterosexual couple bond prevalent during this period no doubt involved a similar concentration of sex/affective energy. Thus, we need not assume that Victorian women's lives were devoid of sex/affective gratification in comparison with Puritan women or contemporary women; or that women had "given up" sex in order to get control of mothering. What is needed is a further amplification of the concept of sex/affective energy in order to conceptualize more clearly the conditions under which it is expressed/satisfied versus conditions under which it is frustrated. For example, Victorian women may have gained power in sex/affective production, compared to Puritan women, by emphasizing nonsexual but intensely affectionate relations with children and other women. But in changed historical conditions it also seems true that the twentieth-century sexual revolution, particularly the lesbian feminist validation of sexual relations between women, contains a revolutionary potential for increased sex/affective energy gratification for contemporary women (Ferguson, 1981b). This is true despite the fact that much of the theory and practice of sexologists and advocates of sexual freedom have been male dominant (Christina Simons, 1979; Campbell, 1980).

*Class and Race Differences in Motherhood and Sexuality.* I have argued that the romantic/Victorian ideology of moral motherhood was a tool used by northern, white, middle-class Protestant women to aid in the transformation of sex/affective production in a way that increased their power over the production and distribution of sex/affective energy and also increased the relative quantity of sex/affective energy they received from children and homosocial networks. But by the end of the nineteenth century, the moral motherhood ideology was almost universally accepted by white working-class families as well. This was ironic, since the emphasis that the romantic/Victorian ideology placed on women being at home where their standards of sexual purity could be enforced on husbands and taught to children legitimized sexual violence against working-class women who were forced, for economic reasons, to work outside their homes.

For black women the moral motherhood ideology has two dimensions of racist control: the background of slavery, and economic necessity. The historical background of slavery in which black women were raped by white owners in order to produce more slaves created the material base for a racial-sexual stereotype of black women as bestial and sexual. Motherhood for them was not, like that for "full" (white) humans, a chosen career, but a natural, involuntary process as it is for all beasts of burden. The image is created of black people mating like dogs. Under this stereotype, black women could not be expected to be moral authorities like white mothers. Rather, they could care for the white mistress's children under her moral supervision. The second part of the slavery stereotype of black women as mothers, then, is as servants caring for (white) children, rather than as mothers in authority caring for their own children. The racial/sexual stereotype thus sets up the dichotomy *white* (good, virginal mothers) versus *black* (evil, sexual, bestial whore).

One explanation for working-class acceptance of the moral motherhood/cult of domesticity is provided by Hartmann (1981b). According to her, late nineteenth-century organized trade union movements led by skilled male workers attempted to create a "family wage" in order to protect their challenged interests as family patriarchs. A family wage, i.e., a wage which allowed a wage-earning husband to support a non-wage-earning wife and children, performed two functions for patriarchal control: It cut competition from women wageworkers, and it allowed men to keep their wives at home to provide personal services, services that are not so easily forthcoming when women have to deal with the problems of the second shift. The family wage and protective labor legislation for women and children were a "bargain" struck by male capitalists, upper-middle-class women reformers, and male unionized workers, which served each group's interests—the capitalists' because their new concern to reproduce a skilled labor force led them to emphasize public schooling and home childcare for children, care most economically provided free by working-class mothers.

It is important to note that contemporary changes in the married women wage-labor force have changed the historical dynamic in which women could in fact gain power as mothers by remaining home with children. Working-class white women historically gained power as mothers by the institution of the family wage and protective legislation, but they also lost the power that being economically independent/less dependent on men brings to women who are waged. Black women, however, never gained any power from family wage legislation, for black men were largely excluded from unions. So black male unemployment and/or low wages was one of the reasons so many black married women worked in wage labor.[12]

*Period III: Public (Capitalist) Patriarchy.* Our contemporary American society is a social totality containing a mode of economic production, welfare state corporate capitalism, and a patriarchal mode of sex/affective production we can call "masculinist" (Ehrenreich and English, 1978). The shift between the first phase of industrial capitalism and our present stage began to occur during the progressive period of the 1890s and has been increasingly consolidated since then by the growth of the welfare state.

In terms of sex/affective production, the content and social relations of women's mothering in the home have changed significantly with the advent of the consumer economy. First, many of the tasks associated with "mothering" maintenance work (e.g., sewing, mending, cooking, gardening, nursing children and old people) are now no longer done primarily at home by mothers. Ready-made clothes, store-bought foods, and fast-food restaurants have lessened mothers' domestic work in these areas, although the increasing drain on the male breadwinner's wage that consumerism brings has caused a steady rise in women's wage work in the twentieth century.

The fact that mothers' work as health care workers and isolated mothers in the home has been diminished by the shift to public schools, hospitals, and nursing homes has not brought women a great equality or control in the societywide sexual division of labor providing these services. Rather, as Ehrenreich and English note, the rise of the male-dominated medical profession in the late nineteenth and early twentieth centuries diminished the control women had in health care, childbearing (by eliminating midwifery), and child nurturing. As male experts came to define what was healthy medicinally (the proliferation of the drug industry), emotionally (child development "experts"), and sexually (Freud and the sexologists), women lost the "moral expert" status re children they had gained with the adoption of the moral mother ideology.

Contemporary childbirth and reproductive practices are increasingly a form of "alienated labor" in the market sense, as a male-controlled medical technology is used to limit women's reproductive control (e.g., involuntary sterilizations, and making mothers passive, drugged objects in childbirth) (Rich, 1976; Jaggar, 1983).

The increasing dominance of the public school system and the growth of suburban and urban living patterns has meant the isolation of mothers from supportive networks of other women. This has meant an increasing loss of control over their children's emotional and social environment. The nineteenth-century concept of children as private property of their parents is increasingly unbelievable (Ferguson, 1981a). Not only do major socializers of children beside the family (teachers, peers, TV, and the mass media) contribute to personality formation of young people, but the welfare state with its social workers of all kinds has increasing legal power to intervene in family affairs (McIntosh, 1978; Donzelot, 1979).

Contemporary motherhood creates an ambivalent relationship between mother and child that is extreme. Children are no longer apprentices to parents nor may their adult lives be much like those of their parents, so it is hard for mothers to see their children as products reproducing their interests and skills. From the child's point of view, parents become increasingly outmoded authorities whose only value lies in their access to money to pay for children's wants. Children form intense social bonds with their peers that often supplant parents as the objects of sex/affective energy.[13]

Within the nuclear family context itself, the influences of the sexual revolution for women have not so much increased the sexual satisfaction afforded to women as undermined their power as mothers. The late 1920s and 1930s saw the popularization of Freudian ideas by the development of a new liberal ideal of the "companionate marriage" (Christina Simons, 1979). This involved a new domestic ideal of "mom" as sexy housewife. Mental health within the family required that mothers balance their affectionate involvement with their children by an equally intense, sexually intimate, and affectionately involving relationship with their husbands. Women who attempted to resort to nineteenth-century methods of controlling sexual intercourse by resisting husbands' advances could now be labeled "frigid" and "castrating women." Women who preferred the company of their children to that of their husbands were "narcissistic," had "separation problems," were causing sons to become homosexuals by tying them to their apron strings, and in general were damaging their children's health by excessive "momism" (Ehrenreich and English, 1978). Finally, women who prefer homosocial friendship networks to social time with their husbands, a practice taken for granted in the nineteenth century, can now be stigmatized as "sexually repressed" or, even worse, as *lesbians,* a concept which didn't exist in the nineteenth century (Ferguson, 1981b; Weeks, 1979, 1981).

It is not surprising that motherhood has become devalued in late twentieth-century capitalist countries. Now that the percentage of women in the United States who are wageworkers is over 50 percent and the number of married mothers with children under eighteen who do wage work has increased dramatically in the last ten years, the second-shift problem has become acute for working mothers. The United States in particular has handled the problem of working mothers in a totally inadequate way: Only one out of six children whose mothers seek public childcare is able to find an available slot. Why have the problems of motherhood increased while its consequent social status has decreased?

One explanation is provided by Carol Brown (1981), who argues that since children are no longer economic assets to the family, due to the development of public schooling and child labor laws, men have lost interest in economically supporting children. Thus, what seems to be an advance or even a victory for women, the change from "father right" characteristic of nineteenth-century divorce law to the "mother right" typical of twentieth-century cases (lesbian mothers of course not included!) is, in actuality, a breakdown of paternal obligations toward children. Women have won a "right" to child custody that merely guarantees an added unequal burden compared to fathers: not only the total burden of the sex/affective work involved in raising children, but in addition being the "breadwinner" (if only via welfare payments) as well.[14]

Carol Brown's argument has a rather excessive economistic emphasis on the economic costs and benefits of children. From the sex/affective production paradigm we can frame an additional explanation of why fathers have ceased to accept the "family wage" bargain of the nineteenth century and the role of primary breadwinner for wives and children. This is that the "victory" of the nineteenth-century mothers using the moral motherhood ideology in gaining control of the sex/affective energy exchange between parents and children dissociated fathers from direct control and production of this sex/affective good. Thus men don't want to contribute to the support of children to whom they do not experience a close sex/affective connection.

Another reason why the status of motherhood has declined under public patriarchy is, ironically, the partial success of the sexual revolution for women. Women's increasing economic independence from men and increased sexual permissiveness (partly as a result of the commoditization of sex through the influence of consumerism) have weakened men's ability to impose sexual double standards on women.

A frustrated male backlash to greater sexual freedom for women has been male recourse to sexual violence (rape, incest, domestic violence) (Easton, 1978) as well as the increased sexual objectification of women (pornography, sexual advertising) (Dworkin, 1981). In sharp contrast to the nineteenth-century split between the moral mother and the whore, many men now experience women simultaneously as both mother and whore, thus devaluing motherhood (Hooks, 1981).

The increasing crisis of motherhood in the United States is exacerbated by the phenomenal increase in the divorce rate in the twentieth century (up to two-fifths of all marriages) (Bureau of the Census, 1977). Since marriage is no longer for life, women cannot rely on a stable family household and support from a male breadwinner in exchange for mothering and housework. Even though it is easier for divorced women to remarry now that the social stigma of divorce is lessening, many white mothers find divorce creates a crisis in self-identity, in part because single motherhood has been so devalued in white culture. This is an important difference between black and white culture, for American black culture has always valued motherhood, married or not, more than white culture has.[15]

The major increase in alternate families, particularly single motherhood and families formed by remarriage, is creating new social problems. Stepchildren often resent their new social parent (or mother's new lover), and lack of social precedents for how to facilitate conflicts often keeps the new family from developing equitable decisionmaking processes. This creates special problems for women, for as mothers and stepmothers, and despite the patriarchal image of the "wicked stepmother," women are expected to be the ones to heal the conflicts within the family and to nurture everyone involved.

Racism has kept motherhood a very different experience for American white and black women in the past. Nonetheless, twentieth-century changes in multisystems domination relations are developing a particular form of white-supremacist capitalist patriarchy. Noncapitalist-class white and black women's lives as wageworkers, welfare recipients, single mothers, and sexual objects are much more similar with regard to sex/affective production than they used to be. Four key factors are the rise in single motherhood for both black and white women; the general rise in impersonalized violence against all women (rape); the rise in physical mobility of families and individuals, which causes the loosening of extended family networks; and, consequently, the increasing isolation of motherhood for all women.

Political strength and emotional survival under these conditions require for both black and white women a *chosen* as well as a blood kinship networking with other women to handle the fact of motherhood. This is not to deny that racism and classism oppress women differently. Rather, it suggests that with respect to motherhood, issues of sex/gender class in sex/affective production (e.g., conflicts between men and women over parenting, sexuality, and nurturance) are becoming structurally similar. Black and Third World feminist organizations are thus developing within different racial and ethnic communities as an attempt to resolve intracommunity the social crisis of the family and personal intimacy presently occurring across racial/ethnic lines. Influential members and groups within the white women's movement are presently seeking to make coalitions with black feminists, in part by dealing with the racism within the white women's movement.

The women's movement has created a rising consciousness of the social inequalities forced on mothers by our current social arrangements of parenting (masculinist sex/affective production). Lesbian feminism arose in the early 1970s as one way to turn the sexual revolution toward egalitarian sexual relationships for women. As a result, many young women who might have married and had children in an earlier era have become lesbians. Many women, lesbian and heterosexual, have coped with the problem of motherhood today by choosing not to become mothers. For them, the problem becomes how to challenge the patriarchal ideology that a woman is not successful (indeed has not achieved adult status) until she becomes a mother. Other women are resorting to nontraditional ways of becoming mothers: artificial insemination, the "one-night stand," adoption, etc. In addition to the economic, legal, and social difficulties that single women face in trying to become mothers, there are continuing legal problems of child custody rights faced by lesbian mothers.

It would take another paper to develop in detail the political implications of conceptualizing motherhood as a part of a sex/affective production process. Briefly, however, we can say that, failing a fascist takeover of state capitalism, the New Right will not be able to reconstruct the patriarchal nuclear family of nineteenth-century husband patriarchy. Families of choice, viz., social families with alternate egalitarian structures, are here to stay. Rather than accept the terms of the debate posed by the New Right (the family versus lesbian/gay rights, traditional mothers versus career women, etc.), the women's movement needs to continue to build an oppositional culture and politics that validate social, egalitarian parenting, parenting characterized by close, non-possessive social networks of women and children (social motherhood), or men, women, and children (social parenthood) (Ferguson, 1981a; Allison, 1980). Only in this way can we strengthen ourselves as women and mothers to use the current contradictions between masculinist sex/affective production based in the family and the ongoing development of state capitalist society in a struggle to challenge public patriarchy as a system of male domination.

## Conclusion

I have argued that male domination can best be understood as perpetuated by the social relations of parenting, affection, and sexuality. These social relations involve different modes of the production and exchange of "sex/affective energy" and the production of gendered producers of this energy. Although different societies have had different modes of sex/affective production at different times, a cross-cultural constant is involved in different modes of bourgeois patriarchal sex/affective production. This is that women as mothers are placed in a structural bind by mother-centered infant and small child care, a bind that ensures that mothers will give more than they get in the sex/affective parenting triangle to which even lesbian and single parents are subjected. The ensuing double consciousness explains the internalization of oppressive structures of parenting in a way that avoids the static, deterministic emphasis of feminist neo-Freudian analyses like those of Nancy Chodorow. Furthermore, the concept of modes of sex/affective production can be applied to historical changes in parenting in American history to pinpoint changes in the concepts of motherhood and consequent strategies of resistance to male domination.

Historically, there are three main modes of sex/affective production in modern American history: father patriarchy (the colonial period), husband patriarchy (the romantic/Victorian period), and public patriarchy (the twentieth century). The multisystems approach shows that each of these periods is characterized by different power relations between men and women in parenting and sexuality, relations which also vary by race and class. Consequently, the *meaning* of motherhood, as a strategy of resistance to male domination or as a capitulation to it, varies in different periods, classes, and races. Further analyses are needed of areas within capitalist patriarchy where different domination systems functionally support each other and where they are in contradiction. Only by such concrete analyses can we develop specific feminist strategies for change in motherhood that make it clear what sorts of families of choice (social families) rather than birth (biological kin networks) we must conceptualize.

## Notes

Thanks to many friends who gave me criticisms of earlier drafts of this essay, including Sam Bowles, Barbara Ehrenreich, Nancy Folbre, Sandra Harding, Annette Kuhn, Elaine McCrate, Linda Nicholson, Francine Rainone, and Iris Young. Special thanks to Liz, Francine, Kathy, Connie, Sarah, Lisa, and all the mothers and daughters who have provided the nurturance in which this article was born.

This chapter was previously published in Joyce Trebilcot, ed., *Mothering: Essays in Feminist Theory*. Totowa, N.J.: Rowman and Allanheld, 1984. Copyright © 1984 by Ann Ferguson. Published by permission of the copyright holder and publisher.

1. Adrienne Rich's classic *Of Woman Born* (1976) raises important issues for further thought. I chose these two quotes to begin this essay not because I totally agree with them but because they raise important theoretical questions. The first quote privileges the *biological* bond between mothers and daughters, thus raising the question of whether *social* mothering (adoptive mothers, step- and foster mothers, older sisters, other mother surrogates) involves a secondary or different kind of mother-daughter bond. The second quote is ambiguous on the question of whether the actual *process* of mothering a child, as opposed to having been a child, makes an important difference to one's self-concept and perspective on life. I disagree with one of the implications of this quote, which suggests that actual mothering is irrelevant to one's self-concept. Rather, I maintain that actual mothering, whether biological-social or nonbiological social (e.g., adopting, communal living, etc.), does make a difference to one's self-concept, which is not simply one of status in patriarchal societies.

2. The connection between gender identity and sexual preference (sexual identity) is problematic. While some theorists seem to assume an automatic connection (Chodorow, 1978a, b), the gay and lesbian liberation movements of the twentieth century have hypothesized sexual identity as quite separate from gender identity (Ferguson, 1981b). Compare also the view of sexologists and gays of the late nineteenth and early twentieth centuries that gays constituted a "third sex": "Uranians" (Weeks, 1979).

3. I use the word "patriarchal" in a generic sense to refer to many types of male dominant sex/affective production processes, and not in the specific sense in which it refers to a *father* patriarchal family where wife and children are economic and legal dependents.

4. In an earlier paper (Ferguson, 1979, reprinted as Chapter 2 of this book), I argue that in patriarchal sex/affective production systems, unequal labor time exchanged by men and women in housework, sexuality, nurturance, and childcare is exploitative in the classic Marxist sense: Men appropriate the surplus labor time of women in appropriating more of the human goods

produced. In a subsequent paper (Ferguson and Folbre, 1981) the argument is advanced that increasing contradictions between patriarchy and capitalism are creating women as a new sex/gender class that cuts across family economic class lines. I owe many of my ideas on the analogies between economic and sex/affective production to Nancy Folbre (Folbre, 1980, 1982).

5. I develop the concept of sex/affective energy to improve on the concept of libido introduced by Freud and further developed by Reich (1949, 1973, 1974). I have two objections to classic libido theory as developed by Freud and Reich: (1) They posit it as a bodily *drive* or type of *instinct* rather than an *energy*. This suggests a fixed quantity of energy held in check by the psychological mechanisms of repression. Foucault (1978), among others, has creatively criticized that image of sexuality and has suggested, to the contrary, that sexuality is an energy that can be brought into existence, focused, and augmented by social discourses. On this point I tend to agree with Foucault. (2) Freud's and Reich's use of the concept of libido seems to assume that *genital sexuality* is the highest expression of this drive: that other forms of sexuality are either stages of arrested development or sublimated forms. I do not wish to assume that any one form of sexuality or affection is a "higher" or more basic expression of the generic form, nor do I wish to imply that affection is simply sublimated genital sexuality. Hence, I use a slash in the concept: sex/affective energy.

6. A much-quoted passage from Engels's *Origin of the Family* is richly suggestive and ultimately ambiguous on the question of how to conceptualize sexuality, nurturance, and human reproduction:

> According to the materialistic conception, the determining factor in history is, in the final instance, the production and reproduction of immediate life. This again is of a two fold character: on the one side, the production of the means of existence, of food, clothing and shelter and the tools necessary for that production; on the other side, the production of human beings themselves, the propagation of the species. The social organization under which the people of a particular historical epoch and a particular country live is determined by both kinds of production; by the state of development of labor on the one hand and of the family on the other (Engels, 1972, pp. 71–72).

The quote would seem to suggest that modes of the family are part of the material base of a society. Unfortunately, neither *Origin* nor *The German Ideology* deals seriously with changes in the "production of people" except as a direct function of the production of things (viz., the economy). So, other passages from *The German Ideology* suggest that Marx and Engels thought that the family in capitalist production is no longer part of the material base of society but has become part of the superstructure. This is a position which *reduces* the domination relations involved in the patriarchal production of people to a straight function of the domination relations involved in the production of things. The concept of sex/affective production, on the contrary, is meant to avoid this consequence.

7. Sara Ruddick argues (1980) that the maternal perspective involves a constant adjudication of one's own needs in reference to the child's because of three features of mothering work: concern for the physical survival, social acceptability, and growth (developmental needs) of the child. Her insights here are somewhat flawed by the apparent assumption that these concerns are not seriously altered by (a) the relation to the father, (b) other children or adult parent surrogates, and (c) the responses and options of the child, e.g., whether or not the child accepts mother's directions in these areas.

8. Marge Piercy's novel (1974) raises all sorts of interesting questions about whether the biological differences between men and women in human reproduction should be totally eliminated in order to permit gender-free childrearing.

9. The history of forms of the Afro-American family differs from these dominant family forms because of the institution of slavery and subsequent attempts by the black family after slavery to cope with the effects of institutionalized racism in the wage-labor force. Since the black family has always had a different and more egalitarian internal structure than white family forms, sexism in the Afro-American community needs to be seen as a reflection of dominant white cultural forms (e.g., the sexual division of wage labor, macho images in the media, etc.) rather than as an autonomous structure of the community itself.

10. The theoretical method in use here differs from that followed in Nancy Chodorow's influential work, *The Reproduction of Mothering* (1978a), in several respects. First, the claim that mothering in bourgeois nuclear family systems can be seen in terms of a sex/affective triangle involving father, mother, and child(ren) places more emphasis on the historically constructed system of parenting and sexual roles than does Chodorow. The nature of the mother-child bond and masculine/feminine gender identities is determined not simply by the fact of primary mother infant care but by the manner in which the father controls or intervenes, the parents' treatment of sexuality, and the part played by other siblings in the child's interaction with parents. While Chodorow maintains that gender identities are fixed in childhood, she can account neither for the changing conceptions of sexual identities nor for gender identities caused by peer oppositional cultures of the contemporary lesbian/gay and women's movements. In conceptualizing parenting as a historical process that interacts with a historical set of sexual practices, my approach can take into account race, ethnic, and class differences in motherhood. Its emphasis is more dynamic and agent-centered than Chodorow's, for the aim is to show that women have struggled to redefine motherhood (and consequently gender identities) within the parameters of the sex/affective triangle, given the opportunities afforded by changing economic, political, and cultural variables.

11. The gradual transference of parental authority from fathers to mothers and the intensification of the mother-child relationship would seem to have had contradictory effects for middle-class children. Children became economic dependents of the family, as the length of time spent in school increased while the practice of apprenticing children decreased. As mothers came to feel children to be their exclusive products, children may have felt at once powerless

to escape mothers, yet encouraged to develop some autonomy because of the new permissive childrearing practices coming into fashion. We can thus suppose that certain forbidden sexual practices (masturbation, homosexual play) actually increased among children, in part as a psychological distancing and resistance mechanism. This is quite a different explanation for the increased attention to adolescent sexuality evinced by eighteenth- and nineteenth-century writers than that provided by Foucault (1978). According to him, bourgeois sexual discourses (including religious confessional writing, sexual purity writers, and sexologists) created a new bourgeois concern with sexuality not as a response to any changing material conditions but simply as a spontaneous change of direction in "discourses." My explanation assumes, on the contrary, that a material change in power relations between bourgeois children and parents created new sexual practices, including asexuality among wives and sexuality among children, which then spurred new regulatory discourses.

12. Black women have consistently worked outside the home since the Civil War in proportions that were three to four times higher than for white women. In 1880, for example, about 50 percent of black women were in the labor force, compared to 15 percent of white women. The percentage of married black women working compared to married white women is similarly high. In the 1880s, for example, no more than 10 to 15 percent of white native and immigrant wives worked in wage labor (less in certain immigrant groups, e.g., Jews and Italians). Yet in New Orleans in the 1880s, 30 percent of black wives worked, and in Cambridge, Massachusetts, Nashville, Tennessee, and Atlanta in 1886 the figures were from 44 percent to 65 percent (Degler, 1980, p. 389).

13. Many sources discuss the alienation of contemporary mothers. The classic is Friedan (1963). Others are Wandor (1974) and Bart (1970).

14. Most divorced fathers cop out not only on direct childcare work but on financial contributions toward child support: 90 percent of divorced women do not receive regular child support payments from fathers, and those who do, do not receive the full payments the legal settlement entitled them to (Women's Agenda, 1976a). Welfare mothers are also subject to a male-headed bureaucracy whose interference in personal life and demeaning regulations attempt to reduce women to menial status.

15. This may be why a recent study of black women found that single black mothers had much higher self-esteem than single white mothers, in part because the latter did not compare themselves with married women but with other single black mothers in assessing social status (Myers, 1980).

# A Feminist Aspect
## Theory of the Self

The contemporary women's movement has generated major new theories of the social construction of gender and male power. The feminist attack on the masculinist assumptions of cognitive psychology, psychoanalysis, and most of the other academic disciplines has raised questions about some basic assumptions of those fields. For example, feminist economists have questioned the public/private split of much of mainstream economics that ignores the social necessity of women's unpaid housework and childcare.[1] Feminist psychologists have challenged cognitive and psychoanalytic categories of human moral and gender development, arguing that they are biased toward the development of male children rather than female children (cf. Chodorow, 1978b; Gilligan, 1982; Miller, 1973, 1976). Feminist anthropologists have argued that sex/gender systems, based on the male exchange of women in marriage, have socially produced gender differences in sexuality and parenting skills which have perpetuated different historical and cultural forms of male dominance.[2] Feminist philosophers and theorists have suggested that we must reject the idea of a gender-free epistemological standpoint from which to understand the world. Finally, radical feminists have argued that the liberal state permits a pornography industry that sexually objectifies women, thus legitimizing male violence against women (cf. Dworkin, 1974, 1981; Barry, 1979; Griffin, 1981; Lederer, 1980; Dworkin and MacKinnon, 1985; MacKinnon, 1987).

Though each of these feminist approaches to understanding the social perpetuation of male dominance is insightful, they are based on overly simplistic theories of the self and human agency. As a result they tend to give us misleading ideas of what is required for social change. For one thing, they don't allow us to understand how women who are socialized into subordinate gender roles nonetheless can develop the sense of self-respect and the personal power necessary to be strong feminists able to effectively change institutional sexism. In order to grasp what is necessary to develop a strong and powerful sense of self, we must have the correct theory of what the self is. I shall defend an aspect theory of the self in this essay.

## Developing a Sense of Self

Most feminists would take it to be a truism that women's sense of self-worth, and consequently our personal power, has been weakened by a male dominant society which has made us internalize many demeaning images of women. Thus, part of every feminist program must involve a process of feminist education which allows women to develop—some would say, reclaim—a self-integrity and self-worth that will provide each of us with the psychological resources we need to develop full self-realization. Since individuals who lack a sense of self-worth are timid and afraid to take risks, women face the problem of contributing to our own subordination because of not even trying to achieve goals we really want, thus falling victim to the adage "Nothing ventured, nothing gained." But how do we conceive of the process of constructing self-respect? In what follows, I am going to present three different theories of the self which feminist theories have presupposed. I shall give the answers they give to the question of how women can develop a strong sense of self, critique the first two, and defend my own view.

## The Rational Maximizer Theory of the Self

There is a view of self prevalent in American society today which derives from the views of such classical liberal philosophers as John Locke and Thomas Jefferson. This view, characteristic of many contemporary Americans of both liberal and conservative bent, holds that the self is a unified rational thinking subject, possessed of free will and the ability to choose life goals and means to achieve them, as long as fate or external social coercion does not interfere. Examples of such social coercion include government legal restrictions against certain actions or strong social groups (e.g., large corporations or community groups) whose actions or policies restrict one from certain courses of action.

On this view of self, which I call the rational maximizer view of self, humans are unified selves, rational maximizers, who operate to maximize their own self-interest as defined by their goals, within the external constraints laid down by force of circumstance, government, or society. Social oppression of a group, for example women or black people, is then explained by external constraints placed in the way of individuals achieving their goals. These constraints can range from the personal prejudices of employers and potential friends and lovers to the institutional sexism involved in lesser pay for work defined socially as "women's work"; or the fact that housework, defined as women's work, is unpaid labor, which makes the exchanges between men and women in the household economy unequal.

In the rational maximizer view of self, women do not differ from men in terms of personal identity and the human ability to choose reasonable goals and means to them. Thus, if men and women make different choices as to how to develop what economists call their "human capital," that is, their skills and abilities, including their degree of formal education and job training, this is due not to innate gender preferences and skills (e.g., that men are more competitive and aggressive and women more nurturant and submissive). Rather, it is a result of the realistic options that society and the individual circumstances of women provide. Thus, more men than women choose to pursue graduate studies, or careers in management and other high-paying careers in business, politics, and medicine because women choosing as men do would have to face much sexism and would have to work twice as hard and be twice as lucky to succeed. In a male dominant society, it is not rationally maximizing for women to make the same choices as men, especially since most women want to be wives and mothers— whether this is socialized or innate—and these goals are more difficult to combine with the typical high-paying masculine career.

The explanation of women's lesser sense of self-worth in this view is that women lack the skills that are highly valued in our society as well as access to the wages that are necessary to achieve status and economic independence in our society. Furthermore men, because of their comparative social and economic advantage, treat women as inferiors.

In the view that both men and women are rational maximizers, there are two social conditions necessary to develop a better sense of self for women. First is a feminist social policy that makes it less worth men's while to continue their sexist treatment of women, and second are feminist education programs which compensate women for the lack of skills society has denied them by encouraging the development of those skills necessary to compete in a man's world.

Affirmative action programs are a good example of feminist social policy that provides opportunities for qualified women to learn the skills hitherto reserved for men, in higher education and in on-the-job training. Such opportunities help those women involved to change their self-concept. Men will be persuaded to overcome their sexist attitudes when they see that women can do men's jobs as well as women, and will stop treating women as inferiors.

Another kind of training need is psychological retraining: Women need consciousness-raising types of education, like assertiveness training and counseling programs which advocate the goal of economic independence for women. Such programs can provide the survival skills to replace those self-denigrating traditional skills that are characteristic of most women under patriarchy, those which involve habits of deference to men and the myriad skills of indirect manipulation which we have been taught to create the greater likelihood of "catching a man," and in gaining indirect power through men's favors in a patriarchal world.

Since most women want to be wives and mothers, feminists must support state legislation providing affordable, quality childcare centers. At the same time, feminist education must combat the traditional prejudice against combining a career with motherhood. The most important feminist goal should be to create social structures that help women learn to become more like men—in motivations, personalities, and job skills—so that we can get ahead in the system and thus achieve economic parity with men.

## Difference Theory

The second theory of the self that I want to discuss is that of those I call the difference theorists. Unlike rational maximizer theory, which argues that men and women are basically the same underneath though we develop different skills and goals as means to achieving social success, this theory argues that there really are extreme personality and skills differences between the genders. These differences, whether originally innate or socialized in early infancy, are so much a part of the identities of men and women that they cannot be changed. People's identities are not analogous to little atoms of consciousness which can, chameleon-like, take on or shed their personal properties as it is expedient. Rather, since human personal identity is essentially relational, a personal identification with one's gender is an essential characteristic of personal identity. Men and women essentially define themselves in relation to different social standards learned in childhood. Since a man or woman's sense of self-worth is essentially connected to success or failure in meeting gender-related standards, women's sense of self-worth cannot be ultimately achieved by imitating men or by adopting masculine goals and skills. Rather, women must find collective ways to socially revalorize feminine-identified values and skills in order that individual women can reclaim a sense of self-worth denied by patriarchy.

There are two schools of thought among difference theorists on the question of the inevitability of gender differences. One school, the biological determinists, e.g., those such as Mary Daly (1978), Mary O'Brien (1981), and others (Beauvoir, 1952; Holliday, 1978; Barry, 1979) maintain that it is inevitable that masculine traits and inner sense of self be different from feminine ones. Testosterone makes men more aggressive than women, while women's reproductive biology not only creates womb envy in men but makes women more nurturant and altruistic in relation to others (Rossi, 1977; Konner, 1982; Holliday, 1978; Rich, 1976). Thus, universally, men have a motivation to dominate women and the nasty personality skills capable of doing so, while women have a motivation to relate more to children than to men (thus setting up a universal conflict in male and female motivations), as well as to each other (as like understands and empathizes better with like). Thus, given these biologically based gender conflicts, systems of compulsory heterosexuality are set up for the benefit of men to keep women from bonding with each other and children to the exclusion of men.

The social schools of difference include feminist psychoanalytic theory as well as some radical feminist theory (Chodorow, 1978b; Mitchell, 1974; Gilligan, 1982; Raymond, 1979). These theorists argue that the personality differences between men and women, though they are central to personal identity and difficult to change, are not biological. Rather, they are socially produced through the sexual division of labor, particularly in parenting. This sexual division creates in women a more altruistic and relational sense of self than men, who are produced with a more oppositional and autonomous, hence more competitive and self-interested, sense of self.

The biological determinist school of feminism tends toward a separatist solution for women. Men, after all, are incorrigible! Indeed, in one of her books, Mary Daly goes so far as to suggest that they are tantamount to a separate species from women, and consequently women owe them no personal or political obligations (Daly, 1982). Women should learn to value our authentic selves by relating to each other as friends and lovers, thus dropping out of and thereby challenging the dominant patriarchal culture by providing an example to other women of a freer life—one more in tune with women-centered values.

Not all difference theorists believe that such an extreme separatism is the political solution for feminists. Jan Raymond, in *A Passion for Friends* (1986), maintains that women have an authentic Self (her capital "S") different from men's. Thus if women are to be true to themselves they must prioritize being for other women. This means that we should prioritize friendships with women rather than accept the socially constructed patterns of what she calls "heteroreality," all of which socialize women to define our selves and our meaning in life in relationships with men.

Though Raymond wants a certain kind of cultural separatism for women, she does not advocate a "drop out" separatism. Rather than dropping out of the world, women must strive to change the political and economic priorities of a patriarchal society by working in careers that have hitherto involved only males and male-defined values.

It is never made clear in Raymond's book whether she thinks women's authentic Self is more like other women's than like men's for biological or for social reasons. Other difference theorists who clearly reject the biological gender difference argument are Nancy Chodorow, Dorothy Dinnerstein (1976), Carol Gilligan, and Sara Ruddick (1980). These thinkers argue that the psychology of women differs from that of men because women rather than men mother. By "mothering" they do not mean childbearing, that biological function that women cannot share with men, but mothering in the social sense of the nurturing and direct physical care for infants in early childrearing. The fact that women and not men mother in this sense creates a different sense of self in little girls than in little boys. Girls have an immediate role model for what it is to be female: one who is engaged in the concrete chores involved in housework and regular nurturant interaction with children. Consequently, the girl defines a sense of self that is relational or incorporative (i.e., I am like mom in these ways). Girls also must identify with, rather than absolutely oppose, that aspect of mother which is resented and feared: the fact that she can never meet all of the infant's myriad needs. This tends to make females turn anger originally directed at mother inward on themselves in ways that weaken self-esteem.

Gender identity for the boy comes out differently. Society teaches him that to be male is not to be female, and due to the relative or complete absence of his father he lacks a male role model as immediate for him as is the mother for the little girl. Thus he learns to define himself oppositionally instead of relationally (I am not-mother, I am not-female). He can thus project infantile anger not only on mother but on the class of women in general. Thus, the cross-cultural constant, the asymmetrical parenting of women, explains the cross-cultural male depreciation of women.

Carol Gilligan argues that women tend to have a different style of moral reasoning than men—what she calls a different "moral voice." When presented with hypothetical moral dilemmas, females tend to find a contextual solution while males formulate abstract principles and prioritize justifying one solution rather than the other.

The idea that women have a different moral voice than men's is pursued by Sara Ruddick, who argues that the socialization for, and actual experience of, mothering creates a maternal thinking in women which prioritizes the life preservation, growth, and social acceptability of the child under her care. When women generalize from the values embedded in this concrete mothering experience, they develop a more care-oriented ethic, concerned with peacemaking and concrete life preserving, than men. These latter, with their gender identity and masculine training in the abstract skills necessary to do well in competitive male groups and careers, are more likely to fall prey to the militaristic thinking of the sort that justifies war, the arms race, and other life- and species-endangering activities.

Social difference theory has two conflicting tendencies within it in regard to the question of how individual women can reclaim a personal power denied by the standards of femininity built into heterosexual desires. Feminist psychoanalytic theory suggests that women should have recourse to feminist therapy to undo the damages of being denied the proper nurturance for self-autonomy in early childhood. The collective strategies of radical feminism, however, tend to reject this individual solution in favor of a collective process in which women bond with other women to revalue feminine work and values, thus allowing women's self, based as it is on the worth of the feminine itself, to gain power. Thus the importance of comparable worth campaigns and women-only peace protests which reclaim the value of maternal thinking as opposed to militaristic thinking.

The general strategy of this line of difference thought is opposed to the strategies of those liberal feminists who assume a rational maximizer theory of self. Rather than striving to make women more like men so we have a better chance of succeeding in a male dominant world, the feminist empowerment process involves affirming the socially insufficiently recognized value of the feminine. Indeed, ideally, men should become more like women by committing themselves to learn so-called feminine skills. Only by so identifying with the feminine can they cease their deprecation of women. Further, only by an individual commitment of this sort, for example, the commitment to learn mothering skills by co-parenting, can a man create the kind of love relationship with a woman which will allow her the maximum opportunity of obtaining a sense of self-worth.

But it is at this point that difference theory can provide us with no clear answers on how and why men are going to be motivated to make such a dramatic change in the conception of masculinity. And even if they were, how can they be expected to succeed in learning feminine skills if these demand a permeable, or incorporative, personality as opposed to an oppositional one? And, given these problems, why and how can women who are concerned to increase their sense of self-worth work with individual men to encourage change?

## Problems with the First Two Theories of the Self

Although both the rational maximizer and difference theories of the self have important insights, they are inadequate in other ways. Though the first explains why women remain oppressed because of the external constraints that society places on them, it cannot explain why those few women in economically and socially privileged positions in society still defer to men. Why, if a woman is independently wealthy, would she be content to be a wife and mother rather than embarking on a professional or political career which would give her an even greater social effect on the world? Why do some such women even allow themselves to be battered wives? Such behavior does not seem to be rationally maximizing! Why then do these women who are economically independent continue to pursue less rewarding lives that require deferring to men? And why do many women who can afford higher education choose less well paying careers in literature, nursing, and elementary school teaching rather than business, physics, medical school, or engineering? In short, the rational maximizer theory underestimates the way in which people are not rational maximizers when it comes to their ultimate goals in life, which for most are gender-defined and socially engineered.

Though the difference school can answer this question—women after all are constructed with essentially different senses of self, skills, and desires from men—this group is overly deterministic about the static nature of this social molding. Consequently, they cannot answer the historical question of how and why a women's movement should have arisen just now in American history. If women are so different from men, why should women now be demanding the opportunity to enter male spheres? Why should the idea of developing independence and autonomy, long considered the special purview of masculine identity, suddenly be a goal for feminists as well?

My view is at odds with both the rational maximizer and the difference theories. Both of them are *static* and *essentialist*. That is, they conceive of the self as a given unity with certain fixed qualities, though they disagree about what those fixed qualities are. Thus, they both have *atomistic* views of the self. Whether the self is a rational calculator or a phenomenal center that defines itself in relation to others, the self is seen as having an essence fixed by human nature or by early childhood.

Many difference theorists maintain that there is a split between the authentic and inauthentic parts of the self. This model does suggest that radical change is possible by spurning the inauthentic self. But their claim that there is such an authentic aspect of self, and speculations as to the nature of its preferences and interests, are wildly metaphysical and unprovable. Indeed, they have seemed elitist and culture bound to some. For example, since most women continue to prefer men to women as love-mates, how can it be proved that it is more authentic for those women to prefer women, as some difference theories maintain? How do we decide whether the authentic female self is a lesbian, heterosexual, pansexual, or asexual?

## The Aspect Theory of Self

My alternative theory, which I call the aspect theory of self, rejects the idea that the self is an unchanging, unified consciousness which has a two-tiered set of properties: those that are necessary and essential, and those which are accidental. Rather, conscious selfhood is an ongoing process in which both unique individual priorities and social constraints vie in limiting and defining one's self-identity (Ferguson, 1986b, 1989a).

Humans may be rational maximizers if placed in the sort of social practices which encourage such a type of thinking strategy. But that is only one aspect of a self which is more like a bundle of parts or aspects than it is like a unidimensional means/ends calculator. Gender differences in personality, in life choices, and in moral reasoning are characteristic of only one aspect of a complicated human psyche that is often at odds with itself and, therefore, cannot be thought, comfortingly, to have only one essence.

If we think of the self as having many parts or aspects, some of which are in conflict, we can make better sense out of Gilligan's claim that there is a dichotomy of masculine and feminine moral voices. Most male and female psyches, created in standard gender-dichotomous childrearing practices, have at least one characteristic difference that is reflected by a difference in moral voices. But many adult women who engage in similar social practices with adult men, e.g., as business or professional colleagues, may also share with them the so-called masculine voice of moral reasoning. And men influenced enough by feminist women to attempt co-parenting may develop a feminine voice of moral reasoning due to this practice. These men and women will have both so-called masculine and feminine aspects of self as developed by their ongoing social practices, and while they will be likely to find these opposing perspectives incongruous, and indeed inharmonious, there is no reason to say that they are thus "denying their essence" in the social practice in which they are doing the gender anomalous job.

If the self is seen as having many aspects, then it cannot be determined universally which are prior, more fundamental, or more or less authentic. Rather, aspects of our selves are developed by participating in social practices which insist on certain skills and values. Furthermore, the *contents* of masculinity and femininity vary with the social practices they are connected to. A woman defending her child against attack (for example in the movie *Cudjo* or *Aliens*) is supposed to be showing her feminine, protective maternal instinct. But a similar aggressive, perhaps violent act against a man who has made deprecating sexist remarks is not considered feminine.

Where different social practices encourage skills and values that are in conflict, those participating in them will develop conflicting aspects of self. And where certain social practices are taken to be paradigmatic of one's personal identity (as in self-effacing mothering activities for women in our society and self-aggrandizing aggressive or competitive activities for men), then those who develop gender anomalous aspects of self can be disempowered by attributing the inharmonious combination of the two aspects to a personal neurosis. Though the feminist strategy of conceiving of certain aspects of self as inauthentic (for example, manipulative skills or heterosexual charm) is a more empowering approach than this, it does not follow that the view of self as having an authentic core and inauthentic outer layers is correct. Rather, one's sense of self and one's core values may change at different times and in different contexts. How then do we understand what it is to increase a sense of self-worth and personal power when the self is conceived of, as the aspect theory suggests, as an *existential process* in which incongruities and lack of power are due to participation in conflicting social practices? Let us take a concrete example to discuss.

Professional women in the helping professions are a good example of those whose concrete social practices are in conflict. Those in jobs in higher education, nursing, and social work must develop our ability to empathize with concrete others—students, patients, or clients—to do our job well. But since most of us work in large bureaucratic settings where impersonal rules of the game apply to job hiring, promotions, and allocations, we must develop a competitive, impersonal, meritocratic set of values and principles in self-defense. Thus one aspect of our jobs encourages the caring ethic connected to a contextual concern for concrete others that Gilligan claims is typical of the feminine role, and another aspect requires adopting the masculine ethic characterized by a universalistic rights/justice approach. Thus we have two moral voices, both in unhappy and inharmonious juxtaposition in our consciousness. What is alienating is not that our authentic self is thus denied, but the psychological incongruity of having to operate with conflicting values.

This contradiction in ways of thinking and valuing is a feature not only of women's work in the helping professions but of the work of those in male-dominated fields like business, politics, and the law who face the second-shift problem as working mothers.

Ironically, the juggling of incorporative aspects of self in nurturant work at home with oppositional and individualistic ways of being in such careers is also a problem for some men who, in sharing housework and childcare with feminist partners, find their modus operandi different from their more conservative male colleagues at the office. Black and other minority women, no matter whether employed or not, could be expected to develop a rights/justice orientation in self-defense against the social opposition of racist whites, toward whom they cannot afford to take a simple caring orientation.

The way to understand personal empowerment of an oppressed group faced with social practices which involve conflicting values is to combine the insights of the rational maximizer and difference theories of self with a historical perspective. The traditional sexual division of labor in public and private spheres is breaking down for many women and some men. Where it is no longer clear what exactly is men's and women's work, gender identities defined in terms of the different standards of self-worth attached to men's and women's work are put in crisis. It is precisely this developing conflict in gender roles, in conjunction with the American democratic ideology of the right of equality for all based on merit, that has spawned both the women's movement and the possibility for greater empowerment for women. Though the initial phase of capitalist development in America perpetuated male dominance by relegating women to the private, less socially valued, dependent, and relatively powerless sphere of the home, advanced capitalism and consumerist standards of living have been pulling women into part- and full-time labor. Though this has created the second-shift problem for working mothers and the incongruity of women, brought up to do individualized, caring work, placed in impersonal and uncaring bureaucracies and anonymous institutions, it has also allowed many women to gain economic independence from men.

An existential process of resolving this incongruity of personal identity can take many forms. A New Right woman may decide that homemaking in economic and social dependency on a man is a better way to resolve the incongruity in her life than to strive for a career and economic independence from men. As Phyllis Schlafly notes, most women would really rather cuddle a baby than a typewriter!

If the aspect theory of the self is correct, the feminist cannot challenge the New Right woman's choice by claiming it is inauthentic, for there is no way to prove what the authentic female self would choose. Nonetheless, due to the social crisis in gender roles, all women in the United States today are likely to have developed rational maximizer as well as incorporative (i.e., traditionally feminine) aspects of self. This is so because when traditional life-styles are no longer rigidly followed, individuals are forced to a more self-conscious means/ends calculation of what in the long run will serve their interests.

Feminists can appeal to the rational maximizer aspect of women to argue that women who take the New Right solution to the gender crisis face a high risk of failing to achieve their goals of security and well-being. This is so because of the rise in divorce rates, low welfare payments, low-paid wage-labor work for most women, and the small amount of child support most women receive from former husbands. Thus a woman who places all her eggs in the homemaker basket is increasingly likely to end up a single mother who is one of the statistics in the feminization of poverty.

With respect to women's traditional feminine identification as nurturers, feminists can argue that the only way to really have these values be effective today is not to retreat to private motherhood but to influence public policy by gaining individual and collective power in careers and politics that will allow for a public challenge to a militarism spawned by an excessive masculine thinking. Only by gaining public power as women can we have the collective power, through unionizing women and feminist political networks, to demand that those feminine values of caring and contextual moral decisionmaking be incorporated into the rules of the game of our economic and government institutions. In the long run, only a more decentralized worker- (and client-, patient-, and student-) controlled type of decisionmaking can incorporate the caring and contextual considerations needed into the more abstract meritocratic but often inhumane rules by which our public institutions operate.

Such a feminist program will require radical structural changes in the present relation between public and private. We will need to educate the American public to the idea that the raising of children is not a private luxury but a public responsibility. Employers should thus be required to reorganize wage work so as to allow flex-time jobs, with no career penalty for mothers and fathers of young children, as well as maternity and paternity leave and quality affordable childcare.

Our ultimate goal must be the de-genderizing of every aspect of social life. Only this can empower women to develop our potentials as unique individuals not constrained by a social definition which sees our essential nature to be to serve men. However, we cannot achieve this goal without a collective, public process which first empowers women by creating a higher public value for feminine skills and interests. Though assertiveness training and economic independence are key for women, they must be supplemented by comparable worth, Social Security for homemakers, and other such campaigns which set a higher value on women's traditional work.

While feminist collective networking and public feminist political campaigns can start the empowerment process that allows a woman to redefine a core sense of self that can perceive itself as valuable and able to control her life independently of men, there are many other private issues that remain to be negotiated if she is to develop full personal empowerment.

For example, should a woman cut herself off from, or just try to ignore, her parents if they are very sexist? Should she pursue motherhood, given the social costs and dangers of motherhood, indeed the likelihood of being a single mother in a sexist world? Should she give up a heterosexual life-style and choose a woman lover in order to create a more equal context for love? Should she choose an alternative living arrangement with a man which does not involve marriage, to avoid the sexist social and psychological expectations that may be involved? Or should she eschew sexual love relationships altogether and prioritize platonic friendships with women (and perhaps men)?[3]

There is no general answer as to which of these paths a woman should take to personal empowerment. Only trial and error and the experience of juggling the various aspects of her self by trying out different private commitments can lead to what is most personally empowering to different women. The aspect theory of the self, based as it is on the view that the self is an existential process whose integration may be different for different women, must assume an ethical pluralism on such matters of personal choice.

The position of ethical pluralism is a consequence of the rejection of the essentialist idea that all women have the same inner and authentic self which can only be empowered by the same choices. But, nonetheless, we can still draw a few important generalizations about what this empowerment process must minimally entail for women in the contemporary United States: first, collective networking with other women around feminist campaigns; and second, prioritizing friendships with other women that value personal autonomy and the elimination of self-definitions that define self-worth exclusively in terms of relationships with men, whether they be fathers, employers, sons, workmates, friends, husbands, or lovers. Given the fragmented aspects of self and the general deprecation of the feminine that pervades all our social life, these steps are necessary to empower both the rational maximizing aspect of self, which gains when women find ways to gain material equality with men, and the incorporative aspect of self, which finds empowerment when it finds a secure yet self-affirming way to ally one's self-interests in nurturing and supportive connections to others.

## Notes

This chapter is reprinted from Marsha Hanen and Kai Nielsen, eds., supplementary vol. 13 of *Canadian Journal of Philosophy: Science, Feminism and Morality*, by permission of the University of Calgary Press. Copyright © 1987 by the University of Calgary Press.

1. For a survey of this literature, see Sokoloff (1980), Hartmann and the responses to Hartmann in Sargent (1981b), Delphy (1984), and the Gardiner, Weinbaum and Bridges, Hartmann, and Davies articles in Eisenstein (1979).

2. Perhaps the most original and influential article of the new feminist anthropology is that by Gayle Rubin, "The Traffic in Women," in Rayna Reiter, ed., *Toward a New Anthropology of Women* (1975). Other important contributions are the rest of the articles in Reiter as well as those in Rosaldo and Lamphere (1974). See also Sanday (1981).

3. For a discussion of some of these feminist ethical questions, see Ferguson (1989a) and the articles in Ferguson, ed. (1986).

# SIX

# Racial Formation, Gender, and Class in U.S. Welfare State Capitalism

For quite a while socialist-feminists have been saying that racism needs to be given equal weight with patriarchy and capitalism as a social domination system (cf. Spelman, 1988; Moraga and Anzaldua, 1981; Joseph, 1981; Hooks, 1986). But no one has as yet developed a theory of racism that allows us to appreciate that it has an independent dynamic. A recent book by Omi and Winant (1986) is a good start in this direction. In this chapter I attempt to develop some of the implications of their views.[1]

Marxist analyses tend to reduce racism to a divide-and-conquer tactic of the economic elite (Reich, 1981), whereas U.S. mainstream analysis, both liberal and conservative, insists on fitting race identity and discrimination into an ethnic and immigrant model (Glazer and Moynihan, 1970). Neither of these models is satisfactory, Marxism because it is too reductive[2] and immigrant models because they cannot explain racism as it affects Afro-Americans and native Americans who are not immigrants. The notion of sex/affective production presented in earlier chapters of this book sees different forms of patriarchy interacting with capitalism and racism but provides no analysis of different forms of racism. We need a theory of racism with the analytic power of Marxism[3] that does not reduce racism to economic domination. One way to do this is to introduce Omi and Winant's concept of the racial formation of a society.

The concept of a racial formation, like that of a gender formation, is based on the more general concept of a social formation. A racial formation is a historically specific set of economic, political, social, and cultural practices that defines and enforces the "rules of the game" for the society that allow dominant races more power and options than subordinate races.

A racial formation is never a static structure; rather, it involves what Omi and Winant (1986) call "racialization," that is, a process of struggle to define and enforce the social categories connected to race, on the one hand, and challenges to these meanings and practices of power by those who are dominated, on the other. Thinking of social relations as processes rather than fixed conditions allows us to see our society as a series of forces and counterforces that are often in tension. Racialization processes involve both those institutional constraints on subordinate groups set up by dominant racial groups to maintain social control and privileges as well as institutional tendencies and counter-cultural forces developed by subordinate groups to challenge the power of racial dominants. For example, victories by the 1960s civil rights movement ensured the passage of the 1964 national civil rights acts as well as federal affirmative action programs.

These laws and policies undermine racism in the economic sector, thus challenging the racist practices of discrimination on the basis of skin color. A New Right backlash, however, partly institutionalized by the Reagan administration, created massive social service cutbacks that diminished public-sector job opportunities for racial minorities and impacted disproportionately on people of color, thus continuing to stigmatize them, albeit by poverty and homelessness rather than overt discrimination. Both of these tendencies, the racially progressive and the retrogressive, exist side by side in U.S. social formation today, creating an ongoing struggle for control of the state by racist and antiracist forces (Winant, 1990).

One of the basic ways in which a racial formation reproduces social control and privileges for racial dominance and oppression for racial subordination is by a social and legal system of race marking. This is necessary to distinguish those who will qualify for high racial status from those who will not, as race, like gender, is not a purely biological concept. Though race and gender have as necessary conditions observable biological differences between many members of a racial or gender group and a contrasting group or groups, the biological characteristics that count and what their social meanings are vary from culture to culture. Just as societies have various concepts of masculinity and femininity encoded in different gender formations,[4] so complex societies consisting of a mix of peoples brought about by migration, conquest, colonialism, or slavery have different socially institutionalized concepts of race in distinctive racial formations (Harris, 1964; Fredrickson, 1986).

A society involved in a racial formation has three dimensions in which the meaning and value of race and its social effects are defined and contested. First are its *economic practices,* such as imperialism, slavery, or a racial division of labor, all of which involve an unequal exchange of labor and goods between one race and another (Hogan, 1984). Second are the *political and legal practices,* such as legal definitions of race, legal arrangements creating unequal racial property relations (for example, sharecropping), and massive political coercion (for example, the wave of lynchings of black men that took place in the South in the construction of a post-slavery racial segregation system). Finally, there are associated *cultural practices,* such as racial segregation, sexual interactions between white female indentured servants and African slaves, and miscegenation involving white male planters and female slaves.

Racial concepts are not only socially constructed, they also vary in different societies and in different historical periods in the same society. For example, in North America the predominantly English-influenced development of the institution of African slavery developed legal definitions of race that involved the principle of "hypodescent": Any genetic ancestors from those of the subordinate group define a person as a member of that group. Thus until as recently as 1982 in this country, legal definitions of race predicated that any Negro ancestry at all defined one as wholly Negro (Omi and Winant, 1986). This corresponded to a rigid two-color caste system in which whites of all economic classes were in the higher caste and blacks or other nonwhites—Asians, native Americans—were in the lower caste regardless of economic status. In Latin America, on the other hand, the predominantly Spanish and Portuguese system of slavery developed a three-caste (and in some cases more than three-caste) system based on degrees of wealth as well as color (white, brown, black). In societies governed by this process of racialization, individuals from the same biological family could be of different races, depending only on their observable skin color. The principle of race marking in these societies is thus based on the converse of North America. Instead of being defined by association with the subordinate race, status is conferred by degree of similarity to the dominant race in a status continuum of race (Harris, 1964).

In U.S. history, processes of ethnicization have overlapped those of racialization at certain periods and been dropped in others. Though Asians, as a biologically different race, were obvious nonwhites who faced discrimination, other white or racially mixed immigrants have also been classed as nonwhite and been discriminated against in work, housing, and political life. Latin and Mediterranean immigrants, for example, have been loosely classified as nonwhite, as were the Irish in the nineteenth and early twentieth centuries. Though today the

Italians and Irish seem to have made it into the white race, Latins and Jews still retain an ambivalent racial identity, even when they are clearly white in appearance. When we speak of a racial formation, then, it should be understood that this includes both race and ethnic categorizations as they relate to dominant and subordinate social status and opportunities.

## Racial Gender

Gender, racial, and class formations interpenetrate. That is, the social definition of proper masculine and feminine behavior varies by class and race, as does the degree of power men and women have over each other, both within classes and races and between classes and races. Thus, in order to understand any one of these systems, one must connect them to aspects of the others. None is causally or structurally primary. Rather, we should see each system as maintaining an independent effectivity but subject to change with changes in the other systems.

In systems of racism in which one race has established hegemony over one or more racially or ethnically distinct peoples, there is often a complicated process of genderization. Men and women of the dominant race are often defined by gender roles, statuses, and powers that are not automatically assumed to apply to men and women in subordinate races and classes. Thus in the period of colonial American history I have called father patriarchy,[5] white men as husbands had control over their wives and as fathers, control over their children's marriages and access to familial property, but Afro-American male slaves had no such patriarchal rights.

This example demonstrates that gender, class, and racial formations articulate one another. Father patriarchy in the antebellum and Reconstruction South was connected to both race and class privileges for white males of the planter class as opposed to poor whites and black slaves. White male planters had access both to white women and black slaves, whereas poor whites were denied access both to white women of the planter class and to black slave women, who were not their property. As husband patriarchy became the dominant mode of sex/ affective production in the late nineteenth and early twentieth centuries, sexual mores for white males of all classes allowed them access to both black and white women of sharecropper and working classes as sexual partners but did not accord the same privilege to black men across the color bar. To the contrary, in the South a black man could be lynched for suspicion of flirting with a white woman.

The combined processes of genderization, sexualization, and racialization in a society at a particular time are often inconsistent: That
is, they may set certain standards for proper masculinity and femininity
that can be attained by the dominant race and economic class but not
subordinate races and classes. This may be because of material conditions. For example, economic realities in the nineteenth century
required most black women of all classes and white, working-class
women to work in the fields or factories, yet the ruling gender norm
specified that proper women should not work outside the home. This
is an example of how the mode of sex/affective production of the
dominant economic class can stigmatize those of subordinate classes
and races even when their sex/affective kin, bonding, and sexual
relations are not organized by that mode.

Another factor creating gender inconsistencies across race are racialization processes that attempt to control the sexuality of subordinate
races by setting different sexual mores for dominant and subordinate
races. In either case, the conflict between the dominant mode of sex/
affective production (that which applies to the dominant class and race)
and subordinate modes of sex/affective production set up by racialization and class realities can act as a site of struggle by feminists and
antiracists to challenge the gender formation as well as the racial
formation. Examples of this include Sojourner Truth's challenge of the
gender identity of woman as frail dependent of man in her "Ain't I
a Woman?" speech and Ida B. Wells's attempt to enlist both black and
white feminists in defining the antilynching campaign she spearheaded
as a feminist issue (Aptheker, 1983). Conceptualizing black slaves as
involved in a subordinate mode of sex/affective production allows us
to understand ways in which mothering can be seen as an act of
resistance rather than compliance with the dominant culture, as Toni
Morrison's novel *Beloved* develops in a particularly graphic way.[6]

The disparity between the gender norms for the dominant and
subordinate races and ethnic groups of a particular social formation
account for differences in personal identities that make identity politics
based on a common sense of gender difficult. For if the contents of
gender are socially constructed differently by race and class, then a
white, middle-class women's movement may be mistaken to assume that
all women will share enough of a gender identity as women to band
together to fight male dominance (Spelman, 1988). Instead of a concept
of sisterhood based on a shared gender identity, it may be more helpful
to posit different racial gender positions, and possibly different class
gender positions.[7] Processes of racialization in U.S. history have created
at least ten gender identities informed with racial difference if we

consider the various subordinate races: black, Latino, native American, and Asian, as well as the dominant white race.[8]

Though there have been attempts during the first- and second-wave women's movements to build a feminist politics stressing the common gender oppression of women, the difficulties of building a coalition politics around racial/ethnic gender positions have ultimately weakened these movements. For example, it has been difficult for white women to acknowledge that black, Asian, Latin, and native American men have been oppressed because of their gender, as that connects inextricably with their race. In the case previously mentioned, Ida B. Wells found that few white women in the nineteenth century could see lynching as a feminist issue (Aptheker, 1983). Similarly, challenging the stiffer legal penalties for nonwhite men accused of rape as compared to white men has not been defined as a feminist issue by the majority of white feminists today, though black feminists such as Angela Davis (1981) have agitated for its inclusion within feminism.

The first-wave women's movement faced a similar problem in connecting women across economic class. For example, as Kraditor (1965) points out, the middle-class theorist Charlotte Perkins Gilman made an analysis of housework as inefficient, unproductive work that made women as a sex class dependent housewives. She argued that housework should be socialized, thus freeing women to go into wage work without the second-shift or double-day problem (Gilman, 1966). Working-class housewives disagreed, arguing that women's work in the home was necessary to free husbands to work in wage labor; thus that the male breadwinner–female housewife family was an equal exchange (Kraditor, 1965). In the second-wave women's movement, many wage-earning black women have disagreed with the white radical feminist critique of this sort of family arrangement, which they see as a white bourgeois privilege that they would prefer to the second-shift problem (Spelman, 1982). This shows that different racial genders, based in different economic class positions, have caused disagreement on what count as feminist issues (Kollias, 1975; Ladner, 1972; Dill, 1975, 1983; Palmer, 1983; Hurtado, 1989).

Though gender identities are likely to vary by race and economic class for the reasons suggested above, at least two transhistorical features of gender may, in the appropriate historical circumstances, lead to cross-class race and ethnic women's movements. First, in all societies we know of, women's roles are contrasted with men's, even though the content of these roles varies across culture, race, ethnicity, and class. Second, in all societies where male dominance is a part of the dominant culture, women are expected to perform the function of serving and caring for men and children, even though the men and children this applies to may merely be those in their race, class, and kin group (cf. Frye, 1983).

Thus, though women may have more or less social, political, and economic power vis-à-vis men, depending on their race, ethnic group, and class, there is a general tendency to assume that women should defer to the male peers in their social context.

This *gender deference principle*, as we might call it, has some general implications. First, it generates a tendency in men to react to assumed deviation from female deference by violence against women. Second, social laws and economic opportunities tend to restrict women's full option to choose to have children because their social role is connected with mothering. Granted, reproductive rights for women will be variously restricted in different race, class, and historical contexts. For example, abortions are now permitted, but medicare benefits to pay for them are not assured, and forced sterilization is still a problem for minority women. Nonetheless, if the issues are framed in a cross-race and -class way, a common gender identity with respect to reproductive decisions can ground a mass women's movement on these issues.

In summary, the concept of genders as racially specified and racial identities as gender specified requires us to avoid assuming either that women in a racist society have nothing in common because of racism, or that we have everything in common in a sexist society because of sexism. Rather, to say personal identities involve racial genders is to say that there are economic, political, and cultural practices through which race identities and gender identities get defined. Further, in some of these practices white women and women of color are defined differently as women because of their race, which may set up a political antagonism. In other practices, women are defined similarly as women in spite of their race.[9]

Similarly, racism in this society means that white and nonwhite men are defined differently as men because of their race, yet cross-racial sexism means that individual men in consensual sexual and kinship relations with particular women tend to be defined similarly as men, no matter what their race and that of their partners. Thus the political art of antiracist and antisexist organizing in the United States involves coalitions that stress cross-gender, -class, -ethnic, and -race commonalities in ways that also challenge oppressions based on difference. But before we can develop a political strategy, we need to look more carefully at our contemporary racial formation.

## Racism and Sexism in
## the U.S. Capitalist Welfare State

Contemporary U.S. society is characterized by a sex/affective symbolic code that operates on the following binary oppositions: deserving/

undeserving poor, superior white/inferior black or nonwhite; superior man/inferior woman. Through a series of historical reversals in the code, the welfare system, first set up to protect the deserving poor (widows, children, old people) from the breakdown of family support systems caused by capitalist development, must now support those who are considered undeserving because they are primarily both black and unmarried (but not widowed) poor women.

"Being on welfare" has become a basic social stigma that defines for racists and sexists those who constitute the lowest of the social order. Unfortunately, given the way our welfare system is structured and the lack of jobs or job training, those on welfare, mostly women and children and a high percentage of black single mothers, have little choice but to be there and little opportunity to escape. Thus the current welfare system, because of its inadequacy to ameliorate the structural oppressions of capitalist, patriarchal, racist society and vulnerability to manipulation by white males and capitalist elites, is one of the primary perpetuators of sexism and racism.

Our present racial formation is a response to the civil rights movement of the 1960s, some liberal state reforms, and a New Right backlash against these reforms. Let us look more closely at three aspects of this social formation: patriarchy, racism, and classism.

## THE PATRIARCHAL STATE

Capitalist development in the United States has eroded the family's motivation and ability to care for children and old people. This has occurred in part because women, the personal caretakers in the family, have increasingly entered into wage labor on a permanent basis. The huge demand created for affordable childcare and care for old people has not been met by the development of an adequate supply of such services by market forces. This is part of the dynamic that led to the establishment of a welfare state, with Social Security benefits for retired workers and aid to dependent children to support poor women in taking care of children at home (Folbre, 1987a). The other part of the dynamic is that stressed by Ehrenreich and Ehrenreich (1979): that an alliance between middle-class and working-class organizations during the Progressive period in U.S. history forced the state to take on a mediating role between labor and capital and to make concessions toward welfare provisions in order to curtail the disastrous effects of laissez-faire capitalism on public health, occupational health and safety, and workers' material security.

Capitalist social relations have supported an ethic of individualism and consumerism. This in turn has ensured women's increasing permanence in the labor force, both to contribute higher income to the family as a whole and to give individual women more economic independence. These developments have weakened family-based patriarchy, or the power of male kin to enforce an unequal exchange of labor, goods, and options on female kin. This is attested to by the rise in divorce rates and the growing number of single-mother households.

But the increase of woman-headed households, though it has eliminated the material base for family patriarchies centered on husbands' and fathers' power over wives and daughters, does not mean that male dominance is disappearing. Rather, an alternative base for the social control of women has developed through the creation of "public patriarchy," that is, a shift in the perpetuation of male power over women from the family to public institutions, such as the workings of the economic marketplace and the welfare state, both controlled by male elites and an unequal sexual division of labor. As a result, we see the rise of the feminization of poverty, connected to the rise of the poor single-mother household and the second-shift problem (working mothers also expected to do a full day's shift of housework and childcare). These problems, in conjunction with the persistence of the sexual division of wage labor in which women earn only 61 percent of what men earn, continues to ensure social inequality for women of all economic classes in relation to men of those classes (cf. Ferguson, 1989a).

## RACISM

Welfare state racism has arisen gradually since the Great Depression as a less virulent but still racist way to deal with the aftereffects of earlier forms of racism. It supplants the state racism of the southern states based on sharecropping and separate and inferior segregated institutions.

An important aspect of the social practices of any racialization process is "sexual racism," solidified by sexual codes that eroticize and taboo relations between dominant and subordinate races. Our contemporary form of sexual racism is embedded in patriarchal welfare state racism. Minorities, particularly blacks and Latinos, are stigmatized because most of them are part of a permanent economic underclass. This underclass is perpetuated by a racial division of labor, ghettoized communities, and a welfare system that supports systematic underemployment for nonwhite males at the same time it fosters the development and impoverishment of minority single-mother households.

The sexual racism of our system types welfare state clients who are minorities, single mothers, or both as undeserving poor. Dominant ideology suggests that their plight is due to an "oversexed blackness" and the laziness and lack of initiative associated with it. Conservative responses to the AIDS crisis follow a similar logic: They assume that the initial victims of AIDS, gay men and IV drug users—the latter group consisting disproportionately of racial minorities—deserve to get the disease because of their sexual and social excesses.

Though the dominant ideology of our society continues to support racism, there is an undercurrent of challenge to this ideology that has been created by the black civil rights movements of the twentieth century. The massive influx of blacks into northern cities and industrial labor after the Great Depression created a large pool of laborers. Continued discrimination in the white-controlled labor movement and divide-and-conquer tactics by employers set the stage for the civil rights movement of the 1960s. This movement successfully challenged "separate but equal" discriminatory laws and also won federal affirmative action laws setting quotas for minorities to be hired or admitted in any business contract or academic program funded by the federal government.

There were costs to these formal victories, however. Though these steps won blacks formal civil rights and increased the possibilities for "advantaged" blacks to benefit from affirmative action programs (Wilson, 1978; Marable, 1981), for the most part such laws were not used to counteract the institutional economic racism that put many black men at a disadvantage as relative newcomers to industrial wage labor, locked them out of most white-dominated trade unions, and subjected them to the "last hired, first fired" rule of economic recessions. This explains why, because the majority of new jobs have shifted from the industrial to the service sector and the majority of unskilled jobs in this sector are typed as women's jobs, the unemployment ratio of black men to white men has stood at 2:1 since 1956.[10]

The notion of racial gender is helpful in explaining why black men tend to share a particular kind of oppression in our patriarchal and racist social formation. The increase of black male gangs reacting to the meager employment opportunities, the rising level of violence of black men against each other, in part because of forced criminal activity, puts black men in the underclass at physical risk out of all proportion to the percentages of blacks in the larger society. Furthermore, the individual and institutional racism that continues to prevail across economic class means that even middle-class black men do not attain the class privileges that would otherwise be theirs by right in a classist society (Dyson, 1989). Though black men may be able to exert patriarchal privilege in their private interactions with black women, in the larger society their masculinity is challenged by the withholding of the same patriarchal privileges that white men have over white women, and indeed all women.

If black men suffer in the racist United States, black women suffer in comparable but different ways. Even before the Reagan cutbacks in welfare, the state had not succeeded in equalizing economic opportunities in welfare for women and minorities. Most black women are still working as caretakers and servants, though the service economy has shifted the majority from domestic work in private homes to comparable work in the public-service sector. Most work as maids, nurses, waitresses, salesclerks, or secretaries, or, if they are on welfare, they take care of their own children for the pittance that Aid for Families with Dependent Children (AFDC) supplies. This sex/affective labor, because it is women's work, is defined as low status, and even more low status where it is primarily women of color who do it. Half the black women wage earners in New York City today are working in the public-service sector, where they have little power, tend not to be unionized, and have white male bosses.

Women of color are disproportionately victims of the feminization of poverty. In 1983 two out of three poor adults were women, and one out of five children was poor. Women head half of all poor families, and over half the children in female-headed households are poor: 50 percent of the white children and 68 percent of black and Latino children. Women over sixty are twice as likely as male counterparts to be poor. Nearly one-third of black families live below the poverty line. For elderly black women over sixty-five living alone, the 1982 poverty rate was 82 percent (Ehrenreich, Stallard, and Sklar, 1983).

As piecemeal reforms, welfare measures have created a division between those eligible and those ineligible for welfare services. This is supplemented by a pervasive view that those who receive welfare, medicare, food stamps, and special educational or job-training programs are undeserving. The U.S. ideology of capitalist individualism is partly to blame, for it encourages the idea that anyone who works hard and is ambitious can have social mobility in the marketplace without government aid or interference. But there is also a logic of divide and conquer at work, for welfare and entitlement provisions make families with male breadwinners working full time largely ineligible but single mothers and retired old people eligible. Thus poor but employed white, working-class members come to see themselves as a group in opposition to welfare recipients, rather than as jointly oppressed by capitalist development.

## UNDERCLASSISM

By "underclassism" I mean state and economic policies that perpetuate a poor class that does not get its main income from wage labor but is forced to subsist on crime, the informal economy, or state welfare programs. There are three important ways in which U.S. welfare state policies perpetuate racism, sexism, and classism by maintaining a class of poor disproportionately made up of racial minorities and women. First, as I said above, since their inception welfare programs have made a distinction between the "deserving" and the "undeserving" poor. In early welfare programs, states provided for elderly and widows but not for other poor men, women, or children—for example, divorced women with families. The National Social Security Act of 1935 institutionalized differences in benefit levels for the elderly and for mothers with dependent children. Federal funds to the elderly were to match state funds dollar for dollar up to a maximum of $30 per month per recipient; mothers with dependent children only got one federal dollar for two state dollars up to a maximum of $18.

In 1939 amendments to the act further distinguished between the "deserving poor" (widows with children), who were left under Social Security, and the "undeserving poor," who were to be paid much less. In those amendments, Aid to Families with Dependent Children was created for divorced and unmarried mothers. Application for this money was usually not open to two-parent poor families. This restriction, coupled with the lack of sufficient wage-labor jobs for low-income men, has led to the growth of single-mother families among the poor (Folbre, 1987a).

A second mechanism for reproducing a sense of inferiority among welfare recipients is the organization of the social and medical services, which are hierarchical and patronizing, headed by white men. The services objectify, dehumanize, and infantilize clients and patients, creating a sense of powerlessness. Those served have no democratic control or input into the decisionmaking process. They are made to feel unworthy, passive, and stigmatized (Foucault, 1977; Donzelot, 1979).

A third stigmatizing feature is the lack or total inadequacy of services available to certain groups of people. Because middle-class people can afford health care, the poor's need for it is ignored. The absence of a guaranteed right to comprehensive health care or subsidized childcare effectively implies that only those who can pay for it have a right to it or deserve it.[11] Furthermore, no state programs, including Comprehensive Employment and Training Act (CETA) job-training and placement programs (now defunct), have adequately dealt with the unemployment problem among black youths, an important factor in the nonmarriage rate of black teenagers.

In summary, clients of the welfare bureaucracy are made to internalize a feeling of undeservingness because they are treated as second-class citizens. Thus not only do welfare categories stigmatize those who are forced to rely on it for survival, but the welfare system makes their lives miserable by coercive supervision, arbitrary regulations and paperwork, and generally alienating behavior toward its clients. Under these conditions, it is only through populist grassroots social movements that members of the underclass can unite to overcome the social stigma, isolation, and passivity the welfare state creates.

## IDEOLOGICAL CONSEQUENCES OF PATRIARCHAL WELFARE STATE RACISM

Feminist analyses of pornography, sexual advertising, and gendered media images have discussed in detail how women are presented as sexual objects and men as sexual subjects (Dworkin, 1974, 1981; Griffin, 1981; Root, 1984). A parallel and supporting set of racial and class symbolic codes portrays whites and those in the middle class as erotically desirable, and nonwhites and poor people in general as ugly and erotically dangerous. This racist sex/affective code connects with the idea of welfare recipients as undeserving poor to perpetuate a sexual ideology of racism in two more specific ways: by the myth of the (sexually out of control) black rapist and that of the promiscuous (sexually out of control) welfare mother. This is the twentieth-century version of the previous century's slave and Jim Crow ideology that portrayed blacks as having uncontrollable and bestial sexuality.

There are contradictory trends in popular culture, particularly in pop music (much of which comes from black musical roots). Michael Jackson and other MTV video stars, Tina Turner, the Pointer Sisters, Aretha Franklin, the Huxtables on "The Cosby Show," and TV talk show hostess Oprah Winfrey spring to mind as positive symbols of blacks whose appeal does not reduce to a merely tabooed sexuality. But the co-optive element is also present in these images, for the black singers feature more white than African racial features (remember Jackson's nose jobs?) or are presented with an interracial band, giving a utopian image of an interracial culture absent in social reality. Furthermore, the decline of both integrationist and black nationalist aspects of the civil rights movement has left a vacuum into which a resurgence of popular white racism has stepped, as evidenced by a rise in racial violence (for example, the development of racist white skinhead gangs who are explicitly pro–Ku Klux Klan and pro-Nazi).

What are the possibilities for challenging the patriarchal welfare racist system? To answer this we need to consider both the general features of racial formations and the specific material and cultural factors that are undermining the present structure. Racial formations are like economic systems in that they can be seen as dynamic. We may say a particular historical process of racialization is stable when the social power of racial dominants has succeeded in offsetting the resistances of racial subordinates, and that it is in crisis when these latter, in connection with popular social movements, have upset or seriously challenged the ruling system of racial values and have forced the dominators to make institutional adjustments in response.

Thus, in spite of the depressing picture I have painted above of patriarchal welfare racism, its dominance as a system is by no means assured. There are both material and cultural reasons for the system's instability.[12] The Reagan years of cutbacks in welfare programs are only symptomatic of growing stresses on the U.S. empire. The United States can no longer afford to be the capitalist world's policeman, to maintain the excessive wealth of the U.S. capitalist class, and also to preserve the labor aristocracy that keeps the U.S. working class privileged in relation to workers and peasants in the Third World. Something has to give, and under both Republicans and Democrats the welfare state is likely to shrink rather than grow, thus exacerbating the problems of the poor and the underclass.[13]

The gap between the ideology of equal opportunity and the reality of racial oppression in this country has fostered a rebellious consciousness among many in racial minorities. The 1960s civil rights movement and the development of Jesse Jackson's Rainbow Coalition have been welcome signs of an undercurrent of resistance that may eventuate in a counterhegemonic culture that can channel frustrations and defeated expectations of racial minorities, the underclass, and segments of the working class proper into a popular movement to force a modification of our racial formation.

## Hegemonic and Counterhegemonic Racial Cultures

What is involved in creating a counterhegemonic culture? A dominant racial culture achieves what has been called a *hegemonic* status (Gramsci, 1971) when it is at least partially consented to by those in the subordinate group, even though it may be resisted in other ways, for example, by a subordinate subculture, or culture of resistance, which partially reverses the dominant culture's racial values. The hegemonic status of racial ideologies, however, means that they have become psychologically internalized on some level by most of those in the subordinate group. Thus for a racist ideology to be overcome requires more than simply pointing out its logical flaws. Rather, the subordinate culture of an oppressed group must become a *counterhegemonic* culture, in Gramsci's term: That is, it must develop its own intellectuals and social movements that create an alternative vision of the social order maintained by hegemonic culture.

What are the characteristics of a counterhegemonic culture? For one, the alternative vision of such a culture must be historically relevant, must connect to some of the values from contemporary society while rejecting others and must sketch how the chosen values can be better achieved by a restructured society. The vision and proposed structure must also speak both to the special interests of the oppressed groups it organizes and the universal interests of the citizens of the future society. In this way, it can act as a reference point for psychological integrity for those in oppressed groups; it can provide an alternative group identification based on legitimacy and potential social power rather than inferiority and powerlessness.

A racial subculture of resistance redefines the racial categories and rationales of the dominant view so as to provide a new set of values and a rationale for challenging the existing order. When the economic, political, and social resources of the dominant race group are strong, the subordinate race or races may only be able to wage what Gramsci calls "wars of maneuver" from the margins of society (e.g., Indian wars, slave revolts, ghetto riots). Even then, however, there are possibilities of hidden cultures of resistance and folk heroes of the oppressed.

The cultures of people of color in the United States have all incorporated cultures of resistance. Legends of native American leaders such as Geronimo and Sitting Bull were passed down to succeeding generations; those thought of as Mexican "bandits" after the U.S.-Mexican War of 1848 were celebrated as folk heroes in Chicano songs (*corridos*). Afro-Americans have had a sustained culture of resistance in different forms since the beginning of slavery in the United States: Black Christian spirituals have a hidden set of symbols of escaping to freedom, and Nat Turner and Harriet Tubman, leaders of slave revolts and escapes, were slave folk heroes. Though racial segregation in the southern states after Reconstruction eventually became institutionalized into oppressive segregation laws, the separation of the races was actually initiated by blacks, who set up their own hospitals, schools, and churches to reject the inferior treatment accorded them in white institutions, and to recapture a sense of pride in black culture (Marable, 1985; Fredrickson, 1986).

The civil rights movement was a high point in the development of a contemporary black culture of resistance. Aside from civil rights organizations such as the Southern Christian Leadership Conference (SCLC) and the Student Non-Violent Coordinating Committee (SNCC), there were also black trade union groups such as the Coalition of Black Trade Unionists. The black nationalist movement in the 1960s, insisting that "black is beautiful" and validating African elements of black American culture was certainly an attempt to redefine and re-articulate[14] a culture of resistance in order to openly value blackness and thus to weaken the power of white sexual racism. The civil rights and Black Power movements have been slowed recently, however, by the New Right backlash. In spite of the promise of the Rainbow Coalition, the endemic racism of the 1988 presidential campaign demonstrates the continuing power of institutionalized racism to offset challenges from below (Strickland, 1989).

The theory of multiple racial genders in our racial formation explains how difficult it has been to build an antiracist and antisexist coun-terhegemonic culture in the United States. For such a culture would have to challenge the racist work and living structures that separate whites from blacks and other people of color in wage labor. It would also have to challenge the sexual division of labor that perpetuates sexism at home and at work. The organized labor movement has historically been both racist and sexist in its chosen strategies of organizing workers. An encouraging sign of change has been the incorporation of feminist and affirmative action demands into some trade union platforms.

The existence of racial genders also explains why it has been so difficult for the two historical waves of the U.S. women's movement to deal with racial, ethnic, and class differences among women (Kraditor, 1965; Davis, 1981; Aptheker, 1983) and for black civil rights movements to deal with feminism (Wallace, 1979; Evans, 1980). Because white, middle-class women have been in the relatively privileged position of being able to focus on gender oppression independent of race and class oppression, the feminist cultures of resistance that developed around mainstream feminism tended to support autonomous women's networks that were mostly white and middle class. Nonwhite and working-class women's racial and class genders tended to develop a feminism that was much more race- and class-specific, as the cultures of resistance they identified with were those of racial minorities struggling to challenge racism and working-class communities organizing around issues of class oppression (such as trade unionism, homelessness, and so forth).

This is not to say that no cross-class and -race coalitions of feminists have occurred. The first-wave women's movement arose originally out of a coalition between white, middle-class women and some former slaves who were fighting as abolitionists. Though the U.S. Progressive movement of 1880–1920 involved settlement-house and consumer-protection movements run by middle-class feminists who were often overtly racist and classist, the Women's Trade Union League organized middle-class and working-class feminists across the color line (Flexner, 1972).

The contemporary women's movement, though initially classist and racist in its formulation of feminist issues, has developed left-wing and socialist feminist groups that challenge this. One example is the expansion of the notion of what is involved in reproductive rights for women. Thus, the demand in the 1960s that women should have the right to control their bodies through choosing abortion has been broadened to include a right against forced sterilization, the right to affordable abortions, the right to raise children in economically sufficient circumstances, and the right to choose a gay or lesbian life-style without having one's right to parent restricted. Another example is an attempt by local socialist feminist coalitions to link "take back the night" marches (against violence against women) to opposition to racial violence.

Though feminist coalitions that are sensitive to race and class oppression are by no means automatic, there is an opening today to create these because of the ambiguity in our contemporary gender formation's gender roles. Advanced capitalist societies create a universal dispersion of gender norms that stem from white middle- and ruling-class culture via the mass media and public schools. This causes ambiguity as to whether gender norms applicable to the dominant race and privileged economic classes are norms for everyone, a situation that only heightens the ideological conflict between the *ideal* of social equality touted by U.S. culture and the *reality* of gender, class, and race privileges. Women and men increasingly find themselves subject to conflicting demands vis-à-vis gender norms, particularly if they come from the working class or are people of color. The existence of such a conflict in gender norms, together with the economic and racial crises in our society, is part of what creates the opening for the building of an antiracist, socialist, and feminist alliance in this historical period.

The political implications of this analysis suggest that fighting welfare state racism, sexism, and classism requires a pluralist coalition and networking strategy among and between minority nationalist groups, minority and white feminist groups, and working-class groups of various races. The counterhegemonic culture we need to wage what Gramsci called a "war of position" does not yet exist, though countercultural groups such as the Rainbow Coalition could build networks to form such a culture. An important emphasis would be a coalition of social service providers who insist on prioritizing needs rather than profits and challenge the business-as-usual mentality of welfare state workers.

The political conditions in the United States are unlike those of European and Latin countries where a high class consciousness exists. It is a mistake to expect, as does Gramsci (1971), that the working class here can act as a "vanguard" to exercise "hegemony," or direction, over the other cultures of resistance represented in an antiracist, feminist, and socialist-oriented coalition. This is not to say that the trade union movement is not a key site for feminists and antiracists to network with and within. But a sufficient condition for radical social change that challenges racism is building an interracial cross-class counterculture that is explicitly anticapitalist and antisexist. One intellectual move toward such a counterculture is in seeking creative ways to analyze our contemporary racial and gender formation to show how the interests of all the diverse elements in our coalition can be met by altering the status quo. I hope that this essay is one helpful step in this direction.

## Notes

1. In Chapter 4 I claimed that we needed a multisystems approach to social domination. But there and in the rest of the essays in this book, I consider only systems of economic class, gender, and racial domination, thus effectively reducing my working perspective to a trisystems approach. There are, of course, social dominations based on other discriminations, for example, sexual preference, age, and physical ability. Though I deal with heterosexism in Chapters 6 and 7, I do not have the space to consider other systems in this book. The others are certainly important as well, though my own view is that race, class, and gender are more central to the dynamics of our contemporary social formations than the others.

2. It is tempting to offer a reductive functional explanation for the origins of racism in this country, as colonialism and slavery, the domination systems on which our country was founded, functionally require ways to segregate and control subordinate peoples. This is a task that importantly involves control of subordinates' sexuality and sets the stage for the sexual aspects of racism. Because allowing miscegenation runs the risk of a racial assimilation that would reduce the power of racial dominants to mark off, in order to exploit, subordinate peoples, racial dominants must either forbid miscegenation or else find ways to keep mixed-race peoples from challenging the existing colonial or slave system. The creation of racial discourses, or "power/knowledges" (Foucault, 1977, 1978), which define nonwhite and mixed races as inferior and assign unequal legal rights to such groups, is a means to achieve this end.

Though the origins of institutional racism can be given a functional explanation, it is not so clear why racism persists even after colonialism and slavery end. Though racial power/knowledges, institutionalized in economic, legal, and cultural practices, underwent an upheaval after the U.S. Civil War, in altered forms they continue to maintain racial domination. Thus it is more plausible to acknowledge that the social mechanisms for controlling interracial interactions persist and take on a life of their own as influential in shaping dominants' and subordinates' conceptions of their interests as are economic considerations.

3. By a theory with the analytic power of Marxism, I mean a theory that can give us a general approach for analyzing systems of social domination in historically specific contexts. Even poststructuralists such as Foucault, who deny the possibility of universal historical narratives or totalist explanations, assume a general analytic method. In Foucault's case "genealogy" takes on the analytic notions of "regimes of truth," "power/knowledges," and a theory of different forms of power, which are then historically specified. Though some have borrowed Foucault's method to understand racism (cf. West, 1986), I think that the notion of racial formation can suggest a general way to view racial domination in all racially mixed societies. This Foucault's genealogical method cannot do, as it can only give us a history of the present that explains the origins of racial formation in our own society.

4. Most also include some socially institutionalized ways for individuals to cross gender categories, for example, by cross-dressing, performing opposite gender occupations, homosexual activities, and so on.

5. It is important to note that father patriarchy may have been the dominant mode of sex/affective production, but it was not the only mode in operation. African slaves, propertyless workers, and indentured servants had different kinship relations, as did native Americans. In general, however, the dominant economic class of a society is able to impose its mode of sex/affective production as the dominant mode, by its control of the legal, economic, and educational systems. And because the dominant economic class is mostly composed of the dominant race (often one ethnic group as well), the racial/ethnic culture of the dominant class is used to stigmatize and punish the subordinate modes of sex/affective production of racial and class subordinates. Thus, when propertied white English settlers controlled the economic system of early colonial America, the family arrangements and sexual mores of native Americans, indentured servants, and African slaves were stigmatized and (in the case of the latter two groups) controlled by the father patriarchy of the propertied. This of course did not eliminate alternative sex/affective practices, but it did minimize their effectiveness in empowering subordinates to resist. The dominant sex/affective codes of the time were in varying degrees internalized in subordinates, thus creating what W.E.B. du Bois called a divided or "double consciousness" (du Bois, 1961).

6. Paula Giddings (1984) also mentions the use of abortion by black slaves as a refusal to produce babies for the white owners.

7. I owe the idea of racial genders to Leonard Harris, as well as the idea that both men and women of racial minorities may be oppressed because of their gender. Black men lynched for the supposed crime of flirting with white women, of course, were oppressed both because of their gender and their race: A black woman was not subject to lynching for flirting with a white man!

8. In January 1989, as I was writing the first draft of this chapter, there had just been another two days of rioting in Miami brought on by the death

of two black (Afro-American) motorcyclists at the hands of a Latino policeman. The question of the biological race of that policeman was not even raised in the media coverage: His Latin background was sufficient to classify him as in a different racial minority (brown) from black Americans, whether or not he was of Caucasian or Negro biological descent. During the height of the Black Power movement in the late 1960s and early 1970s, however, there was a tendency for black Latinos and West Indians to feel a mixed identification with the native black community. Obviously, the black versus Latino racialization process is subject to change in the future.

Oma Narayan has pointed out to me that there are further ambiguities within this set of racial gender positions. Where do Arabs fit? Or Indians? Are Persians distinguished from Arabs? All Asians are lumped together whereas Latin Americans are distinguished from, say, Italian-Americans as being a different race, when it would seem more plausible to suppose they are merely different cultural groups. Furthermore, native Americans (Indians) from Latin America are of a different racial and cultural stock from Hispanic-Americans yet are not distinguished in our current racial categories. What this demonstrates more clearly is that these categories are historically created to deal with changing immigrant populations and shifting alliances in the dominant racial groups themselves and are subject to change again as the population changes.

9. It is tempting to argue that gender is specified equally by class and race in our society. Although some practices distinguish between "ladies" of the middle and upper classes and "women" of the working and poor classes (cf. Kollias, 1975), however, the mystification of class in the contemporary United States ensures that women will tend to identify more around race and across class than they will around class across race. For this reason I have concluded that in our current social formation, class gender is a less central distinction in personal identity than racial gender.

10. The Great Society welfare programs were instituted by the Johnson administration in the late 1960s in response to civil rights agitation. They increased welfare benefits for poor dependent children and single mothers and created Head Start preschool educational programs and youth job-training programs. Unfortunately, these programs have only succeeded in perpetuating and stigmatizing the growth of the black underclass of poor. This is in part because Johnson did not push for an increase in a progressive income tax on the wealthy to provide adequate funds for these programs, in part because the vagaries of capitalist development did not create sufficient job opportunities for minorities in city ghettos and in part because welfare programs were seen to be giveaway programs that did not benefit poor white, working-class families whose heads had full-time jobs but whose income was at or below the poverty level. Thus they were perfect targets when the New Right successfully pressured the Reagan administration to eliminate and drastically cut entitlement programs.

11. Mention should be made of the AIDS crisis and how because the most at-risk populations of this disease have been gay men and intravenous drug users, of whom a majority are black and Latino, the federal government has not responded as fast as it should to this national health crisis. As these

populations are labeled sex/affective deviants, they are assumed to be "undeserving" sick and thus not worth the expense necessary to treat and research this disease. Not until it became clear that AIDS was a danger to the white, heterosexual population as well did federal money start being released for AIDS research (cf. Patton, 1990).

12. Social change in racism is most likely when a racial formation is in flux, that is, when some important economic or political change—capitalist development, economic depression or recession, war, the introduction of a different labor force—has aroused reaction from conservative forces or rebellion from oppressed groups. I shall call this time when old institutionalized practices are no longer working or are in question a "break" period. When stability has been reestablished, usually by the institutionalization of a new set of economic, political, and social practices of racialization, a racial formation can be said to have achieved "redefinition."

Our contemporary society is in a break period with respect to its racial formation. The civil rights movement of the 1960s challenged the status quo and succeeded in getting some new rules of the game—affirmative action, civil rights laws, social entitlement programs—mandated. These procedures, however, were challenged via the Reagan and Bush administrations and the New Right. Thus there are contradictory forces at work today, some empowering nonwhites and some undermining the newly institutionalized antiracism laws of the 1960s.

13. I owe this point about the crisis of U.S. empire to William Strickland (1989).

14. The notion of "re-articulating" a social identity is borrowed from Omi and Winant (1986). The idea is that a culture of resistance must redefine in a positive way social identity concepts connected to oppression.

# *Part Two*

# FEMINIST POLITICS AND VISIONS

# SEVEN

# Is There a Lesbian Culture?

What is lesbianism? Is it a universal, cross-cultural state of being or is it historically specific to that period in which industrial societies develop? Do lesbians have a culture that cuts across the cultures of race, class, and society? If so, is it co-extensive with women's culture? If not, how does it differ? Is being a lesbian like being Jewish or Afro-American? That is, is it like an ethnic identity, a social aspect of self that is deeper than a mere "preference" that can be changed by individual whim? Or are homosexual desires a part of every human unconscious even though repressed by the majority? Finally, is it plausible to argue that being a lesbian is a political act, an act of resistance to patriarchy? If so, how is it related to feminism?

Feminist theoretical answers to these questions have presupposed a continuous, discontinuous, or deconstructivist approach to understanding lesbianism. Each of these approaches, though it has an important insight, is limited in not allowing for historically specific understandings of different lesbianisms. The dialectical theory offered here of lesbian cultures as cultures of resistance avoids this shortcoming. Systems of social domination in different countries support different forms of patriarchy, class-divided production, racism, and ethnicism. Thus there is at present no international lesbian culture, though in every society there are women who primarily love and have sex with women. Lesbian feminist theory and politics must acknowledge this discontinuity in our sisterhood before we can change it.

An international lesbian culture cannot be just defined or wished into existence, in the manner implied by some radical feminist theorists (cf. Cook, 1977; Daly, 1978, 1982; Rich, 1980). Rather, the very concept of an international lesbian culture is politically problematic. Due to the cultural and material resources of First World industrial societies,[1] the most likely content of such a universal would be modeled after lesbian subcultures in Western nations. This would smack of cultural imperialism, of Western lesbian liberation movements importing notions of the proper values for a lesbian culture of resistance into other societies. Rather than taking as our political project the creation of an international lesbian culture, we would do better to work for the construction of international lesbian, feminist, and gay liberation *movements* that develop a radical democratic form for promoting the development of indigenous national and local lesbian, feminist, and gay oppositional cultures in their particular locales, social classes, and racial and ethnic groups.[2]

In order to develop the view that there is no international lesbian culture and the political implications this has for lesbian and feminist theory, let us consider different ways of conceptualizing culture and of framing lesbian history. After that we will take a look at cultural differences between women who engage in same-sex sexuality, the barriers this creates for building a democratic, grassroots, international lesbian movement, and some suggested strategies to overcome these.

## Lesbian Culture

### WHAT IS A CULTURE?

Lesbian feminist theorists have claimed that there is a universal women's culture hidden under patriarchal cultures (Burris, 1973). Some say women's communities preceded patriarchal societies (cf. Reed, 1973; Grahn, 1984; Cavin, 1985). Within women's cultural networks, others argue, women-loving women form an even more invisible lesbian culture (Cook, 1977; Rich, 1980). Still others see separate women's institutions and communities—convents, Chinese marriage resisters, contemporary lesbian communities—as examples of "gyn/affectionate" women's oppositional cultures without labeling them "lesbian" (Raymond, 1986). This is at odds with Judy Grahn's view, because for her a distinctive social group of women, say spinsters, can be defined as lesbian and as part of a gay culture independently of whether they identify as such, just in case they perform what she calls a "gay office." But other lesbian feminist theorists (MacKinnon, 1987) suggest that neither an authentic lesbian nor a women's culture exists in male dominant societies, for gender identity and sexual desires are patriarchally constructed. To assess these opposing claims we need to understand what constitutes a culture.

Anthropologists have studied different societies using a very broad concept of culture, as a cluster of activities by which a social group is distinguished from and distinguishes itself from other social groups: common language, values, habits, rituals, arts, religion, philosophy, and so forth. Clifford Geertz (1973) argues that culture involves a public sharing of symbols, which Fern Johnson (1987) divides into three interrelated systems of meaning: language and communication, artifacts, and abstractions. This is, of course, a different sense of culture than that in which culture (fine arts, science, and philosophy) is opposed to nature, and women's activities such as domestic chores and child-rearing are belittled as not cultural but natural (Ortner, 1974).

In Geertz's sense of culture, the gender division of labor between domestic household activity and public market or organized state activity can ground differences in values, artifacts, and personalities and thus produce different "gender cultures" in every human society. That is, because those in one gender in every known human society tend to develop different skills, values, and even recognizably different language habits from those in the other gender, then men and women, besides sharing the common culture of their specific society, are participants in different gender subcultures. Certainly the work by Chodorow (1974, 1978a, 1978b), Gilligan (1982), Lakoff (1975), and Johnson and Aries (1983) suggests that women's personalities, ethical thinking, and language, all important elements of culture, may differ from men's.

There is a problem, however, with the characterization of culture as a shared symbol system. Languages, values, and production of artifacts may overlap so that people can be members of different cultural systems at the same time. For example, people can be said to be in subcultures connected to gender, race, ethnicity, religion—even occupation—as well as in a dominant culture defined by nationality, for example, citizens of the United States. How do we decide when people's shared activities are sufficiently similar to constitute a common culture? Afro-American female slaves, for example, cared for planters' children as well as their own. And until recently, a large number of Afro-American women were employed as domestics in other people's homes. Maybe such activity constitutes a common women's culture uniting black women and white women slaveholders in the care of white children.[3] But this ignores the way in which black and white women may also see themselves in different, indeed antagonistic, racial cultures.

These examples point up two ways of defining membership in a culture or subculture. First, there is an "objective" sense of culture, defined by the theorist as sufficient social attributes in common for members to constitute a distinctive social group. This includes shared social artifacts and material practices, that is, common rituals and a system of production and distribution of material and human resources that requires members to function together in a cooperative fashion. Second, there is the "subjective" sense of culture, involving a consciously held identification of others as members, along with self, as part of a particular group.

This second sense of culture, which we can call the "identity sense," requires that one be recognized, both by oneself and by others in one's society, as being a part of a social category. Without such a recognition, as, for example, in societies who lack one of the several Western conceptions of race that developed with the institutions of imperialism and slavery[4] (Harris, 1964), any so-called natural similarities between people, even when they involve shared tasks and values, will lack social implications for an individual's sense of self.

A theorist who characterizes culture in the first sense attempts to show that a group of people indeed engage in enough common activities, or perhaps some core formative activities, to share a symbol system and hence a culture. Such an approach is common to Barry, Grahn, Gilligan, Ruddick (1984), Ortner, Johnson, and Rich.[5] A problem with this objectivist approach is the political conclusions that some theorists draw from assuming a group has a common culture. They hold that if a social domination system such as male dominance, capitalism, or racism oppresses the group, it has a common interest to unite and fight the system. Such an analysis often ignores other social activities and structural positions of individuals that may keep them from feeling any identification, hence shared political cause, with one other. For example, feminists who have argued that women are a "sex class" because of a similar gender division of labor in the market and in the household that oppresses women across race and economic class lines tend to ignore the ways in which race, class, and other cultural differences keep women from sharing the same values or priorities, and thus from identifying themselves as members of a common culture or special interest group. Indeed, my own early work has been accused of this fault (cf. Ferguson, 1979; Delphy, 1984; Wittig, 1981).[6]

The identity sense of culture assumes that members of the same culture do consider themselves as such. That is, every individual assumed to be a part of a culture or subculture must consciously accept, at least on reflection, this characterization of herself or himself. In this view it is problematic to assume that nonwhite and white women share a common women's culture in racist societies. Rather, such a sense of common culture must be struggled for and created by feminist and antiracist movements in which women acknowledge their other social differences, privileges, and oppressions vis-à-vis one another.[7]

The identity approach has another important consequence: It allows us to point out the asymmetry of gender cultures in patriarchal society and thus note the negative consequences for women. Some of the objectivist theorists of culture tend to ignore the effects of domination in limiting the possibilities of women's culture. For example, Gilligan's theory that there is a woman's moral point of view assumes that men's and women's ethical voices are complementary, not antagonistic. But patriarchal culture does not allow such a conclusion; because dominant public culture is controlled by men, men both identify themselves with such a culture and exclude women as contributing members. They thus do not recognize the value of women's cultural activities. Women, then, because our social activities tend to be devalued and less visible, are less able to identify ourselves proudly as members of a cultural group that produces significant artifacts, has its own distinctive language and values (Miller, 1976). In this sense MacKinnon (1987) is correct to question the extent to which patriarchal cultures have allowed any independent women's culture to exist. And Daly (1982) and Rich (1979) argue that an important part of our task is not to uncover a hidden women's culture but to create it, which they (Daly, 1988; Rich, 1978; Wittig, 1971, 1986) have set out to do.

A problem with the identity sense of culture when applied to those who share in lesbian culture is that it defines out of existence "false consciousness," that is, women whose sexual and affectional preferences are for other women but because of internalized homophobia refuse to acknowledge themselves as lesbians. Is it not an arbitrary solution to the political issue of who should "come out" to eliminate the issue by a mere definition of the term *lesbian* that implies that women can never be mistaken about whether or not they are members of this culture (cf. Zita's critique of my earlier work: Zita, 1981; Ferguson, 1981b)?

The shortcomings of both the objectivist and identity senses of culture seem to create a dilemma for lesbian theory, for the objectivist theorist can pick out any set of social activities shared by individuals and label that a "culture," regardless of whether the participants accept that designation. And as we shall see in more detail below, lesbian theorists who take an objectivist approach come up with different continuity qualities that characterize lesbian culture cross-culturally but offer no clear way to tell what the real lesbian or gay culture is. On the other hand, the identity sense of culture suggests that most human societies have been lacking a lesbian culture in the self-conscious sense. For though innumerable women in many societies have engaged in lesbian sexual practices and many have prioritized women over men in their lives, it was not until the late nineteenth and early twentieth centuries that a distinctive self-identified lesbian subculture arose. Is lesbian theory forced to choose between a notion of lesbian culture that is so broad as to include any woman who challenges gender roles or so narrow as to exclude us from any authentic lesbian history before the nineteenth century?

A way to avoid these pitfalls is to change the nature of our search: Instead of looking cross-culturally for common subcultures involving women, we should be looking at cultures of whole societies in a more historical and dialectical way. If we do, we may be able to identify lesbian and feminist oppositional and proto-oppositional subcultures, that is, those which, in their historical context, generated or have the possibility to generate a political resistance to patriarchy and compulsory heterosexuality. Complex societies in which economically and politically dominant groups impose a hegemonic culture on other subordinate groups spawn, under certain social and material conditions, oppositional cultures, or countercultures. A culture of resistance is one that challenges the social roles and valuation given to it by the dominant culture.[8] It is when such an oppositional culture has arisen, or is in the process of arising, that individuals can make and be asked to decide whether they are members of the culture or not.

Contemporary lesbian feminist theorizing has emerged in just such a historical situation, as a tool of lesbian, gay, and feminist social movements seeking to reevaluate and reconstruct existing lesbian, gay, and feminist subcultures so as to forge them into a unified culture of resistance to a dominant culture seen as patriarchal and heterosexist. A dialectical historical approach can explain our historical uniqueness without sacrificing a broader sense of continuity to other actual and potential lesbian and gay cultures of resistance in other settings.

## FEMINIST THEORIES OF LESBIANISM REVISITED: CONTINUITY, DISCONTINUITY, AND DECONSTRUCTIONIST APPROACHES

The argument about how to define *lesbian* has political implications about the best way to conceive of lesbianism in order to advance the cause of lesbian/gay liberation and feminism. Thus it is important to look for the sometimes hidden political agendas and disagreements of those who enter the fray.

My dialectical and historical approach to the lesbian history debate assumes that different theories of lesbian history are themselves historically situated. In assessing them, we must assume a theory-identity connection. That is, theorists tend to use different strategies to defend and valorize the existing subcultures with which they identify. Thus as lesbian and feminist activists, to assess the different strategies we must consider not merely the view of history offered but the political viability, both of the culture that gave rise to it and the culture of resistance that the theorist aims to promote.

To examine the political implications of theoretical differences, let us now revisit the debate about the definition of *lesbian* engaged in by a number of lesbian scholars since 1977.[9] In my 1981 dispute with Rich I put forth three criteria for evaluating a successful definition that Rich and others seemed to assume: (1) that a definition should valorize the concept of lesbianism by freeing it from clinical and pejorative associations with deviancy, sinfulness, and psychological sickness and neurosis; (2) that a definition should help us with a new approach to the project of lesbian history, which could help us uncover evidences of past lesbians so that present lesbian culture could have a sense of belonging to a valuable if hidden tradition that (3) could help us to grasp the magnitude of the underground resistance to the institution of compulsory heterosexuality.[10]

Looking back on this debate, I think that it is not possible to characterize lesbians so as to fulfill these three criteria—indeed I think this is a misguided task. What strikes me now is that there are two conflicting emphases in these definitions that connect to two opposing needs of contemporary self-identified lesbian communities. On the one hand, there is the need for historical *continuity:* We seek to identify with foresisters who also deviated from the strictures of compulsory heterosexuality in their age and society. On the other hand, there are also good reasons to stress historical *discontinuity:* There have never been gay liberation movements of the contemporary sort before, nor have there been lesbian feminist movements like those in advanced capitalist societies today. What does this tell us about our historical uniqueness, both as political subjects and as warriors against hetero-sexism and patriarchy? We need to pay attention to our historical context in order to develop an effective political strategy for our place and time.

*Continuity Approaches to Lesbianism.* There are three major overlapping continuity approaches employed by lesbian feminist theorists. The first identifies lesbians cross-culturally and transhistorically with "woman-loving women," those who prioritize relations with women (cf. Radicalesbians, 1970; Cook, 1977; Sahli, 1979; Faderman, 1981). An advocate of this approach is Lillian Faderman, who defines lesbian as "a relationship in which two women's strongest emotions and affections are directed toward each other. Sexual contact may be a part of the relationship to a greater or lesser degree, or it may be entirely absent. By preference the two women spend most of their time together and share most aspects of their lives with each other" (Faderman, 1981, p. 74).

A second approach, articulated by Adrienne Rich, places all women on a lesbian continuum, with respect to those of their practices that resist compulsory heterosexuality and dependence on men. A third approach, developed by Judy Grahn (1984), assumes that gayness is connected to a universal gay social role, or office, to convey cross-gender information to human societies, which, as they are otherwise gender-segregated, lack access to this integrative function. This view maintains that women who reverse gender roles—"mannish" women and those who cross-dress—are examples of lesbians, and societies that institutionalize such possibilities for men and women, such as many native American cultures, are more "permissive" to homosexuality.

Though these continuity approaches overlap, they also involve implausible and incompatible conclusions. For example, Rich, Cook, and Grahn assume that all woman-loving women are patriarchal resisters. But though this may be plausible as a psychological description of such women, it may be questionable as a political judgment, depending on the historical context. So in the nineteenth century in Western Europe, Britain, and the United States, when the prevalent ideology of true womanhood held that women were more spiritual and less sexual than men, women's romantic friendships were not seen as a challenge to patriarchal ideology but rather a confirmation of it. And what of the "mannish" women that Grahn describes in many native American cultures who cross-dressed and reversed gender roles? Are they challenging patriarchal assumptions of bipolar gender roles or just further supporting them? Even though these women married other women, and thus were woman-loving in this sense, they also bonded with men in the gender division of labor in which they were accepted as men. Do they then count as woman-loving in the political sense?

Another disagreement concerns the status of men who reversed or challenged gender roles, for example, the *berdaches,* or holy men, of some native American cultures and those who cross-dressed did women's work and married other men (cf. Grahn, 1984; Roscoe, 1988). Were they patriarchal resisters, members of an oppositional gay culture, and precursors of a unified feminist and gay liberation movement? Or were they simply breaking one general rule of patriarchal societies—the gender division of social roles based on biological sex—in order to validate a more important rule: that of male bonding by all possible means (Frye, 1983)?

Lesbian historian Judy Grahn tends to equate any same-sex activity, whether by men or women, with a challenge to patriarchy. Interestingly, she and others who identify as part of a subculture with gay men are either older lesbians who banded together in mixed gay bars and gay organizations in the 1940s and 1950s (cf. Nestle, 1987) or younger lesbians whose political work, such as organizing around AIDS or opposing radical feminist views of pornography, connects them more primarily with the mixed gay community than with lesbian separatist or feminist subcultures.[11] On the other hand, those who identify with lesbian separatist and feminist subcultures seek a lesbian history that dissociates lesbian from gay male culture past and present (e.g., Rich, Frye).[12]

It is important to note that Adrienne Rich's "lesbian continuum" has the political effect of broadening the concept of lesbianism to include nonsexual and heterosexually active women as long as they resist patriarchy. This undercuts lesbian feminist separatism,, for it prioritizes an identification with a feminist subculture, not all of whose members identify themselves as lesbian, as those for whom "lesbian herstory" is being written.[13] On the other hand, Grahn's broadening of the concept, though in some ways equivalent to Rich's, seems to have an opposite political emphasis. Her insistence that spinsters, though neither sexually active nor identifying themselves as lesbian, are really a part of gay culture because they perform a gay office (that of modeling an alternative way of being for women) suggests that gay culture is prior to feminism. Otherwise, why not just categorize them as nonsexual feminists?

These disagreements among continuity theorists demonstrate that no one common characterization of "lesbian" applies transhistorically and cross-culturally. Instead, each of these approaches involves an implicit appeal to an objectivist sense of lesbian culture that picks out one cluster of commonalities between gender-rebellious women or women and men and re-articulates[14] for contemporary lesbians one possible historical set of past women to identify as part of their self-conscious lesbian community. But the competing clusters are not coextensive, and there is no objective way to resolve the issue.

*Lesbianism as a Deconstructive Category.* One way to avoid the problem of assigning a specific denotation to *lesbian* in order to do lesbian history is to argue that there is no such denotation because of the logic of the term itself. In this view, *lesbian* is a sliding signifier with no fixed positive content; rather, it is a deconstructive concept that can be applied to any woman who violates assumptions of gender dualism that are themselves historically specific. ("Deconstruction" refers to a technique of challenging dominant either/or categories by discovering items to which both terms fail to apply.)

Monique Wittig develops this idea of lesbianism in her essay "One Is Not Born a Woman" (Wittig, 1981). According to Wittig, *lesbian* challenges the gender binary categories of compulsory heterosexuality. A lesbian is an anomaly in terms of these categories: someone who is not-woman/not-man. No wonder, then, that lesbian existence is invisible in dominant culture (Frye, 1983). The possibility of lesbianism challenges the naturalness of the category "woman" as it is defined socially by systems of compulsory heterosexuality. Lesbian as a category challenges the essentialism of the idea of the eternal masculine versus the eternal feminine defined as natural complements but does not itself have a fixed content or essence. It is merely a negative category and as such empty of specific positive expectations. Nonetheless, it creates the possibility of a radical third gender—presumably "gay male" would be a fourth gender (cf. Butler, 1987)—to challenge the dual gender systems of compulsory heterosexuality and male dominance.

Wittig and Frye imply that the logic of the concept of lesbianism is part of a system of gender language used to impose social dominance on resistant women. It is used in systems of compulsory heterosexuality in a normatively negative way, to characterize someone biologically female who refuses to act her expected sexual role. The deconstructive implications of the concept can be used in productive ways to challenge heterosexist and patriarchal values (cf. Hoagland, 1988).

There are, however, two problems with this deconstructive analysis of the concept. The idea that *lesbian* is used in a normatively negative way implies that it does have a denotation in our society and thus that it is false that lesbians are invisible. There are, rather, quite visible lesbians, for example, working-class butches, those who appear to act like men as well as to have sex with women. Insofar as this role is viewed as a type of deviant womanhood, it is on the same level as prostitution: Both lesbians and whores are women, but they are "bad" or "failed" women. In neither case does the existence of "bad" women threaten the hegemonic characterization of "good," "true," "natural" women as nonpromiscuous, heterosexual, and, eventually, married and mothers.

Second, even if Wittig is correct that compulsory heterosexuality in our society reinforces patriarchy by promoting a gender dualism that makes the concept "lesbian" a challenge to the concept "woman," her point does not necessarily apply to other historical types of patriarchy, compulsory heterosexuality, and gender dualism. For example, it might be argued that those cultures such as the native American ones cited by Grahn that institutionalize forms of homosexuality do not have exact equivalents of our words *lesbian* or *gay*. Instead, they have terms that translate more like "woman who does not want to marry" and "woman/man." If so, any deconstructive and hence patriarchy-challenging use of that concept in our society does not necessarily carry over to those and other non-Western societies. Furthermore, it begs the question to suppose that such cultures, because they have a type of gender dualism—after all one must dress either as a man or woman, regardless of one's biological sex—must be male dominant, and that the term most nearly equivalent to *lesbian* must carry negative connotations that challenge the term *woman.* Rather than assume this a priori based on the logic of *lesbian* in Western societies, we must do further empirical research on the social relations of these societies.

The deconstructive strategy is ahistorical in another way. It doesn't focus on the question why, just at this historical moment, have lesbians, typed as failed women by patriarchal categories, suddenly become so visible? To understand this, we need to turn to the discontinuity approach.

*The Discontinuity Approach: Lesbianism as a Historically Developed Identity.* Whether or not one is willing to grant sufficient commonality to structures of male domination across race, ethnic group, class, and culture to allow the univocal use of the term *feminist* to name women who resist patriarchal structures, the concept of lesbianism seems more historically discontinuous. Perhaps this is because capitalist development has led to the historical separation of kinship and economic organization in a way that creates a much more open sexual economy for women. Wage earning allows the possibility that unmarried women can live independently of kin, thus that for some women living with and engaging in sex with women could take the place of heterosexual marriage. *Lesbian* acquires a unique meaning as networks of female homosexual practitioners are enabled to create their own networks and subcultures facilitated by available wage labor and the development of urban centers. Key features in such urban centers are the possibility of living separate from kin in boardinghouses and apartments, and the development of gay bars, which allows for a sexual economy permitting a cultural area and set of rituals for women to engage in lesbian sexual exchanges.

Another important factor is the success of late nineteenth- and early twentieth-century sexology in promoting a theory of essential self-identity based on sexual identity. The theory promoted by Krafft-Ebing (1892), Ellis (1936), and Freud (1963a) of sexual inversion as a particular type of deviant psychological personality becomes a hegemonic cultural idea (Foucault, 1978; Weeks, 1979, 1981, 1985; Adam, 1987). In the process, the new concept of a distinctive homosexual *identity* that is not simply reducible to homosexual sexual *practices* allowed the development of a sense of group identity and the possibility of a self-conscious subculture.

This oppositional culture found ways to incorporate and reconstruct a more positive notion of homosexual identity. This involved, first, the notion of the "gay" identity that opposed heterosexual puritan attitudes toward sex and in contrast valued a positive attitude toward the possibility of nonmonogamous sex with the same sex (Adam, 1987).

A somewhat later development for lesbians was the "woman-identified woman"—a way of seeing lesbian love that resists the merely negative pathological implications of the sexologists (Ferguson, 1981b).

The idea of gay and lesbian as distinctive, historically developed identities connects to the identity sense of culture discussed earlier. It has the obvious advantages of allowing us to explain how and why the new social movements of the 1960s and 1970s in the United States and Europe led to radical gay liberation movements. For though there were gay political organizations in these countries before the 1960s, the idea that institutional racism infringes on the civil rights of racial minorities enabled the development of the notion of an analogous structure of compulsory heterosexuality, or heterosexism, which infringes on gays and lesbians as a sexual minority. Thinking of gays as an oppressed social minority rather than a set of individual deviants was made historically possible by the existence of a gay and lesbian bar culture, social clubs, and friendship networks that constituted a segregated subculture in some ways similar to the U.S. Afro-American subculture produced by slavery and social segregation.

One advantage that the idea of a historically unique lesbian identity provided to U.S. feminism is a way to understand the connection between new lesbian subcultures and sexual liberation for all women. Though the mere existence of such networks of sexually defined women existing independently of heterosexual marriage theoretically attacks the ideology of female sexuality as a mere passive complement to aggressive male sexuality, such networks cannot pragmatically challenge the dominant ideology of female sexuality until lesbians develop political power as a self-conscious community.[15] Though political lesbian community-building began in the United States in the 1940s and 1950s by lesbian and gay organizations such as the Mattachine Society and the Daughters of Bilitis (DOB), it was the consciousness-raising techniques of the 1960s women's movement and the view that the personal is the political that allowed lesbians to denounce the homophobia in women's groups like the National Organization of Women. The women's movement's redefinition of the female orgasm as not reducible to the vaginal orgasm (Koedt, 1970) suggested that lesbian sexual practices might actually be more "woman-identified" than standard heterosexual practices. This set the stage both for the demand that women's liberation goals include the right of women to "woman-identified" and lesbian sex (Ehrenreich, Hess, and Jacobs, 1986) and for the more radical development of lesbian feminist separatism, which argued that the true feminist or "woman-identified woman" was a lesbian (Radicalesbians, 1970).

Though the discontinuity approach to lesbian identity is helpful in understanding the unique aspects of contemporary women's history, some of the political appropriations of this approach are problematic. For one, many people assume that the new homosexual identity is analogous to an ethnic identity, that is, one that though socially constructed is nonetheless fixed for those defined by it. Such an assumption is used to base an identity politics, namely, of acknowledging one's inner "essence" as a lesbian or as a gay man, of "coming out," and of defining one's interests as centrally involved with promoting those of the lesbian or gay community. This is the deterministic pole of identity politics: that individuals should not try to escape what they "really" are in order to avoid social repression. As such, it is characteristic of much of "old" lesbian and gay politics of the 1950s in the United States and Europe as well as much of contemporary gay politics in these countries that centers on gaining civil rights for gays (cf. Plummer, 1981; Epstein, 1987).

The other pole of identity politics is implicitly antideterministic. This was, ironically, a feature of both early lesbian feminist separatism (cf. Myron and Bunch, 1975) and radical humanist lesbian and gay liberation (Dworkin, 1974, 1978; Altman, 1974). Early lesbian feminist separatism stressed that because heterosexuality is itself socially constructed, all women can choose to be either lesbian or heterosexual.[16] Thus women should opt for lesbianism as the vanguard of feminism. Radical humanist gay liberation, on the other hand, stressed that all humans have unconscious homosexual tendencies, so coming out will ultimately allow the development of a bisexual or pansexual orientation for everyone. According to this view that we are all homosexuals as well as all dual gendered, the best strategy is a nonseparatist sexual liberation movement that attacks homophobia and sexism within and without its ranks (Altman, 1974; Escoffier, 1985). This view, like the corresponding ideal of androgyny in the women's movement (Ferguson, 1977) has now been discounted as utopian by most feminist and gay liberation activists (Raymond, 1979; Altman, 1983). The problem is that assuming that human nature is pansexual or androgynous is still an essentialist position (although it does rule out the idea that some individuals are more "naturally" attracted to one sex rather than the other or more bent on "masculine" rather than "feminine" ways of approaching the world). Not only can such a view of human nature not be proved, but it is utopian to assume it in our strategy of sexual liberation, for we are already socially constructed in non-pansexual, nonandrogynous ways.

The discontinuity approach, though it suggests an identity politics, gives us no way to adjudicate between the politicization of conflicting identities (Weeks, 1985). For example, though some lesbians consider themselves a vanguard against patriarchy, others make common cause with gay men in a struggle against heterosexism, for example, by working against the homophobia engendered by the AIDS crisis. Because lesbians and gays do have a common interest in fighting heterosexism, why not then identify ourselves as part of a mixed lesbian/gay community?[17] Even though sexual identity politics tends to imply that we must politicize our sexual identity, it is not clear why we must assume that lesbian practices support only one kind of identity: We seem to have the choice of defining ourselves as lesbian feminists and/or as lesbian/gays and/or as bisexual/androgynous lesbian humanists!

Barbara Ponse (1978) presents a related critique of discontinuity theory of lesbian identity. She argues that the prevalent image of lesbian identity accepted by both theorists and the majority of self-identified lesbians is ideological, not empirical. That is, instead of *describing* how individuals actually identify themselves and the relation between this and their sexual, gender role and other social practices, the identity image *prescribes* or sets an ideological norm based on the idea of the essential, authentic self that has a fixed, unified sexual identity. But if we are to capture the more complicated reality of those associated with the self-conscious lesbian community, we should acknowledge that instead of a uniform identity of its members, there are at least four identity/activity combinations: (1) women with a lesbian identity who engage solely in lesbian sexual activity; (2) women with a lesbian identity who engage in either heterosexual or bisexual activity; (3) women with a bisexual identity who engage solely in lesbian sexual activity; and (4) women with a heterosexual identity who engage solely in lesbian sexual activity.[18]

U.S. lesbian feminist politics often assumes that women in the second, third, and fourth groups are involved in false consciousness, are denying their true sexual identities. But such a presupposition itself is bound up with some of the ideological assumptions of compulsory heterosexuality, namely, the logic of what Ponse calls the "heterosexual paradigm" and "the principle of consistency." The first is the view that all people's core self-identities must be infused with their sexual interests. The second assumes that one's gender identity, gender role, and sexual identity must follow the logic of bipolar opposites: Feminine people are attractive to masculine people. Applying this principle of consistency to those with lesbian and gay identities and practices has led mainstream theorists to infer, first, that one must be either a heterosexual or a homosexual and, second, that if one is not a heterosexual, one must be an "invert," that is, one who is engaged in the reverse gender identity and sexual direction. Why, if lesbian feminists want to insist that heterosexual norms are socially imposed on individuals, should we accept the inevitability of a connection between one's identity and one's sexual practices or of a bipolar opposition between heterosexuality and lesbianism?

## A Dialectical Approach to Lesbian Cultures

In the review of continuous, deconstructive, and discontinuous approaches to lesbian history, I have argued that none gives us a totally satisfactory approach to understanding lesbianism and what constitutes a lesbian culture, although each is helpful to focus on certain political questions of concern to lesbian feminists. Rather than continue with interminable arguments on a definitional issue that cannot be resolved by empirical research, I suggest that the historical reconstruction of lesbian history must be in terms of lesbian *pasts,* not one lesbian past. That is, there have been a number of types of female homosexual/erotic or what I call sex/affective practices, none of which amounts to a unified lesbian culture of resistance. Each can be said to have contributed in some ways to challenging patriarchal and heterosexist assumptions but to have been co-opted or ineffective in other ways. Thus none can provide the definitive answer to the political question of the best way to reconstruct a lesbian identity and culture of resistance today.

The alternative approach I recommend, a dialectical and historical approach to the question of lesbian culture, assumes that there is a historical discontinuity between societies in which women have a high status and homosexuality is legitimated and those whose forms of patriarchy involve some type of compulsory heterosexuality for most women, though types of male homosexuality may still be permitted (e.g., Hellenic Greece, various Middle Eastern cultures[19]). Lesbian practices that are legitimated because they are connected to the religious rituals of priestesses or cross-dressing women who are given an accepted social status (e.g., in Mohave and other native American societies) do not constitute a lesbian culture in the dialectical sense in which I am interested.[20]

The dialectical approach focuses on lesbian cultures that are, or have the potential to be, oppositional subcultures, that rise or continue as a feminist practice of resistance in a primarily patriarchal society. Some interesting cases involve those peoples who have developed a mixed culture with both patriarchal and women-empowering elements because a conquering, more patriarchal group has failed to completely eradicate women-centered practices from the culture as a whole. More empirical work needs to be done on Grahn's theory that there was in

the British Isles a real human culture of fairies, which was a women-
centered and homosexually permissive society. Grahn's view is that
these people were conquered by the Celts and incorporated into Celtic
culture, creating a mix of patriarchal and women-empowering elements.
This would account for the features of Celtic society that allowed for
warrior queens like Boadicca to exist alongside male warriors, gave
women many more rights to property than in more patriarchal societies,
and included religious rites involving lesbian practices.[21]

After the Roman conquest of the Celts and the imposition of the
patriarchal and heterosexist Roman Catholic religion on the populace,
an oppositional lesbian culture probably formed from the remnants
of Celtic culture, connected to witchcraft and pagan nonpatriarchal
religious practices that also involved some men engaged in gay religious
rites (cf. Dworkin, 1974). This would explain why the Inquisition
regularly charged witches with lesbian sexual practices and why Joan
of Arc was targeted as a part of a heretical woman-centered culture
because she insisted on wearing men's clothes, thus challenging patriarchal privilege as well as the Catholic male clergy's right to interpret
the will of God. It would also explain the elevation of the Virgin Mary
to high status in an otherwise patriarchal religion, as an attempt to
co-opt some of those who would otherwise have rejected Roman
Catholicism for more woman-empowering pagan religions.

The thesis that lesbian subcultures tend to form when a mixed
culture composed of dominant patriarchal and subordinate matrilocal
and more woman-centered peoples has developed also makes sense of
the lesbian culture in Mombasa, researched by Gill Shepherd (1987).
In this society the Swahili, who long ago merged with invading Islamic
Arabs, have a patriarchal religion and familial gender ideology but a
more bilateral and matrifocal social reality. Thus women are veiled,
have limited legal autonomy, are expected to marry and be obedient
to their husbands, and stand to inherit only half as much property as
their brothers. Nonetheless, the high divorce rate and the practices of
leaving children with the divorced mother and of divorced women
leaving property to their daughters have created a situation where 50
percent of Swahili women live independently of provision by a husband.
There is a lesbian subculture consisting of lesbian couples living
together—usually a high-status, wealthy woman with a low-status,
dependent woman—and a social life of salons of lesbian women who
meet regularly in one another's houses. A sexual economy permitting
such lesbian relationships is based on the higher status a poor woman
achieves by being paired with a wealthy lesbian than by being a
dependent first or second wife of a poor man.

A sign of the matricentered nature of Mombasan society in spite of the patriarchal Islamic culture imposed on married women there is that lesbian women do not need to cross-dress to have high status; rather, this is achieved by wealth, which allows them to outdo married women in feminine finery at the all-women activities surrounding marriages and funerals. Also, poor homosexual men achieve status by cross-dressing and being accepted into the salons of wealthy lesbian women.

Shepherd suggests that lesbianism is accepted in Mombasa because lesbian relationships do not break rank rules, that is, they are not egalitarian. Rank is more important as a social marker than male dominance, she suggests, so lesbian relations, as they are hierarchical, do not fundamentally challenge the most important social dominance relations in Mombasa, which are based on birth and wealth. If Shepherd is correct, we should expect that the Mombasan lesbian subculture would be unlikely to accept Western lesbian feminist views of egalitarian relationships or to challenge male dominance involving married women. It thus will be unlikely to grow into an oppositional culture that fundamentally challenges the patriarchal aspects of Mombasan Islamic culture. But Shepherd may be assuming too easy a fit between the lesbian subculture and dominant cultural views of status. For example, the contradictions between this subculture's high valuation of independence for women from men and the dominant Islamic culture's insistence that women should be subordinate to men might surface by lesbian women's uniting with heterosexual women to challenge the necessity of marriage as a marker of adult status for women.

A dialectical approach to lesbian culture can explain the development of two distinctive lesbian subcultures in the United States, based on economic class distinctions between women. Two examples of this are the split between working-class and middle-class lesbians in the "old lesbian" culture of the 1930s to 1950s and, second, the split between old lesbian culture and the lesbian feminist culture that developed out of the women's movement of the 1960s.

What there was of public lesbian culture in the earlier period had centered on bar culture and was based in the working class (Davis and Kennedy, 1986). Then in the 1940s and 1950s, the Daughters of Bilitis decided that to be acceptable to the majority of Americans, lesbians must have a life-style presentable to middle-class Americans in every way except their sexual preference. This meant dissociating public lesbian culture from working-class bar culture (Van Staveren, 1987). To convince the public that lesbians, though a sexual minority, were decent people who deserved to have civil rights, DOB created a speakers bureau to address churches and women's clubs. They developed an assimilationist approach based on the idea that gays were a minority group, on the order of blacks and Jews, who couldn't help their sexual orientation but should be accepted as individuals. The Mattachine Society also cultivated this politics for the combined lesbian and gay communities (Escoffier, 1985).

By the time the lesbian feminist movement came on the scene in the early 1970s, the old lesbian culture was split between the working-class bar dykes and the upwardly mobile middle-class politicos who claimed to represent them. Lesbian feminism threatened to impose a new order of politicos on existing lesbian culture: a primarily middle-class, college-educated group that claimed that patriarchy, not homophobia, was the real enemy. The new lesbian feminists were even more insistent than DOB had been that the butch/femme roles of old lesbian culture were part of the problem, not the solution. The easy merging of gay male and lesbian bar cultures, particularly in small towns and cities where there was only one gay bar, was questioned. It was argued that gay men, with their compulsory promiscuous sexuality and phallocentric culture, are really more a part of patriarchal culture than true feminist culture, which is equated with lesbian culture (cf. Rich, 1980; Frye, 1983).

At the same time lesbian feminist culture challenged old lesbian culture, it also claimed to be the vanguard of the women's movement. Its most extreme moment involved the political split between straight feminists and lesbian separatists. Though the split arguably had the positive result of forcing the women's movement to confront its homophobia, it also destroyed the sense of community between straight and lesbian feminists in many local areas. The question was raised whether there could be one feminist culture that respected straights and lesbians as equal contributors to the fight against male dominance. This is another example of politicos who, by insisting that only those like them could be a part of the "true" radical culture, end up destroying, at least temporarily, the sense of community necessary for such a culture to exist.

Though a look at the history of political ideological splits in the U.S. lesbian community connected to economic class shows important cultural differences, there is at least the potentially unifying feature of social spaces—bars, women's bookstores, lesbian magazines and newsletters—that allow any woman regardless of class, racial, or ethnic background to find a common identification as lesbian. With a coalitionist politics that is sensitive to race, class, and ethnic differences, then, there is the possibility of a minimally unified lesbian oppositional culture in the United States.[22] But this is not necessarily so in many Third World lesbian subcultures.

This is not surprising if we acknowledge that there are different forms of patriarchy and compulsory heterosexuality in different societies. Thus patriarchal marriage customs and the power of patriarchal churches are stronger in Latin America, parts of Africa, and the Middle East than in First World countries like the United States. This means that the average woman's ability to have some geographic mobility and independence of patriarchal kin is greater in the latter countries, where the development of independent lesbian communities is therefore much more likely.

Furthermore, though most existing societies could be said to have some degree of compulsory heterosexuality, this condition is enforced by a number of mechanisms. Because these can vary in strength depending on the context, resistance to patriarchy can take any one of a number of different forms that may have no common "core" of cultural practices or self-identifications. Postindustrial capitalist patriarchal societies create the material conditions for a contemporary lesbian feminist culture that challenges gender roles. But such conditions are not present in every society. Thus in some societies and some historical periods, resistance to patriarchy may involve women "passing" as men or women banding together with gay men to identify a common gay culture (cf. Myron and Bunch, 1974b; Katz, 1978). This seems to be true today in societies where marriage is such a dominant institution that even those engaging in lesbian and gay practices must first marry, unless they find religious roles as monks, nuns, or priests or drop to the bottom of the social ranking altogether by becoming prostitutes.

In most Latin American countries, the characteristics of a lesbian or gay identity have until recently been very different from those in First World countries. The key distinction is between *activos,* or those who play the macho role, and *pasivos,* or those who play the feminine role (Adam, 1989). The *activo* men and the *pasivo* women are not considered "real" gays or lesbians, respectively, for they act according to correct gender roles with the exception of their sexual preference. There is a lack of a sense of common gay or lesbian culture: *Pasivo* gays and lesbians identify primarily with straight women and feminists, not a unified gay male or a unified lesbian community in our sense. This has made it difficult for independent gay liberation movements to develop in these countries or for organized feminism to develop a strong demand for lesbian liberation.[23]

These cross-cultural and transhistorical examples make it plausible to argue that there are historically different gender and sexual formations in place in societies—various family structures, economies, forms of the state that embed diverse forms of patriarchy and sexual hierarchy. I call such systems modes of patriarchal sex/affective production. In different sexual formations there will be somewhat divergent ways available to resist patriarchy and sexual hierarchy. Many of these can be associated with lesbian sexual practices that will involve different senses of self-identification, not only between one country or region of the world and another but also within cultures, among different economic classes, racial, and ethnic groups. Our lesbian history thus should conceive of a number of lesbian subcultures rather than one universal lesbian culture.

The politics of a lesbian feminist dialectical approach to lesbian cultures as potential cultures of resistance against dominant patriarchies is coalitionist and nonseparatist. Because womanhood and lesbianism in different racial, ethnic, religious, class, and world cultures are variously constructed, attempts to build one unified lesbian oppositional culture that reconstructs a new gender and sexual identity in the same way (for example, with a specific set of sexual mores) is doomed to failure. Rather, as lesbian activists we need to articulate our particular political goals for resistance to patriarchy and compulsory heterosexuality in our historical time and specific social context. We must study the differences and commonalities among local, national, and international networks of woman-loving women that can act as a base for the development of re-articulated oppositional lesbian cultures and identities. We must reject the comforting image that there is one correct way to construct a model lesbian identity with a specific cultural content that will allow us to build a vanguard lesbian culture of resistance. A more democratic approach would consider an international lesbian culture possible, if at all, only after a long process of networking among those disparate subcultures of women, all of which engage in same-sex sexual practices but whose concept of lesbianism may be very different. We need, as I shall explain below, to view our goal as international political *movement*-building (of interconnected lesbian, gay, and feminist movements) rather than *culture*-building.

## Building an International Lesbian Movement

What is the difference between the goal of building international lesbian, gay, and feminist movements and building cultures? My view is that those who see themselves as building a political movement are more able to tolerate value disagreement than those who see themselves as building a culture. Those who define their task as movement-building will tend to recognize the need for strategic and tactical thinking, which inevitably involves disagreements, experimentation, and changes in political positions as a result of perceived failures in the results of political actions. On the other hand, those concerned with culture-building will tend to fall into the pitfalls of identity politics. That is, they will emphasize the importance of symbolic unity in oppositional life-styles, rituals, social practices—the agreement on all values of the relevant oppositional community—in order to validate a way of living alternative to the dominant culture.[24]

To avoid the weakening of potential sisterhood that lesbian vanguardism involves, we should conceive of ourselves not as building one unified lesbian culture but as building a plurality of lesbian cultures, each with its own set of self-definitions and each of which can, out of its reconstructed sense of its own interest, choose to involve itself with the lesbian and feminist liberation movements but none of which gets to define itself as "the" vanguard of that movement. Then, I hope, we will feel freer to disagree yet to support one another on general campaigns challenging sexism and heterosexism.

This point is even more important for international lesbian feminist politics. Capitalist development in the advanced industrial countries has permitted the rise of distinctive lesbian and gay oppositional subcultures and politics. The partial success of women's, gay, and lesbian liberation movements in some Western democracies, particularly in the United States, has given us access to institutional resources—academic jobs, women's and gender studies programs, and support from parts of the political liberal establishment for gay liberation issues, especially recent education efforts to combat the homophobia connected with the AIDS crisis. We have won the political space for lesbian/gay pride marches on the national level and in many local spaces. The space of gay and lesbian research and some financial resources means that the international lesbian and gay academic conferences and political networks are dominated by Western gay and lesbian sensibilities, and even more by U.S. gay and lesbian consciousness. Not only does this tend to lead us to ignore differences in the histories of lesbian/gay politics in Western countries but to assume that Second and Third World countries should develop lesbian and gay countercultures and politics after the U.S. model.[25]

If, however, we are seeking to construct a democratic international women's culture, which is, presumably, the aim of international sisterhood, we must adopt a model that permits the self-determination of local and national lesbian cultures. Such a process supposes lesbian cultural pluralism and not a cultural imperialism. This presents the paradox for U.S. lesbian feminists: To avoid cultural imperialism we can only aid in the creation of such a culture by not defining international culture-building as our goal! Another way to express this is that aiming for an international lesbian feminist culture is subject to the same problem involved in the paradox of hedonism: The desired result cannot be achieved if directly aimed at.[26]

## Conclusion

In this chapter I have distinguished two senses of culture: an objectivist sense and an identity sense. Because both of these, employed by continuity and discontinuity approaches to lesbian history, involve theoretical and political problems, I have defended as an alternative a historical and dialectical approach which thinks of lesbian cultures as potential cultures of resistance within historically specific patriarchal cultures. I have maintained that no international lesbian culture exists and that the goal of lesbian feminists who seek to promote an international sisterhood opposing compulsory heterosexuality and patriarchy should not be to construct such a culture, but to work instead for the creation of an international lesbian movement that is culturally pluralist in its approach to defending lesbian subcultures.

## Notes

A shorter version of this essay appears in Jeffner Allen, ed., *Lesbian Philosophies and Culture*. Binghamton, State University of New York Press, 1990. Copyright © 1990 by Ann Ferguson. Reprinted by permission of the copyright holder and publisher.

1. Lesbians and gays living in Western industrial societies have access to greater material resources to export information to other nations, and this creates a nonreciprocal influence that can be called culturally imperialist.

2. I owe this distinction between an international movement and an international culture to Cindy Patton.

3. Linguistically there are similarities between Southern "high, white" English and black English.

4. See the discussion in Chapter 6 of the variability of the social construction of race; see also the writings of Harris (1964) and Omi and Winant (1986).

5. Though not all of these authors specifically make the argument about a common women's culture, all are part of a project that supports the approach of those who have been called "cultural feminists" (Donovan, 1985): That is, they are attempting to show that women's common activities lead to personalities and values that are sharply contrasted to men's and thus provide the political basis for a resistance to patriarchal culture. Many cultural feminists are also engaged in creating new lesbian and feminist rituals, such as feminist seders, new moon celebrations, and so on.

6. Marx had a similar problem with his notion of economic class, for he felt that a class "in itself," that is, one that shared a common relation to the means of production, would tend to become a class "for itself," one in which

members identified themselves as having common interests. In Chapter 2 I argue that women are coming to be a sex class in advanced capitalist societies, although I don't assume that this is an inevitable or automatic process. Thus I disagree with theorists like Small (1975) and Delphy (1984) who assume that structural similarities in position automatically create a common identification of interests. As I point out in Chapter 1, the debate within the U.S. women's movement about class, racial, ethnic, and sexual differences among women shows that there is no automatic identification across differences. Rather, such a connection has to be forged politically. But I do think that the historical context in Western countries is ripe for such a feminist coalition to create women as a sex class—only, however, if we acknowledge and respect our differences.

7. It was the failure of white, middle-class women in the first-wave U.S. women's movement to do this, argue Angela Davis (1981) and Bettina Aptheker (1983), that was ultimately responsible for the end of militant feminism during this period. Similarly, black and Third World feminists have taken the second-wave U.S. women's movement to task for its white, middle-class bias (Moraga and Anzaldua, 1981; Lorde, 1984; Combahee River Collective, 1979; Hull, Scott, and Smith, 1982).

8. I am taking the concepts of hegemony and counterhegemony from the work of Gramsci (1971) in much the same way I follow Omi and Winant (1986), in Chapter 6, in understanding the hegemonic and counterhegemonic aspects of racial formations.

9. These theorists include Blanche Weisen Cook (1977), Nancy Sahli (1979), Lillian Faderman (1981), Monique Wittig (1981), Marilyn Frye (1983), Adrienne Rich (1980), Jacquelyn Zita (1981), myself (1981), Judy Grahn (1984), and Susan Cavin (1985).

10. What is missing in this list of tasks for lesbian history is the political dimension; that is, knowingly or not, lesbian feminist theories of lesbianism are used in the contemporary lesbian community as tools in ideological and political debates over who counts as a "real lesbian" and a "real feminist." A clear example of this is Rich's view that lesbian existence should be dissociated from male homosexual values and allegiances (Rich, 1980, p. 65). This strongly implies that lesbians who identify with a mixed gay community rather than a separate lesbian one are lower down on the "lesbian continuum," thus not in the political vanguard of "woman-identified women" she wants to valorize.

11. This identity difference between lesbians shows that neither sexual identity, as defined by the gendered objects of one's sexual desires, nor gender identity, whether one identifies with the social roles assigned to one on the basis of biological sex, can by itself determine what subculture one will identify with. For example, many self-identified sex radicals tend to define their social identity by the type of fringe sexual practice they engage in (e.g., consensual S/M, nonmonogamous sex, pornography consumerism, butch/femme roles, prostitution). Thus they may adopt a social identity across the gender or sexual identity divide. Therefore, any lesbian history that equates being lesbian with specific types of sexual practice will automatically exclude some who identify as lesbian. For further discussion, see Patton (1985) and Ponse (1978).

12. The first model of gay liberation tends to conceive gayness as similar to ethnicity: It is something one is born into and does not choose (cf. Epstein, 1987). Gays, like Jews, are seen to be in minority subcultures oppressed in most human societies. Thus unless we defend the value of gay ethnicity to challenge cultural homophobia, we will never be accepted as individuals. On the contrary, the radical lesbian feminist model may be either *essentialist* in the biological sense—women by nature have superior values to men (cf. Barry, 1979; Cavin, 1985)—or else *voluntarist*—any woman can choose to be a lesbian. Voluntarists maintain that women's developed personalities are superior to men's (Bunch, 1975). In either case, the political and theoretical strategy ends up being what has been called "cultural feminism"; women should separate themselves from men in order to create a superior, and liberated, women's culture.

13. Some lesbians who study the past want to call their study "herstory," not "history," because of the way the latter has excluded women. As yet there is no common usage; I keep it "history" to avoid confusion.

14. I owe the term to Omi and Winant (1986). See the discussion in Chapter 6 of their views in connection with racism.

15. In this way, lesbian networks are similar to networks of prostitutes: Until the group develops a self-consciousness to organize itself to demand status and rights, the contradiction that such groups' sexual practices pose to the ideology of female sexuality can be ignored by writing such women off as bad, sick, or deviant.

16. Later trends of lesbian separatism have been more essentialist, implying that men and women are like separate species in their differences (Daly, 1982). Andrea Dworkin's *Intercourse* (1987) seems to conclude that heterosexual intercourse inevitably favors male domination. Social constructionism among radical lesbian feminists, however, continues to be pursued by some theorists, for example, Celia Kitzinger (1987).

17. If a key political task of lesbian/gay liberation is the re-articulation or reconstruction of a positive sexual identity, why not promote the idea of a pansexual continuum that cuts across heterosexual, bisexual, and homosexual categories? This allows us to claim as allies both bisexuals and transsexuals, rather than having no satisfactory theory for them (cf. Raymond, 1979; Orobio de Castro, 1987; Runte, 1987). Such a move has already begun, for example, with an annual Northampton, Massachusetts, march called the "Lesbian/Gay/Bisexual Pride March." This has, however, caused fierce political disagreements (cf. news coverage of such disputes in spring 1990 issues of *Gay Community News*).

18. The situation is even more complicated than Ponse's categories suggest, for there is confusion as to what counts as "lesbian" sexual activity. Does this mean any sort of sexual practice engaged in by women together, or does penetrative activity, say with dildos, count as "heterosexual activity"? To eliminate this confusion, we could rephrase Ponse's categories to refer to same-sex versus opposite-sex activity, though this doesn't deal with the normative issue raised by sex with dildos.

19. Even the analytic concept of "compulsory heterosexuality" needs to be used with care, for it may lead us to ignore historical differences between our own contemporary social formation and others. For example, a case can be made that the concept of "heterosexual identity" is itself a contemporary one. Previous types of patriarchy—father patriarchy, husband patriarchy—based on kin organization of the economy did not require the self-identification of individuals as having a heterosexual sexuality, as men's sexual control of women was guaranteed by patriarchal marriage and property laws. Thus both men and women could engage in homosexual practices that did not challenge their gender identity as long as they were, or planned to be, married.

20. Though Sappho was allowed to teach young women and practice lesbianism, the context did not challenge marriage or create a permanent lesbian oppositional culture because her school (The House of Poets) taught song, poetry, and dance to upper-class young women for use in marriage and religious ceremonies. It is doubtful, then, that she was a part of a lesbian subculture in the dialectical sense. Most Hellenic women, secluded as they were with female kin, did not have much possibility of lesbian practices, unless they were prostitutes (cf. Nestle, 1987). Hellenic patriarchal philosophy certainly does not assign a value to lesbian sex in the way it does to male homosexuality (see the discussion of Plato's *Symposium* in Allen, 1986). Mervat Hatem (1986) writes of the legitimated male homosexuality in patriarchal Islamic Egyptian cultures, which brought that form of patriarchy into conflict with the Christian patriarchies of the invading English and French cultures. Lesbianism was probably practiced in the harems but not legitimated and could have been the source of an oppositional subculture.

21. Julia Kristeva suggests that certain matriarchal aspects of contemporary Chinese society (the power of the mother-in-law, for example) are subcultural remnants of an earlier matriarchal society that was overcome by a patriarchal one (Kristeva, 1977). Perhaps the marriage-resister subculture of the twentieth century had historical precedents in Chinese matriarchal history.

22. Our lesbian oppositional culture, however, is only minimally unified. For though we have some common social spaces and resources, such as lesbian and gay organizations, magazines, and bars, we also have intense value disagreements among ourselves. Should lesbians engage in butch/femme roles, S/M sex, cruising sex, adult-child sex, bisexuality, penetrative sex, motherhood, pornography, separatist politics? Should we build coalitions with gay men? With straight feminists? With generally progressive groups such as the Rainbow Coalition? Any one of these disagreements has been used as a way to distinguish "real lesbians" from others and thus to deny some self-identified lesbians membership in the "true" lesbian oppositional culture.

23. This distinction is changing because of the influence of First World gay liberation struggles. *Pasivo* gays and *activo* lesbians are now using the example of First World gay cultures to urge their lovers to "come out" as gay (cf. Adam, 1989).

24. This is why "cultural nationalists" in the U.S. black liberation movement and "cultural feminists" in the U.S. lesbian and feminist movements tend

toward cultural "monism"—a rigid set of norms for personal life-styles—rather than a cultural pluralism that would tolerate, even validate, the right of a diversity in personal life-styles and identities within the oppositional culture itself (Omi and Winant, 1986; Willis, 1984). This subjects individual members of the group to the moralism of other members, which can either be a tyranny of the majority or of the intellectual elites who have come to be accepted by the majority as formulating the appropriate cultural norms for the group. Ironically, however, because cultural nationalists and cultural feminists are more concerned with a countercultural symbolic unity than they are with strategic thinking, their middle-class intellectual elites are particularly vulnerable to co-optation, either by the forces of capitalist development—"Black is beautiful" and "Amazons are woman-identified women" are adapted to sell commodities and produce a new class of businesspeople—or by the welfare state or academic establishments.

25. An example of gay cultural imperialism occurred in the early 1970s when gay U.S. volunteers who cut cane in Cuba staged a gay pride march, met with incomprehension and embarrassment by Cuban gays and repression by the Cuban authorities. Because Cuban lesbians are invisible and only the "femme" gay men even define themselves as gay, the gay subculture in Cuba requires a different model for liberation than pride marches. This does not imply that Latin American lesbian and gay cultures will never use such tactics—indeed, some small lesbian and gay public demonstrations have occurred. Rather, it implies that North Americans must be respectful of local lesbian and gay views of the value of such tactics in their contexts.

26. The paradox of hedonism is this: She who seeks pleasure directly or as her sole end will find it difficult to achieve, but she who seeks activities for their own sakes will tend to realize pleasure as a by-product of these activities. Similarly, lesbians who do not seek to impose their values by defining a common culture for woman-loving women from different cultural contexts may succeed better in creating such a culture than those who do. This may be true if we pursue friendships (Lugones, 1986) and minimum agreed-on political goals to defend our perceived common interests as women and as lesbians.

# EIGHT

# Why Feminism and Socialism
# Need Each Other

In previous chapters I have argued that male dominance is based in systems of sex/affective production that, together with economic systems, create different organizations of human sexuality, parenting, and social bonding. Patriarchal systems of sex/affective production perpetuate unequal sexual and parenting arrangements that have been embedded in class-, race-, and ethnic-divided societies.

How does this socialist-feminist analysis of male dominance help us to understand the relation of the goals of feminism to socialism? Is a gender egalitarian society a necessary condition for achieving a class egalitarian (or classless) society, the goal of socialism? Conversely, is a socialist reorganization of the economy a necessary condition for gender equality?

There are at least two ways to go about answering these questions. One is the abstract philosophical discussion of values and definitions: What counts as gender egalitarianism? Does this require that all women have the same material opportunities as all men? If so, this would seem to imply that social classes based on control or lack of control of material goods have been eliminated, which implies socialism.[1] Conversely, if socialism is defined as common ownership and control of production, the implicit egalitarianism of this formula seems to imply that no one social group (such as men or whites) should have more control or benefits than others over and from the organization of production.[2]

Aside from such theoretical issues, however, there are also empirical questions about the connections between feminism and socialism. Does the achievement of public ownership of production, socialism in the narrow sense of the term, automatically cause male dominance to be overthrown? Even if there is no automatic connection of this sort, is the elimination of capitalism at least causally necessary for women's liberation? If so, that suggests that fighting for socialism should be a strategic priority for feminists. But what are the strategic links between social movements advocating women's liberation and those advocating socialism? Should feminists accept the "unite and fight" strategy, advocated by many socialist groups, of joining with men to fight for socialism (the "class first" position)? Or, realizing that men as a sex class have an interest in maintaining male domination, should women insist on if not a separatist, then at least an autonomous, women's movement with its own goals and priorities?

In addition to the empirical question whether socialist transformation is a necessary means to women's liberation, there is the converse empirical question whether feminist goals, processes, and means are necessary means for the achievement of full socialism. Unfortunately, as we shall see, past socialist struggles have not ultimately centered on the necessity of feminism for socialism. Perhaps because the leaders of such struggles have been men, they have focused more on what the socialist struggle had to offer women than what the feminist struggle had to offer socialists.

A historical perspective must be taken to answer the definitional questions about the connections between feminism and socialism as well as the empirical questions of ends and means. Definitional questions always involve values, and the defense of values assumes a historical context. Western socialist feminism defines itself in a historical political culture where both individual freedom and democratic rule are assumed to be intrinsic ends. Thus my understanding of socialism implies both formal civil rights for individuals (freedom of speech, religion, sexual preference) and formal and substantial democracy for groups of individuals. Formal democracy for groups amounts to political pluralism, that is, that social groups having common interests (women; racial, sexual, religious, and ethnic minorities; workers; consumers) have the legal right to form political organizations, factions, and parties. Substantial democracy has been ignored or downplayed in Western capitalist democracies. This is because it refers to material structures that allow everyone as far as possible an equal weight in political decisions that affect their lives, and this requires state restraints on the power of capital to privilege the options of the owning elite at the expense of the few. Substantial democracy involves two components, social democracy and economic democracy. Social democracy requires that the state ensure social services such as education, health, childcare, and transportation that equalize everyone's material opportunity to meet their material needs as well as to participate in political decisions.

Economic democracy requires workers' control of decisions concerning production.[3]

If this version of democratic socialism is accepted, it clearly requires feminism's goal of gender equality. Women as individuals should have the same civil rights as men, and as a group should not be formally or materially disadvantaged compared to men. I have maintained above that feminism's goal of gender egalitarianism must by definition include the goals of socialism (cf. note 1). Thus I have concluded that, on the abstract level, in the Western cultural context at least, socialism and .feminism are interconnected goals.[4]

Settling the definitional issue, however, doesn't really answer an equally important question, the historical and empirical question whether and under what conditions socialism and feminism are jointly achievable. Western feminists have argued that existing state socialist societies, such as the Soviet Union, China, Cuba, and Eastern Europe, and historical socialist movements have in fact never succeeded in placing an equal weight on eliminating sexism as they have put on eliminating capitalism. Consequently, though important initial steps were taken toward gender equalization in socialist revolutions, patriarchal aspects still remain. Furthermore, classical Marxist theory on the "woman question," as it has been applied in practice, has tended to downplay the importance of women's liberation in the international workers' struggle for socialist liberation. Why, then, should feminists struggle for socialism as an important strategic step toward women's liberation?

In my view, it is a mistake to emphasize, as some Western feminists do, only the ways in which socialist revolutions have failed to do away with sexism. After all, socialist transformations have occurred both in underdeveloped, peasant societies (Russia, China, Cuba, Vietnam, Mozambique, Nicaragua) and in industrial societies (Eastern Europe). Even though patriarchal aspects remain in all existing socialist societies, in order to assess how successful socialist revolutions have been in achieving feminist goals, we must contrast such societies with other nonsocialist societies at a similar economic stage of development. Thus Western feminists ought to compare the gains of socialist revolutions in other industrialized countries with their own capitalist industrial societies when considering whether struggling for socialism is necessary to achieve feminist goals in their countries.

There are two general problems that socialist regimes in nonindustrialized societies have had with achieving gender equality. First, peasant cultures have historically been more patriarchal than industrial societies. This is not only because of the greater weight of patriarchal religions in those societies but also because family patriarchies, that is, those in which male dominance is reproduced primarily by the power of male kin rather than by male power in the state, are stronger systems than state or public patriarchies.

Second, in most socialist revolutions in nonindustrialized countries the degree of material scarcity and the low level of productive forces[5] have seriously limited the available resources for socializing domestic work (building childcare centers, canteens, socialized medicine, etc.). It can thus be argued that such societies lack the material resources to free women from the patriarchal mode of sex/affective production based in the family domestic economy.

The situation in industrial countries is different. Here the problem has been not so much the lack of material resources to fund public projects benefiting women, although this has been a major problem for some.[6] Rather, a combination of historical and political priorities has led to a failure to focus attention on such projects. Furthermore, in Eastern European countries the possibilities of autonomous women's movements and other social movements have been restricted by the lack of formal democratic rights in totalitarian socialist societies.

The recent shake-up in Eastern European countries is a welcome sign that previously totalitarian socialist societies can reform from within. But the reorganization of these societies has just begun. Thus it is not clear at this point whether their interest in reestablishing some aspects of market economies will lead in the end to capitalism proper or to some type of market socialism.[7]

One issue of key importance with respect to women's liberation is whether these social upheavals will lead to a continuation or a cessation of the state-supported social programs that have benefited women in many of these countries. For example, if we compare the material situation of East German women before autumn 1989 to women in the United States, a much larger and wealthier country, we find some striking ways in which East German women were comparatively better off because of certain socialist programs. This suggests that socialism, though not by itself sufficient to bring about women's liberation, may well be a necessary step for gender equality.

In spite of the success of East German socialism for gender equality, until the 1989 upheavals there was a lack of a visible women's movement or the kind of cultural and psychological empowerment that Western women's movements have offered women. This stemmed from a general weakness in the classical Marxist strategy of dealing with the woman question. I argue that Western feminism's emphasis on the personal as political is a key precept that must be incorporated into an expanded feminist-materialist perspective on women's liberation. Though both classical liberalism (the emphasis on formal legal rights for individuals: the need for choice) and classical Marxism (the need for material social equality for oppressed groups) must be part of a strategy to challenge male domination, even together they are not enough. They need to be supplemented by a socialist-feminist analysis that stresses not only choice and equality but also self-determination as a process goal for those oppressed by patriarchy, capitalism, and other forms of social domination such as racism and ethnicism. Neither liberalism nor Marxism has acknowledged the independent weight of the social organization of sexuality, parenting, and nurturance in the reproduction of systems of social domination. Consequently, the importance of a revolutionary process of redirecting desires toward egalitarian rela- tionships must be an important aspect of a socialist-feminist strategy.

## Socialism as a Necessary Condition for Women's Liberation

### ALTERNATIVE MODELS FOR UNDERDEVELOPED COUNTRIES

Existing socialist governments in the Soviet Union and the Third World have vastly improved the lot of women, even though the historical contexts in which they took power, as well as failures in theory, have not yet allowed for the full development of social equality for women. But given the intensely patriarchal peasant cultures in which these social revolutions took place, women in these countries could only have attained the degree of social equality they have because of the gender reforms set in place by these revolutions. Among the changes are marriage reforms (including the right to divorce); women's right to property; public access to safe, affordable abortions and birth control; state-supported public childcare; and national health care. Thus pre- vious socialist revolutions, though they have not in themselves been *sufficient* to eliminate patriarchy, were absolutely *necessary* first steps for women's liberation.

The dependence of women's liberation on socialist revolutions can be highlighted by considering the records of alternative social structures. For the so-called underdeveloped countries of the world, there seem to be only three: (1) "modernization," that is, a dependent neocolonial relation with a capitalist state; (2) religious theocratic regimes, such as that in Iran; or (3) some type of socialist economy, often requiring smaller nations (like Cuba) to enter into a client-state relationship with a larger socialist state (such as the Soviet Union). Given these possibilities, the record is clear that the third option has reduced male dominance whereas the other two options tend to worsen conditions for women. Modernization, a euphemism for the development of capitalist imperialist relations of poor producer countries to rich buyer countries, has most often meant the insertion of the cash/use crops dynamic into the sexual division of labor.[8] This has just increased women's workload and economic dependence on men. On the other hand, revolutionary theocracies have compounded male dominance by bringing the power of the state to bear in enforcing patriarchal religious edicts on women.

## CAPITALISM AND FEMINISM

It is not only in the poor countries of the world that socialist development is a necessary condition for the liberation of women. Institutionalized racism and classism in advanced industrial societies and the development of public patriarchy and welfare state racism in the United States make it clear that here, too, the elimination of the social oppression of women requires a radical transition to a democratic socialist society. There is no other way to do away with the feminization and racialization of poverty structurally implicated in advanced capitalist societies. For capitalist societies cannot support full employment, state-guaranteed minimum family incomes, and national health care and childcare without jeopardizing the conditions of reproducing the capitalist system itself, that is, a malleable and needy work force that will accept nondemocratic work structures. And without full national health care, available and affordable childcare, and a feminist reproductive rights national policy, including free abortions on demand, an end to sterilization abuse, and effective sex education in the public schools, women and racial minorities will continue disproportionally to constitute an underprivileged underclass of poor. Capitalism will remain resistant to instituting such radical reforms because it structurally requires unemployment, hence reserve armies of labor—historically made up of women and minority men—in order to avoid major cycles of depression and recession. For this reason, status quo forces will continue to perpetuate sexism and racism by supporting a continued racial and sexual division of wage and home labor that allows women and minorities to be used as reserve armies of labor. Thus the classic socialist-feminist principle that capitalism must be challenged in order to promote sisterhood across race, class, and cultural differences remains true: None of us can be free until all of us are free.

# Conflicting Ideologies on the Woman Question

## CLASSICAL LIBERALISM AND THE CHOICE PARADIGM

In spite of the structural inability of a capitalist economy to create gender equality, the classical liberal ideology that arose in the transition to a market society is one important ideological grounding for feminist movements around the world.

Classical liberals like John Locke, Mary Wollstonecraft, Thomas Jefferson, and J. S. Mill[9] rejected the organic world view typical of feudal societies and patriarchal religions such as Judaism, Christianity, and Islam. The organic world view holds that the role of individuals in society is analogous to organs in a living organism: They are designed to serve the purpose of the whole and get their value from satisfactorily performing their role. Human individuals are created with natural variations—gender, race, inborn abilities—in order to perform different functions within the community, ensuring its harmonious operation. The organic world views of Plato and Aristotle and theologies based on such philosophies justified slavery, male dominance, human dominance over animals, and social hierarchies as part of the purposes of Nature and God.[10]

In contrast to the organic world view, classical liberal ideology developed a theory of the relationship between individuals and community on the one hand and the state on the other that emphasized the right for individuals to make their own choices with respect to life goals: jobs, marriages, citizenship. Individuals' ability to use reason to make their own decisions and the possibility of self-determination (freedom) for personal development were the ultimate values. Thus community practices and state laws should protect individual rights to freedom and self-development.

Classical liberal feminists analyzed the woman question using the ideology of individual rights and advocating the value of freedom and self-development.[11] From this perspective, which we can label the choice paradigm,[12] patriarchal arrangements in the family, the state, and society that assumed women should be legally and economically dependent on fathers and husbands were wrong. These arrangements interfered with women's natural rights to make their own contracts, choose marriages, divorce, work for wages and control their own income, and own property independently of their husbands and male kin.

According to classical liberal feminists, the legal and economic inequalities of women are due both to traditional attitudes based in patriarchal religions and to remnants of feudal economic arrangements. Therefore, the liberal strategy for gender equalization involves education to challenge traditional patriarchal attitudes, at the same time initiating legal reforms to make women equal citizens under the law. Classical liberal feminism, exemplified in the first-wave women's movements in the United States and Great Britain in the nineteenth and early twentieth centuries, argued that these reforms, in combination with a capitalist economy, would guarantee that a gender egalitarian culture could gradually supplant old patriarchal attitudes.

UTOPIAN VERSUS SCIENTIFIC SOCIALISM

Socialist movements in Britain, France, and the United States in the early nineteenth century challenged the classical liberal feminists' choice paradigm and consequent strategy for achieving gender equality. These movements, based on the ideas of Robert Owen and Comte de Saint-Simon, criticized not only patriarchal attitudes based on the organic world view but also the capitalist system. According to these socialists, simple reform in marriage law is not sufficient to liberate women, for the whole institution of marriage is based on the concept of private property. As long as the economy and the family is based on the concept of private property, men will continue to believe that they can own women and both men and women will consider children their private property to do with as they wish. Thus the only way to liberate women is to reform the whole system in which some own private property, whether in goods or in people, that allows them to exploit others. There should be communal ownership of productive property (socialism), love unions should be entered into and dissolved at will, and children should be a collective rather than an individual responsibility of biological parents (Taylor, 1983).

The Owenist emphasis on the whole system of private property and how it reinforces the patriarchal nuclear family suggests the embryo of what Marxist theory would later develop into the equality paradigm of women's liberation: It is not until the whole system of economic arrangements of society is reorganized so as to allow women material social equality with men that women will be fully liberated. But before we develop the implications of the equality paradigm for socialist strategies on the woman question, we must consider the split within socialist ranks that hindered the development of theory and practice on this issue.

Owenist ideas had spawned a number of socialist experiments, ranging from Owen's attempt at cooperative management of his factories by workers to workers' cooperatives and communal living. Unfortunately, the producer cooperative movement in Britain was smashed when the workers' major strikes failed in 1833–1834, and the communes disintegrated because of bad management. The failure of the practice of Saint-Simonism and Owenism led Marx and Engels to label these movements "utopian socialisms" and to distinguish their own view as "scientific socialism." Engels argued that the attempt to establish workers' cooperatives and communal living arrangements as a way to reform capitalism from within was impractical (Engels, 1978).[13] Although his criticism may have been accurate, the resulting split in the socialist movements was unfortunate from a feminist perspective.

With respect to the woman question, Marx, Engels, and the socialist parties based on their theories espoused the view that any egalitarian reorganization of marriage and the family could only take place *after* a socialist revolution had occurred. They therefore dismissed socialist feminists who placed equal priority on the fight for gender equality and for socialism as either "utopian" or else "bourgeois feminists." Ironically, then, the so-called scientific socialists ended up refusing to consider coalition strategies with feminist groups, which might have expanded the socialist movement and helped develop a more sophisticated socialist-feminist theory of women's liberation (Taylor, 1983). For example, Marx went so far as to recommend excluding the U.S. section from the First International on the grounds that their organizers preferred the woman question over the labor question, although the U.S. members insisted that they ranked them equally. Engels attacked the political demand of feminists for equal pay for equal work on the grounds that it, too, was utopian, even though *The Communist Manifesto* had argued that the proletarianization of women and children was an inevitable development of capitalism (Landes, 1989). And Lenin criticized socialist Klara Zetkin for trying to organize German women around the "minor" feminist issues of marriage and sexuality that should be left until after the socialist revolution.

The classic Marxist theory on the woman question is found in Engels's *Origin of the Family, Private Property and the State* (Engels, 1972). From this brilliant, promising, but ultimately flawed work come both the Marxist equality paradigm for women's liberation and a theory of origins of male dominance. Because my theory of sex/affective production has points both of agreement and disagreement with Engels's approach, it is helpful to consider his argument in some detail.

## MARXIST THEORY OF THE ORIGINS OF MALE DOMINANCE

Engels sketches a history of the human family as it transformed from matriarchal to patriarchal organization. Like classical liberalism, Marxism refuses to accept the conservative organic world view that biological differences between men and women make male domination inevitable, natural, and right. Unlike liberalists, however, Engels argues that it is not merely patriarchal attitudes or ideology but the structural economic arrangements of the human family that determine whether women are equal or subordinate to men. Engels posits that early human societies were organized by a natural sexual division of labor based on women's childbearing and childrearing functions. But this division did not automatically create male dominance. Rather, early societies were matriarchal in terms of the matrilineal kinship structures and inheritance practices and involved communal ownership rather than class divisions based on private property.

Even though Engels somewhat confusingly labels them "matriarchal," early societies were more or less gender egalitarian because property was communally owned by the gens, or tribe, and distributed according to need. It was only when a new economic development threatened the matrilineal family that male dominance developed: The domestication of animals and the creation of herding allowed for a surplus in the productive sphere controlled by men. This gave them an interest in changing inheritance rights from matrilineal to patrilineal, in order better to control their wealth by passing it on to their sons rather than to their sister's children. At the same time herding created a use for extra labor to generate more wealth, so slaves began to be taken in battles with other tribes. Thus class society, and private property in both persons and goods, arose at the same time as the patriarchal family. Women were owned and exchanged by men in marriage,[14] a situation characterized by a double standard of monogamy: Prostitution allowed a man to satisfy his sexual lusts outside of marriage, but a woman had to remain monogamous in order to guarantee that her offspring were from her husband's seed, avoiding possible disputes about inheritance rights.

Having posited that patriarchal marriage is the economic base for the oppression of women, one that persists through different class-divided modes of economic production (slavery, feudalism, capitalism), Engels views the development of industrial capitalism as the beginning of the process of women's liberation. Because capitalists seek the cheapest wage labor in order to increase their profits, women will inevitably be drawn into wage labor, at first as part-time, temporary workers (as a reserve army of labor) and finally full time as an underpaid group competing with male workers. Although this process will compound the misery of the working class, it will also destroy the patriarchal family, as women will have some base for economic independence from men.

The classical Marxist strategy for liberation of women (cf. Bebel, 1971; Stalin, 1951) has three components: (1) socialize the means of production (socialism); (2) get women into production (wage labor); and (3) get service production out of the household. After the means of production is socialized by a revolution, goods production is removed from the household. But service production, or housework, childcare, and other domestic labor for consumption of goods,[15] tends to remain in the household after goods production exits. This creates a contradiction for the wife, for "if she carries out her duties in the private service of her family, she remains excluded from social production and unable to earn; and if she wants to take part in public production and earn independently, she cannot carry out her family duties" (Engels, 1972, p. 121). The solution to this is to bring women into public industry, and because no one will be left to perform privatized services in the household, this will require the socialization of service production. Housework and childcare will become public services offered by the state rather than private services offered by wives to husbands and children. With no economic motive to sustain sexism, it will wither away, and women will come to be paid the same wages for their work as men.

Engels's origins theory and the equality paradigm for women's liberation have many important insights. His emphasis on the economic motives for the perseverance of the patriarchal family and its connection to class society is an important corrective to the shallowness of the liberal choice paradigm's target (traditional attitudes) and its inadequate palliative (legal reform to guarantee women's rights). Furthermore, his origins theory has the merit of suggesting that patriarchy is social and historical, thus changeable, rather than biological and inevitable.

Nonetheless, Engels's theories of origins need to be expanded and corrected in the light of subsequent research.[16] His too facile assumption that male dominance is based in the patriarchal family, which will "wither away" in socialism, ignores other sites and economic motives for the persistence of patriarchy that are quite compatible with public ownership of production. For example, I and other writers have argued that advanced capitalism has shifted the site of male control of women from family patriarchy to the state and the sexual division of wage labor, a type of system we call "public patriarchy" (Brown, 1981; Eisenstein, 1984; Ferguson, 1989a). Marilyn Young has used the same term to refer to both advanced capitalist and state socialist societies (Young, 1989). Thus, even though male control of women in the family may weaken, male control could persevere through male bonding in the state political sphere and in public production.[17]

To say that patriarchal power is centered in the state and public spheres does not imply that the family has no role in public patriarchies. Public patriarchies often emphasize the importance of the family in society. Indeed, most state socialist societies have developed an ideology of the family that makes it central to the socialist state. This has tended to create a sex/affective culture that is still sexist and heterosexist. For in a context where there is a continued second-shift problem for wives and mothers because of the persistence of privatized domestic labor, privileging the heterosexual nuclear family directs sex/affective energy to a masculinity that takes male privilege for granted and a femininity that eroticizes a nonreciprocal service of others.[18] Wilhelm Reich, radical Marxist and Freudian therapist, critiqued the Russian Revolution because the Communist party lacked a theory of how sexual repression worked to perpetuate classism and authoritarian regimes (Reich, 1970). Many feminist analyses of existing state socialist societies point out that sexually repressive cultures persist in these countries. Discussing violence against women and outlawed homosexuality is taboo, and the Communist party leadership has no theory of the connection between sexual liberation and human liberation.

How do we explain the persistence of patriarchy in socialist revolutions? Put another way, how do we explain the apparent tendency of socialist revolutions to renege on their initial promise of feminist reforms? Various writers (Rowbotham, 1972; Scott, 1974; Stacey, 1983; Croll, 1978; Albert and Hahnel, 1981; Kruks et al., 1989) have argued that socialist revolutions have involved an initial period of challenging the patriarchal family followed by periods of reaction when state policy seeks to strengthen the patriarchal family. Explanations for this pattern include psychoanalytic theories of gendered sexual conflicts (Reich, 1970, 1973, 1974; Weinbaum, 1978), inability due to material scarcity (Goldman, 1989; Nazzari, 1989; Kruks and Wisner, 1989), failures of Marxist theories and strategies for challenging patriarchy (Taylor, 1983; Waters, Davin, Kruks and Wisner, Einhorn, Lampland, Basu, Eisenstein, all in Kruks et al., 1989), political alliances with patriarchs (Gilmartin, 1989), economic benefits to the socialist state of continuing the unequal sexual division of labor (Scott, 1974; Weinbaum, 1976), and economic benefits to men for continuing patriarchal arrangements in socialism (Hartmann, 1981b; Delphy, 1984; Young, 1989). Let us explore the plausibility of these theories by examining some particular socialist revolutions to see what factors may have been involved in their social policies on the woman question.

## Revolutions in Peasant Cultures and the Woman Question

The Russian Revolution, as the first socialist revolution, has exercised undue influence on subsequent revolutionary strategy, not merely through the force of its example but also through the Russian Communist party's control of the Third International's (Comintern's) official theories and policies on socialist revolution. There are various explanations why the initial promising reforms of the Soviet Union on the woman question in the 1920s were overturned or rolled back in a reactionary manner in the 1930s.

Wendy Goldman's (1989) analysis of the 1920s and 1930s in the Soviet Union gives material scarcity and the need for political accommodation with entrenched patriarchal interests as the reason for the shift. She points out that the 1918 Family Law was the most progressive in the world at the time. It created legal equality for women, eliminated the religious base for marriage, allowed divorce at will for either party, awarded alimony to either partner based on need rather than gender, did away with the concept of common family property in favor of reserving property to each of the partners, and eliminated the concept of illegitimacy. Because the Soviet Union was still a primarily agricultural society where the predominant mode of production was production for use, adoption was outlawed for fear that children would be taken in simply for their economic benefit to peasants. The state, it was felt, should exercise the collective responsibility for children by taking care of orphans.

The Land Code of 1922 was an attempt to give women property rights they had not previously had. Unfortunately, it was a compromise between the previous patriarchal peasant law and a complete guarantee of women's legal equality to men with respect to property and divorce rights. Though it allowed women a right to a share of the household property and a right to leave the household on divorce, it left in place the communal property aspects of the household for those who stayed. Thus husbands couldn't withdraw money legally owed to divorced wives from the communal *dvor* (property-income pool). Consequently, divorced peasant wives were not paid alimony, putting them at a severe disadvantage to men.

The Family Code of 1922 was undermined by the problem of *besprizormiki,* or homeless children. Material scarcity made it impossible for the state to care for these orphans of war in an adequate fashion, and funds put out for their care drained the state coffers for other social services (childcare centers, etc.) relevant to socializing women's home service production. A compromise was reached by the revised Family Code of 1926, which reestablished adoption rights as an incentive to get peasants to adopt homeless children, thus taking them off the hands of the impoverished state. In the process, however, the state reneged on an important feminist demand: that responsibility for childrearing be collectivized. Instead, it reaffirmed the importance of unpaid work in the family to bring up children at minimal social cost. The right of housewives to a claim on their husband's wage, given in the second code, weakened the concept of no common family property of the first family code.

Unfortunately, the alimony and child support provisions of the family code turned out to be unenforceable, as divorced men simply couldn't pay alimony when they were often unemployed, underemployed, or supporting another family. Because women's wages were only 65 percent of those of men, divorce often left women destitute. No wonder that peasant women were opposed to easy divorce on the grounds that women were the ones economically harmed thereby. Feminist leader Alexandra Kollontai's (1975) advocacy of free love unions was certainly not shared by the masses of peasant women! In any case, the influence that leftist feminists *could* have had on the masses or state policy disappeared in 1930 when Stalin abolished the Zhenotel, the Women's Department of the Soviet state that had pioneered in fashioning the family codes and in advocating for women.

Sheila Rowbotham (1972) documents the resistance of patriarchal peasant culture to the Bolsheviks' attempts to institutionalize civil rights for women and material social equality. As in China, initial feminist reforms on the part of the Communist party and subsequent attempts by women to claim these rights were met by massive patriarchal backlash. Women who refused arranged marriages, bobbed their hair as a symbolic gesture, or insisted on their right to divorce were often murdered by their husbands, fathers, or brothers. Thus it is a mistake to place the blame for takebacks of initial gains for women solely on material scarcity or on theoretical failures of the Communist party leadership without noting the political problem of the fierce resistance of the peasant masses to feminist ideas.

In any case, Stalin's decision to forcibly collectivize agriculture in the late 1920s in Russia, though opposed, was eventually successful and did abolish the patriarchal household as the material base of women's oppression. Under Stalin's leadership in the 1930s, however, many of the legal gains for women's civil and sexual rights were reversed. Abortion, which had been legalized in the 1920s, was again made illegal, as Stalinism valorized motherhood as a way to increase the birthrate endangered by World War I and the civil war. Homosexuality was also outlawed, and divorce was made difficult to obtain. The goal of this legislation was to strengthen the nuclear family, which was seen as central to the efficient reproduction of the future labor force. This in turn was to ensure the existence of an important productive force for the building of socialism.

Articles by Christina Gilmartin and Marilyn Young in Kruks et al. (1989) argue that in the Soviet Union and China the consolidated socialist state becomes a public patriarchy for both economic and political reasons. In both, the initial feminist phases of revolution undermine the patriarchal family by instituting legal reforms that provide women with civil, property, and reproductive rights. Thereafter, however, women act as a reserve army of labor, their choices and their material equality with men eroded by patriarchal backlash by party cadres and peasant masses and by party ideological shifts. This reversion comes not merely to pacify patriarchal political allies,[19] but also as part of defining the economic interests of the socialist state in the use of women's reproductive capacity and a reorganization of their role in the family household so as to more cheaply and efficiently aid in socialist accumulation.[20]

But are there real economic advantages, as opposed to patriarchal rationalizations, for socialist states to restrict women's control over their productive and reproductive possibilities? Batya Weinbaum (1976) argues that patriarchy has persisted in the transition to a socialist economy because the socialist state has an interest in maintaining an unequal sexual division of labor in order to further socialist accumulation. Weinbaum claims that the socialist state in China had an interest in continuing the reorganization of the household sphere started by capitalism[21] but for different reasons. We can generalize her theory as follows: Although capitalists want only individual profit, the managers of socialist states want socialist accumulation in the interest of the whole community. Unfortunately, for agricultural economies that hope to industrialize rapidly, the cheapest and fastest way to achieve this goal is to foster an unequal sexual division of labor that perpetuates patriarchal relations between men and women.

Weinbaum argues that as socialism developed in China, women were pushed *out* of the industrial sector into which capitalists had initially drawn them, and *into* the service sectors (health, education, culture, neighborhood collective factories).[22] Workers in these sectors were underpaid compared to industrial workers. Further, urban collectives, which were 80 to 90 percent women, were not financed by state investment and thus saved the state money.

State policy that perpetuated an unequal sexual division of wage labor and encouraged women's privatized service in the household was motivated by several considerations. First, the state wanted as fast a rate as possible of capital development. So, for example, between 1953 and 1957 the state investment of capital in heavy industry was 86.2 percent and in consumer goods only 9.3 percent. This led to demands for higher wages, inflation in consumer goods prices, and black markets in such goods.

The rise of illegal nonstate production of consumer goods created a crisis for state production, solved by the organization of legal housewives' collectives outside the state sector, as well as increased production for use of consumer goods in the homes.[23] This allowed the state to continue its primary investment in heavy industry to speed socialist accumulation yet meet the need for consumer goods and let households acquire supplemental incomes. Unfortunately, it also solidified an unequal sexual division of labor and thus perpetuated patriarchy.[24]

Generalizing from Weinbaum's case study of China, feminists can challenge the classical Marxist argument that women's status will improve as growing productivity raises the economic level in under-developed socialist countries. Rather, as one of the ways to increase productivity and speed socialist accumulation depends on the repro-duction of women's inequality, socialist revolutions in underdeveloped countries are faced with a trade-off: Either speed socialist accumulation at the expense of continuing short-run women's material inequality or choose a slower route to socialist accumulation in order to provide conditions for material equality for women sooner. Thus, to take an example, arguments defending the absence of sufficient childcare facilities in Cuba, on the grounds that material scarcity does not allow the state to fully socialize home service production, ignore the way socialist accumulation in underdeveloped countries benefits from having women not fully incorporated into production.[25]

If our generalization of Weinbaum's views about the economic advantages for Chinese socialist accumulation of an unequal sexual division of labor and household income pooling is accepted, it provides feminists with an important reason to challenge the automatic con-nection between rapid economic development and feminist goals. In a transition to socialism, the *political process* of comparing costs and benefits of different economic strategies of development must become a central arena for feminist input. In this process, the values of gender justice must be weighed against a facile utilitarian argument that would favor faster economic development, ostensibly in the common interest of all, over the material and social equality of women to men.

From a feminist point of view, there are three general problems that have been involved with the political process in existing socialist revolutions. First, because socialist revolutions have occurred in ag-ricultural rather than industrial economies, Engels's strategy for women's liberation—getting women into public industry and socializing domestic labor—is inappropriate in many contexts. For example, Sonya Kruks and Ben Wisner (1989) note that in Mozambique most peasant families are supported by the woman's production for use, whereas the men do occasional wage labor or produce cash crops that supplement the family income. Nonetheless, Engels's classical theory of women's lib-eration is mechanically applied by the Organização da Mulher Mo-çambicana (Mozambican Women's Organization, or OMM), the women's branch of the Mozambique Liberation Front (FRELIMO). According to a 1984 conference document, 58 percent of women are not "economically active" (read: are not in wage labor or producing cash crops), and the OMM must find ways to get more women into industry! Not only is women's productive work downgraded by this analysis, but strategies to include more women in producer cooperatives are hampered by a lack of a contextualized economic analysis of what would empower women in work.[26]

A second problem of politics in existing socialisms is the use of the Leninist "vanguard party" model as a way of organizing socialist struggles (Lenin, 1974). Marxist-Leninist parties, particularly those that have had to engage in guerrilla struggles for years before coming to power, have adopted a democratic centralist model of political process. Mass organizations for particular interests, such as women's, youth, and trade union organizations, have been subsumed to the vanguard party's leadership. Independent organizations claiming to represent particular interests have been repressed, as they are said to lead to "factionalism" and are adverse to the common interest of socialist struggle against the reactionary forces of national and international capitalism.

Though a vanguard party organization may be a necessity in protracted wars for national liberation, its continued use after the seizure of state power is problematic. As recent popular protests in state socialist countries have shown (Solidarity in Poland, student demands for democratic rights in China), a more pluralist democratic political structure is required to ensure that entrenched party elites do not preempt power. This is particularly true for women's interests, for, as we have seen, patriarchal backlash and economic shortcuts to speedy industrialization can impede a gender egalitarian socialist process that defies male privilege and brings about women's material equality with men. Thus women require autonomous political organizations to struggle for their interests, and these must have more autonomy than has typically been the case in the relation between Marxist-Leninist vanguard parties and mass organizations for women.[27] Racism, ethnicism, and the oppression of national minorities might also be alleviated by ensuring the rights of racial and ethnic groups to organize autonomous political organizations to press for their own interests.[28]

The final problem with existing socialist revolutions' political processes has to do with the excessively rationalist approach taken by socialist leaderships that adhere to the classical Enlightenment world view, a view also held by Marxists. The assumption that social classes and privileged groups generally act to promote their own rational self-interests, unsupplemented by any political theory of the human unconscious and the way that its workings may impede movements for social change, does not help us understand either the success of fascism in Germany and Italy or the force of patriarchal backlash against advances by women.

To better analyze the persistence of patriarchy in socialist revolutions we should adapt Freudianism, expunging its conservative and ahistorical elements to understand how sexual repression and the patriarchal coding of sexual desire (Deleuze and Guattari, 1977) interfere with the egalitarian aims of socialist movements. Reich (1970, 1973, 1974) sketched an expanded Marxist theory of social domination incorporating a Freudian perspective. His view was that sexual repression in patriarchal family upbringings created children who unconsciously desired to be dominated by a patriarchal authoritarian leader. He was concerned that the Bolshevik party after the Russian Revolution had no adequate theory or strategy to radicalize sexual mores. This was necessary not only to free women from the patriarchal family but also to challenge what he called "sex negative" culture, which kept desires for domination alive and undermined the achievement of democratic workers' control of economic and political decisions. In *Blood at the Root* (Ferguson, 1989a), I agree with this aspect of Reich's analysis and argue that patriarchal modes of sex/affective production eroticize desires for domination and submission that impede the feminist goal of reciprocal exchanges of sex/affective energy, whether this be in sexual and love relationships, friendships, work relationships, or political structures.

Weinbaum (1978) develops a Freudian-Marxist theory that supplements Reich's perspectives and explains the initial feminist advances and subsequent patriarchal reactionary periods in socialist revolutions. She argues that resistance to the father figures of the bourgeois and feudal political leadership fuels the unconscious motivations of the revolutionary cadres. Thus in the first revolutionary phase, radical men make alliances with radical women in the symbolic role of "brothers" and "sisters" challenging the patriarchal power of the "fathers." Once the revolution is successful, however, and radical men gain power as leaders, they then want to achieve the symbolic role of fathers and to relegate their women comrades to mere "wife" status. That is, they see it as in their interests as men to institute a husband patriarchy after having successfully challenged father patriarchy. Whether or not we accept Weinbaum's general theory, we still need a theory of sex/affective production to explain the insistence of the pattern of initial advance and subsequent retrenchment in socialist revolutions in very different contexts.

One important aspect of sex/affective production in advanced industrial societies, neglected by both Reich's and Weinbaum's theories of unconscious desire, is the existence of unconscious gender identities and sexual desires that undercut patriarchal desires. As I argue in *Blood at the Root,* capitalist public patriarchies create a set of contradictory desires, one aspect of which eroticizes equal sexual and love relationships and the other of which eroticizes patriarchal domination and submission. Presumably, a similar process is at work in industrial state socialisms where egalitarian and patriarchal aspects of economic, political, and sex/affective processes conflict with one another.

What this demonstrates is that women's liberation has a social base from which to develop in both capitalist and socialist countries. To see why feminists in industrial capitalist countries ought to put socialism on our agenda, we need to take a brief look at the situation of women in East Germany. This will make clear both the advances socialism has brought to women and the need for further consciousness-raising there of the sort advocated by current Western feminist movements.

## Gender Equality in Industrial Countries: The United States Versus East Germany

Women in East Germany have been in a more powerful situation vis-à-vis men than they have in Russia, China, or the other industrialized Eastern European socialist countries. They have also been better off than U.S. women with respect to many aspects of their lives, notably their political representation, services that partially socialize domestic labor (public childcare, national health care), and measures that reduce the conflict between wage work and mothering (maternity grants and leave). On the other hand, there has been a taboo on public discussion of such topics as rape and domestic violence against women, male sharing of housework, and issues of sexual autonomy, most notably homosexuality. What accounts for this mixture of empowerment and repression?

Barbara Einhorn (1989) argues that one reason there have been more political and economic structures supporting women's social and material equality in Germany than in other state socialist countries is that the East German Democratic Women's Federation, the DFD, existed as an independent group prior to the socialist transformation of 1949 and maintained relative autonomy from the East German Communist party. Equal pay for equal work was won in 1946.

Further evidence of the power of feminism in East Germany is that women there escaped the cutbacks in social services and reproductive rights of other Eastern European countries. Though Soviet strictures on East German development, involving World War II reparations, forced a concentration on heavy industry over light industry and consumer goods, this direction was never used, as it was in other Eastern European countries (Scott, 1974), as a rationale to cut back on childcare facilities and on women's wage work.

In 1950 the strong Act for the Protection of Mother and Child and the Rights of Women was passed, which set up state responsibility for public childcare centers, mandated generous one-year paid maternity leaves, revised marriage and family law, and initiated measures to gain women access to male-dominated occupations.

Abortion rights were never restricted to increase the birthrate, as happened in other Eastern European countries. In fact, the abortion rights law, passed belatedly in 1972, is the only state socialist law of its kind that incorporates the liberal choice paradigm into its position, acknowledging that individual women should have the right to make their own decisions on reproduction.

East German women have had much stronger political representation than women in any of the capitalist countries and more than other state socialist societies. In the Volkskammer, the national congress, 161 of 500 seats were held by women. (Compare the United States, with only 5 percent female representation in the House of Representatives and 2 percent in the Senate!) In general, many more women in the GDR have been in public political life than have women in the Western industrial states. For example, 25 percent of local mayors and 47 percent of the members of local arbitration commissions were women; county, district, and borough representation averaged 40 percent. In spite of such good showing in most political arenas, however, women were still only 35 percent of the SED (the Socialist Unity party, East Germany's Communist party), made up just 13 percent of its Central Committee, and had no members in the Politburo (Einhorn, 1989).

Women have had much more economic independence vis-à-vis men than their industrial capitalist counterparts. This is in part because 80 percent were in wage labor, facilitated by the nearly universal childcare available. Between 80 and 90 percent of children were in infant school daycare, and 84 percent of 6- to 10-year-olds were in after-school programs. East German women have also made greater inroads into former male-dominated occupations. In 1977–1979 women were 45 percent of all judges, 35 percent of lawyers, and, in 1983, 57 percent of dentists and 52 percent of doctors. Compare this to the United States, where in 1987 women were 8 percent of lawyers, 6 percent of dentists, and 17 percent of doctors; to the UK, where women were 4 percent of lawyers and 16 percent of doctors; and to West Germany, where women were 15 percent of judges and 14 percent of lawyers. From a feminist perspective East Germany has clearly been doing something better.

The downside of these encouraging statistics is that there has been no effort to challenge gender stereotypes in the universal daycare programs for children. Certain professional sectors continue to resist gender equalization, particularly those of very high status, such as university teachers and professors (only 7 percent of college lecturers and many fewer professors are women) and those jobs involving authority over other workers. There is also a continued second-shift problem for women, as they do 80 percent of the domestic labor. Indeed, women are estimated to put in a second day for every day worked: forty hours a week of domestic work in addition to a forty-hour wage-work week.

The lack of gender sharing of housework connects to the standard Marxist-Leninist political practice to achieve the equality paradigm, emphasizing the socialization of domestic labor but ignoring the personal aspects of the political struggle for women's liberation. Hence the official party and women's organization did not create a consciousness-raising culture that would politicize the unequal exchange of domestic labor between men and women. As there was no official theory of how unequal sexual and nurturance exchange in marriage and parenting, sexual repression, and the eroticization of domination and submission in sex contribute to male dominance, there has been until lately no theoretical base from which to launch a feminist initiative in these areas.

Einhorn has argued that in recent years feminist literature has begun to play an important consciousness-raising function in East Germany. The writer Christa Wolf (1978) has suggested that women in the GDR are in a unique situation to reach a new level of self-expression. Because women have been forced to shoulder multiple responsibilities, they are able both to see the limitations of male-identified career hierarchies and to retain a broader socialist-feminist vision of a future society in which mutual respect, nurturance, and cooperation would replace domination and subordination. The development of the East German women's peace movement is one sign that a new feminist movement there may adopt the Western radical feminist notion that the personal is political and use this insight to supplement the classical liberal choice and the Marxist equality paradigms for women's liberation.

This movement has been given much greater impetus since the recent upheavals that have brought reunification with capitalist West Germany. Although more freedom of expression is now allowed to feminist artists and writers, the lack of state funds and subsidies due to the development of a market economy has forced a cutback in a number of the social programs that working mothers have relied on. Many nursery schools have already closed, and other social programs especially benefiting women, such as maternity leaves, job guarantees, and abortion clinics, have been placed in jeopardy. Even the right to abortion is likely to be severely restricted to bring the East German legal code in line with that of West Germany. East German feminist writer Daniela Dahn argued in a recent trip to the States that this means many working women will be forced into the home and many younger women will not be able to enter the work force. Thus the movement is faced with having to fight for programs for material equality that they had under socialism but that are being lost in the transition to capitalism.

The new women's movement is also politically naive. Before the recent overthrow of the government, the independent women's movement allied with the Green party in expectations of congressional representation in return for their support. But of the eight seats the Green party won in the ensuing free elections, none was given to women. At least now East German women recognize their political power and are determined not to let such betrayal occur again.[29]

## Conclusion

I have argued that socialism and feminism are necessary conditions for each other, both conceptually and practically. A democratic socialist vision requires full gender equality, and an ideal feminist society requires the elimination of other social domination structures such as classism and racism, as well as the elimination of sexism. Socialist revolutions in nonindustrialized peasant economies have been hampered in theory, material resources, and political practice from achieving full gender equality for women, but they have still created a better situation for women than have nonsocialist countries with comparable economies and material resources. A comparison of the Western capitalist industrial nations such as the United States and the UK with the socialist industrial state of East Germany shows that state socialism has made women better off in political representation, economic independence, and social services than in the former countries. East Germany, however, has lacked the theory and practice of the personal as political pioneered in Western feminism as a way to continue the struggle for women's liberation. I hope I have shown how the theory of sex/affective production advanced in this book is able to supplement both the choice and equality paradigms for women's liberation by adding a personal political paradigm. Only a socialist-feminist theory that incorporates choice, equality, and personal/political paradigms into its practice can hope to be successful in the struggle for a socialist-feminist revolution. In subsequent chapters I shall discuss in greater detail what a socialist-feminist model of an ideal society would look like, as well as strategies for achieving such a society in the United States.

## Notes

1. It is possible to define gender egalitarianism in a way that does not imply a classless or nonhierarchical society. For example, one could define it as the situation where women of any economic class, race, ethnic, or other social grouping have the same material opportunities and benefits as the men of that group. By this definition, striving for feminism is not creating a sisterhood to challenge social privilege between women. Such a characterization of feminism, though consistent, is not likely to allow for the coalitions across class, race, and other social boundaries necessary to achieve gender egalitarianism in either sense. Thus I shall assume that a viable feminist politics requires a gender egalitarianism that implies the elimination of other social dominations as well.

2. Such a spelling out of the concept of socialism implies that none of the existing state socialist societies has completely attained the socialist ideal, as none has completely abolished gender, class, and ethnic or racial inequalities. Marxist-Leninist theory of the transition to a classless society acknowledged that full social equality was a process that would not automatically occur after the takeover of state power by the proletariat and the public ownership of production.

In *State and Revolution* Lenin posits three stages of postcapitalist development: socialist revolution, state socialism, and communism. Only in the last stage is it possible to erase classes and other social inequalities. In the second stage there will still be classes because people will be paid by the standard "from each according to their ability, to each according to their work." Only after everyone has been resocialized to think cooperatively and not individualistically can communism develop, which will allow pay by the standard "from each according to their ability, to each according to their need."

The development of the Stalinist theory of "socialism in one country" as a stage to world socialist revolution has meant that existing state socialist societies following Marxist-Leninism think of themselves as in the second phase of state socialism, not having achieved the final utopian stage of communism. For them, thus, communism and not socialism is the ideal model of society. Because Western ideology treats all state socialist societies that espouse Marxist-Leninism as communist, it would be misleading to use the terminology of socialism and communism in this theoretical way. Thus I have chosen to develop a concept of democratic socialism as the model of an ideal society, and I am using the concept of socialism in a different manner than it is used in Marxist-Leninist thought.

3. In my view, social and economic democracy will eventually engender the sort of resocialization that Marx, Engels, and Lenin expected could yield a transition from an individualistic "equal pay for equal work" standard (from each according to their ability, to each according to their work/merit) to a

communitarian standard (from each according to their ability, to each according to their need). But, as I see it, the breakdown of the social division of labor that distinguishes between mental and manual work, as well as the elimination of the sexual division of wage labor, will not occur automatically but will require explicit anti-expert and feminist empowerment strategies. I discuss these problems further in Chapter 10.

4. The question whether there can be an international feminism that transcends national historical political cultures is an extremely difficult one. I would argue that we are saved from the specter of an unsolvable relativism about what would constitute the common goals of such a feminism by the development of international capitalism, which, through its spread of markets even to collectivist societies, has advanced the notion of individual rights. At the same time, the conflict between the movement of international capital and national interests of self-determination has raised the question of social equality with respect to the exercise of these rights. Thus, indirectly, two of the underlying values of feminism, the right of individual choice and of gender material equality, are increasingly being mandated as values that all national cultures must struggle for on the international level.

5. "Productive forces" is a concept that refers to available resources, including level of technology, know-how, and ability to exchange products on the international market to obtain needed goods.

6. For example, unlike West Germany, for twenty years East Germany had to pay reparations to the Soviet Union for World War II. Thus much of the productive resources of East Germany were exported and were not available to build up its own economy.

7. Just as there are many different types of capitalist society—from a complete laissez-faire, or unrestricted, market economy to welfare state or corporate capitalist economies such as those of Japan and Sweden—so there are different forms of socialism (cf. Kenworthy, 1990). Three models of socialism are a centrally planned, command economy (e.g., the USSR), a market socialist economy (e.g., Yugoslavia), and a council socialist economy (e.g., the anarchist collectives in Spain before the Spanish Civil War). For more on these models, see Albert and Hahnel, 1981.

8. In some instances, where women have been those initially drawn into wage labor, as in the silk industry in China in the early twentieth century and currently in the textile and electronics industry in much of capitalist Asia, women have benefited as Engels predicted. Their wage labor has made them less dependent on male relatives and more able to resist arranged marriages and other patriarchal decisions. Even where some advantage is achieved by women in wage labor, however, great costs often ensue. For example, occupational hazards ruin their eyesight or health, or simply working (being a "loose" factory girl) ruins their reputation, making them unable to marry and forcing them to turn to prostitution or, ultimately, as un- or underemployed spinsters, dependence again on the earning power of a male relative (Ehrenreich and Fuentes, 1984).

The limited advantages gained by Third World women brought into wage labor obscure the fact that women wageworkers are typically young single women. The fate of married peasant women is worse under capitalist development: The common pattern, especially in Africa and Latin America, is for men to be drawn into production of cash crops or wage labor while women are left doing subsistence agriculture to support their children (hence the cash/use crops dynamic).

9. For their views, see John Locke's *Second Treatise on Civil Government;* Mary Wollstonecraft's *Vindication of the Rights of Women;* Thomas Jefferson's comments on *The Declaration of Independence* and the Virginia *Act for Establishing Religious Freedom, 1786,* and Jefferson's *Letters;* J. S. Mill's *On Liberty;* and J. S. Mill and Harriet Taylor's *Subjection of Women.*

10. In the next chapter, on androgyny, I discuss the natural complement theory of gender roles. This view of the natural relations between men and women is grounded in the organic world view.

11. See Wollstonecraft's *Vindication of the Rights of Women* and Mill and Taylor's *Subjection of Women.*

12. I owe the concepts of the choice and the equality paradigms to Sam Bowles. See his discussion of the need to acknowledge positive aspects of both the classical liberal and Marxist world views (Bowles and Gintis, 1986).

13. Rather, he argued, the economic contradictions of capitalism had to develop to the point where the system could no longer function, at which point the workers would create a revolution, take over all the capitalists' property, and collectivize all productive property, with the force of the state on their side.

14. Indeed, Engels points out that the Roman word *familia* originally meant a man's possessions in persons, whether they were wives, children, or slaves. Gerda Lerner (1986) puts in a somewhat different but related hypothesis. She argues that women were the first slaves, as they could be more easily subjugated by rape and impregnation to develop kinship connections with their owners, which made them less likely to try to escape. Like Lévi-Strauss (1969) and Meillassoux (1981), Lerner suggests that women were the first property, traded to solidify kin ties with other tribes.

15. As Weinbaum (1976) points out, Engels variously calls service production "family duties," "household management," "private housekeeping," and "care and education of children" (cf. Engels, 1972, pp. 120–121; 137–139).

16. Though patriarchy is indeed social and historical, it is too simplistic to suppose that economic motives can fully explain the origins of patriarchy, as Jane Flax has made clear (Flax, 1976). Flax notes that Engels never really explains the economic motive for the transition from matriarchal to patriarchal society. The development of a domestic herding economy and the existent sexual division of labor in which men were in control of the social surplus would not explain why men should have desired to alter kinship inheritance practice so as to have their own biological children inherit their property, thus setting up patriarchal families. Economically, accumulation through inheritance could continue just as efficiently by continuing the matrilineal practice of the sister's children inheriting her brother's wealth. Only if one posits a psychological-cum-metaphysical reason, for example, the desire to perpetuate

oneself symbolically in one's own biological offspring (cf. O'Brien, 1981) does such a shift make sense.

There were patriarchal aspects of many human cultures (wife capture, rape in war, etc.) prior to economic-class-divided societies. This suggests that for the human species, the organization of sexuality and nurturance occurs in systems that are semiautonomous from those that organize the production of material goods. Control of, and access to, sexuality and nurturance is a source of potential conflict in all human societies, independently of the economic consequences of reproductive sexual practices. Further, it seems likely that Engels was wrong on his stage theory of the evolution of patriarchy from matriarchy. Rather than the former evolving from the latter, it may well be that both patriarchies and matriarchies existed simultaneously, albeit in different tribes, and that patriarchal tribes gradually conquered matriarchal cultures, made the women slaves and wives, and thus ended the gender egalitarianism of these societies (Ferguson, 1989a; Lerner, 1986). In any case, feminist anthropologists have made a good case for the view that relative male and female power in human societies is dependent on a number of factors in the way they organize sexuality, parenting, and social bonding, not merely the type of economic system and kinship inheritance they have (Sanday, 1981; Reiter, 1975).

17. Gloria Joseph (1981) has argued that because male bonding does not occur across race in racist societies like the United States, such socialist-feminist arguments are too simplistic. Although Joseph has a point—race does divide men—it does not divide them absolutely. Both racist tendencies for men to bond only by race and sexist tendencies for men to bond across race coexist. In different specific contexts, one or the other tendency wins out. Theorizing public patriarchy is not meant to assume that all men inevitably bond with each other, regardless of race and class difference. Indeed, male intrarace and -class bonding can create a problem for leftist attacks on the structures of public patriarchy and on welfare state racism, as is demonstrated by racism and sexism in SDS, and sexism in SNCC and the Rainbow Coalition (cf. Wallace, 1979; Evans, 1980).

18. Flax (1984) maintains that the Cuban family code, though it is radical in its elimination of the concept of the head of household, still valorizes the family as the necessary "cell" of socialist society. In this way, it supports compulsory heterosexuality and disparages both heterosexual singles and ho-mosexual liaisons. On the other hand, it should be said that the Cuban family code is the only legal code in the world that advocates the equal sharing of domestic labor. And though this has not resolved wage-earning women's double-shift problem (cf. Nazzari, 1989), it has certainly validated the concept of the personal as political in Cuba, and has allowed women a valuable way to challenge male machismo.

19. Gilmartin argues that the Chinese Communist party (CCP) initially prioritized feminist demands, such as for women's right to voluntary marriages and divorces, education, and property rights. The party supported independent women's organizations and schools in order to encourage cross-class collabo-

ration between women. In the period 1925–1927, CCP training institutes for women organizers, particularly among the factory silk workers, involved 300,000 members. But the prioritizing of feminist demands was one of the main reasons the coalition with the nationalist Guomintang party broke down. In the bloodbath by the Guomintang against the Communists on April 12, 1927, women, particularly feminists with bobbed hair, were singled out for particularly horrible sexual violence and murder.

Partly in reaction to these events and to the patriarchal backlash among their own male cadre, on the Long March in 1928 the CCP revised its women's liberation program. It denounced many of the united front feminist programs as bourgeois and counterrevolutionary. In the next twenty years peasant women were encouraged to support the civil war against the Guomintang by traditional women's activities such as sewing uniforms and nursing, but not by challenging the authority of their husbands, as had been the organizing tactic of the 1920s.

Other socialist struggles have had to contend with patriarchal political forces. Israel, which started off with a loose federation of socialist communes or collective farms (kibbutzim), is now a mixed economy with a strong central state. During its long rule, the Labor government, to maintain power, has ceded to the religious Right control over marriage and family law. Now that there is a more right-wing government composed of a coalition of Labor and the Likud, the situation is even more difficult for women. Recently, two different groups of women have conducted prayer services at the Western Wall in Jerusalem. Religious feminists have prayed to assert the right of women to pray in public. Others have prayed to express publicly their opposition to the occupations of the West Bank and Gaza. Both groups have met violent confrontations by right-wing rabbis, and the police have not protected the women from these assaults (personal communication from Batya Weinbaum).

20. Mary Buckley (1989) details the shifts in the Soviet Communist party's ideology of the woman question as different male leaders redefine what women's interests are depending on how women's role in production and reproduction is seen to dovetail with other state priorities.

21. Capitalism in Western Europe, the United States, and China sought to develop a market sector of economies that were organized primarily for use by reorganizing women's household production and drawing them into wage labor there (e.g., textile production). It was primarily daughters who went into wage labor, for others in household production for use would lose either individually (fathers losing control of land, sons losing inheritance) or collectively (if the mother went, her organization of children in the putting-out system of labor was lost, and hence that source of income for the household). The conflict between production for use and capitalist production exacerbated conflicts between women and men, as the female proletariat squeezed out skilled independent male artisans, for example, male weavers (cf. Weinbaum, 1976).

22. This shift in women's and men's sectors in the economy was not brought about because of a concerted patriarchal motive by men in Communist party leadership positions to undercut women. Ironically, Weinbaum sees the move

of men out of agriculture and into industrial work as in part due to the Communist reforms in marriage and family law to give women rights, such as outlawing arranged marriages and allowing women to own property and to retain it after divorce. The resulting instability in peasant households' abilities to aggregate large, stable holdings from arranged marriage caused men to leave agriculture in order to seek a more secure income from industrial wage labor.

23. Thus, to encourage women to make clothes at home, the production of sewing machines went up by 570 percent between 1952 and 1957, whereas the output of finished goods increased only a fraction (Weinbaum, 1976, p. 42).

24. Weinbaum argues that the perpetuation of an unequal sexual division of labor in China also occurs in the organization of communes, for women tend to spend more time in household than commune production and to be given fewer work points for the commune work they do. In addition to developing a less secure relation to wage labor than men, and thus fewer skills (such as learning how to work machinery), women are often organized to do volunteer work for free (e.g., paraprofessional health care work). This keeps the wages of women working in this sphere lower than they would otherwise be.

25. Muriel Nazzari (1989) makes a complementary point. She argues that the Cuban state's turn from moral to material incentives to increase productivity, coupled with the existing differentials between men's and women's wages, gives women incentives to maximize the family income by no or only part-time wage work. Furthermore, generous maternity leave provisions that make women workers more costly than male workers deter state firms from hiring them. These are two economic reasons why both firms and women workers will support an imbalance in the housework load for men and women, thus undermining the goals of the Cuban family code requiring men and women to share housework equally.

26. Another example of a mechanistic application of a Marxist base/ superstructure model is FRELIMO's critique of the patriarchal polygamous family. FRELIMO argues that the patrilocal polygamous family persists because of "feudal attitudes" that must be combated. But this blinds them to an economic analysis of how polygamy is not just a superstructural feature of the family but an actual relation of production. Thus FRELIMO cannot understand why most women want to continue polygamy, which is for an economic not merely ideological reason: In the current sexual division of labor, polygamy allows wives more help in the subsistence work they are expected to do. Consequently, FRELIMO and OMM are hampered in both their educational and economic strategies for challenging the existing patriarchal structures and finding a way to empower women.

27. Until the Sandinista (FSLN) electoral defeat in February 1990, Nicaragua had been involved in a socialist process with a democratic pluralism not seen in previous revolutions. Though the Sandinista party initially conceived of its relation to mass organizations of women and peasants, local block organizations,

and trade unions on the classic vanguard model, recent challenges by feminists and other grassroots activists have been successful in giving the mass organizations more autonomy. For example, while in power the Sandinistas maintained a fragile alliance with the patriarchal Catholic Church by refusing to advocate abortion rights for women. But even before the FSLN's electoral defeat, the Associacion de Mujeres Nicaraguenses Luisa Amanda Espinosa (Luisa Amanda Espinosa Association of Nicaraguan Women, or AMNLAE) stepped up efforts to legalize abortion. Furthermore, there are now independent feminist projects such as the Ixchen family planning and abortion centers, the Masaya and Matagalpa all-purpose women's centers, and a Managua AIDS education group of lesbians and gays. These groups, though supportive of the FSLN, are also critical of its practices of machismo and homophobia. Ironically, because the FSLN has lost governmental power and must rebuild and strengthen its mass base, these popular feminist projects now have more influence on the FSLN to correct these practices in order to make a strong coalition with them. Thus there is a wide open window of opportunity for expanding feminism in Nicaragua at this moment, which nonetheless still depends for its ultimate success on the resurgence of the FSLN as a changed and strengthened coalition that can retake governmental power in the next presidential election.

28. Socialist revolutions have had notable success in attacking racism and ethnicism inherited from previous systems of slavery and colonialism. Cuba is a particularly good example of this (cf. Cannon and Cole, 1978). The Cuban Communist party has revalidated the African roots of Cuban culture. The slogan "We are an Afro-Cuban people" has been backed up by incorporating African music and dance into mainstream education and culture. Because the darkest members of the multiracial Cuban people were also typically the poorest, much racism has been combated by attacking classism through free education, health care, affordable housing, and other welfare state measures.

Socialist revolutions have been less successful in dealing with national and ethnic questions in situations which involve national minorities who have been forcibly included in the state or ethnic groups practicing fundamentalist religions. For example, the USSR includes the Baltic states of Latvia, Estonia, and Lithuania, incorporated in 1939 by the Hitler-Stalin pact and forcible occupation. Since the recent upheavals, these republics have begun fighting for their independence from the USSR. The Bolshevik party was primarily based among ethnic Russians. They opposed both national liberation movements within the USSR and independence for ethnic religious sects. In part this was a consequence of the antireligious views of Marxism, but in hindsight it appears also to have been an ethnicist move to give Russians hegemony and to keep the Soviet Union from unraveling at the seams because of racial and ethnic rivalries. Thus the Soviet Communist party has consistently suppressed ethnic minorities such as Jews, Greek Orthodox Christians, and Moslems who have tried to preserve their religious cultures. Though the patriarchal nature of these religions raises serious questions of how to reconcile democracy for ethnic minorities with feminist goals, vanguard party repression of these elements is not the solution. Albert and Hahnel (1981) argue that Marxist-Leninist theory of socialist revolution must be expanded from its focus merely on economic exploitation to deal with social domination based in racial and ethnic community power, as well as kinship and state power structures.  ·

29. This information comes from a student paper by Steven Berrett, who received it from a talk given by Daniela Dahn, April 1990, at Mt. Holyoke College.

# NINE

# Androgyny as an Ideal
# for Human Development

In this chapter I shall defend androgyny as an ideal for human development. To do this I shall argue that male/female sex roles are neither inevitable results of "natural" biological differences between the sexes, nor socially desirable ways of socializing children in contemporary societies. In fact, the elimination of sex roles and the development of androgynous human beings is the most rational way to allow for the possibility of, on the one hand, love relations among equals, and on the other, development of the widest possible range of intense and satisfying social relationships between men and women.

## Androgyny: The Ideal Defined

The term "androgyny" has Greek roots: *Andros* means man and *gynē*, woman. An androgynous person would combine some of each of the characteristic traits, skills, and interests that we now associate with the stereotypes of masculinity and femininity. It is not accurate to say that the ideal androgynous person would be both masculine and feminine, for there are negative and distorted personality characteristics associated in our minds with these ideas.[1] Furthermore, as we presently understand these stereotypes, they exclude each other. A masculine person is active, independent, aggressive (demanding), more self-interested than altruistic, competent and interested in physical activities, rational, emotionally controlled, and self-disciplined. A feminine person, on the other hand, is passive, dependent, nonassertive, more altruistic than self-interested (supportive of others), neither physically competent nor interested in becoming so, intuitive but not rational, emotionally open, and impulsive rather than self-disciplined. Since our present conceptions of masculinity and feminity thus defined exclude each other, we must think of an ideal androgynous person as one to whom these categories do not apply—one who is neither masculine nor feminine, but human: who transcends those old categories in such a way as to be able to develop positive human potentialities denied or only realized in an alienated fashion in the current stereotypes.

The ideal androgynous being, because of his or her combination of general traits, skills, and interests, would have no internal blocks to attaining self-esteem. He or she would have the desire and ability to do socially meaningful productive activity (work), as well as the desire and ability to be autonomous and to relate lovingly to other human beings. Of course, whether or not such an individual would be able to *achieve* a sense of autonomy, self-worth, and group contribution will depend importantly on the way the society in which he/she lives is structured. For example, in a classist society characterized by commodity production, none of these goals is attainable by anyone, no matter how androgynous, who comes from a class lacking the material resources to acquire (relatively) nonalienating work. In a racist and sexist society there are social roles and expectations placed upon the individual which present him/her with a conflict situation: Either express this trait (skill, interest) and be considered a social deviant or outcast, or repress the trait and be socially accepted. The point, however, is that the androgynous person has the requisite skills and interests to be able to achieve these goals if only the society is organized appropriately.

## Limits to Human Development: The Natural Complement Theory

There are two lines of objection that can be raised against the view that androgyny is an ideal for human development: first, that it is not possible, given the facts we know about human nature; and second, that even if it is possible, there is no reason to think it particularly desirable that people be socialized to develop the potential for androgyny. In this section I shall present and discuss natural complement theories of male/female human nature and the normative conclusions about sex roles.

There are two general facts about men and women and their roles in human societies that must be taken into account by any theory of what is possible in social organization of sex roles: first, the biological differences between men and women—in the biological reproduction of children, in relative physical strength, and in biological potential for aggressive (dominant, demanding) behavior; and second, the fact that all known human societies have had a sexual division of labor.

According to the natural complement theory, there are traits, capacities, and interests which inhere in men and women simply because of their biological differences, and which thus define what is normal "masculine" and normal "feminine" behavior. Since men are stronger than women, have bodies better adapted for running and throwing, and have higher amounts of the male hormone androgen, which is linked to aggressive behavior (cf. Maccoby, 1966), men have a greater capacity for heavy physical labor and for aggressive behavior (such as war). Thus it is natural that men are the breadwinners and play the active role in the production of commodities in society and in defending what the society sees as its interests in war. Since women bear children, it is natural that they have a maternal, nurturing instinct which enables them to be supportive of the needs of children, perceptive and sensitive to their needs, and intuitive in general in their understanding of the needs of people.

The natural complement theory about what men and women should do (their moral and spiritual duties, ideal love relations, etc.) is based on this conception of what are the fundamental biologically based differences between men and women. The universal human sexual division of labor is not only natural, but also desirable: Men should work, provide for their families, and when necessary, make war; women should stay home, raise their children, and, with their greater emotionality and sensitivity, administer to the emotional needs of their men and children.

The ideal love relationship in the natural complement view is a heterosexual relationship in which man and woman complement each other. On this theory, woman needs man, and man, woman; they need each other essentially because together they form a whole being. Each of them is incomplete without the other; neither could meet all their survival and emotional needs alone. The woman needs the man as the active agent, rationally and bravely confronting nature and competitive social life; while the man needs the woman as his emotional guide, ministering to the needs he doesn't know he has himself, performing the same function for the children, and being the emotional nucleus of the family to harmonize all relationships. Love between man and woman is the attraction of complements, each being equally powerful and competent in his or her own sphere—man in the world, woman in the home—but each incompetent in the sphere of the other and therefore incomplete without the other.

The validity of the natural complement theory rests on the claim that there are some natural instincts (drives and abilities) inherent in men and women that are so powerful that they will determine the norm of masculine and feminine behavior for men and women under any conceivable cultural and economic conditions. That is, these natural instincts will determine not only what men and women can do well, but also what will be the most desirable (individually satisfying and socially productive) for them.

Even strong proponents of the natural complement theory have been uneasy with the evidence that in spite of "natural" differences between men and women, male and female sex roles are not inevitable. Not only are there always individual men and women whose abilities and inclinations make them exceptions to the sexual stereotypes in any particular society, but there is also a wide cross-cultural variation in just what work is considered masculine or feminine. Thus, although all known societies indeed do have a sexual division of labor, the evidence is that what behavior is considered masculine and what feminine is *learned* through socialization rather than mandated through biological instincts. So, for example, childcare is said by the proponents of the natural complement theory to be women's work, supposedly on the grounds that women have a natural maternal instinct that men lack, due to women's biological role in reproduction. And it is true that in the vast majority of societies in the sexual division of labor women do bear a prime responsibility for childcare. However, there are some societies where that is not so. The Arapesh have both mother and father play an equally strong nurturant role (cf. Mead, 1963). A case of sex-role reversal in childcare would be the fabled Amazons, in whose society those few men allowed to survive past infancy reared the children. In the case of the Amazons, whose historical existence may never be conclusively proved, what is important for the purposes of our argument is not the question of whether such a culture actually existed. Rather, insofar as it indicated that an alternative sexual division of labor was possible, the existence of the myth of the Amazon culture in early Western civilizations was an ongoing challenge to the natural complement theory.

It is not only the sexual division of labor in childcare that varies from society to society, but also other social tasks. Natural complement theorists are fond of arguing that because men are physically stronger than women and more aggressive, it is a natural division of labor for men to do the heavy physical work of society as well as that of defense and war. However, in practice, societies have varied immensely in the ways in which heavy physical work is parceled out. In some African societies women do all the heavy work of carrying wood and water, and in most South American countries Indian men and women share these physical chores. In the Soviet Union women do the heavy manual labor involved in construction jobs, while men do the comparatively light (but higher-status) jobs of running the machinery ("Political

Economy of Women," 1973). In predominantly agricultural societies, women's work overlaps men's. From early American colonial times, farm women had to be prepared to fight native Americans and work the land in cooperation with men. Israeli women make as aggressive and dedicated soldiers as Israeli men. Furthermore, if we pick any *one* of the traits supposed to be primarily masculine (e.g., competitiveness, aggressiveness, egotism), we will find not only whole societies of both men *and* women who seem to lack these traits, but also whole societies that exhibit them.[2]

Further evidence that general sex-linked personality traits are learned social roles rather than inevitable biological developments is found in studies done on hermaphrodites (Maccoby, 1966). When children who are biological girls, but because of vestigial penises are mistaken for boys, are trained into male sex roles, they develop the cultural traits associated with males in their society and seem to be well adjusted to their roles.

Faced with the variability of the sexual division of labor and the evidence that human beings as social animals develop their self-concept and their sense of values from imitating models in their community rather than from innate biological urges, the natural complement theorists fall back on the thesis that complementary roles for men and women, while not inevitable, are desirable. Two examples of this approach are found in the writings of Jean-Jacques Rousseau (in *Emile*) and in the contemporary writer George Gilder (1973). Both of these men are clearly male supremacists in that they feel women ought to be taught to serve, nurture, and support men.[3] What is ironic about their arguments is their belief in the biological inferiority of men, stated explicitly in Gilder and implicitly in Rousseau. Rousseau's train of reasoning suggests that men can't be nurturant and emotionally sensitive the way women can, so if we train women to be capable of abstract reasoning, to be self-interested and assertive, women will be able to do both male and female roles, and what will be left, then, for men to excel at? Gilder feels that men need to be socialized to be the breadwinners for children and a nurturant wife, because otherwise men's aggressive and competitive tendencies would make it impossible for them to cooperate in productive social work.

The desirability of complementary sex roles is maintained from a somewhat different set of premises in Lionel Tiger's book *Men in Groups* (1969). Tiger argues that the earliest sexual division of labor in hunting-and-gathering societies required men to develop a cooperative division of tasks in order to achieve success in hunting. Therefore, men evolved a biological predisposition toward "male bonding" (banding together into all-male cohort groups) that women lack (presumably because activities like gathering and childcare didn't require a cooperative division of tasks that would develop female bonding). Because of this lack of bonding, women are doomed to subjection by men, for this biological asset of men is a trait necessary for achieving political and social power.

It is hard to take these arguments seriously. Obviously, they are biased toward what would promote male interests and give little consideration to female interests. Also, they reject an androgynous ideal for human development, male and female, merely on the presumption that biological lacks in either men or women make it an unattainable ideal. It simply flies in the face of counterevidence (for example, single fathers in our society) to argue as Gilder does that men will not be providers and relate to family duties of socializing children unless women center their life around the nurturing of men. And to argue as Tiger does that women cannot bond ignores not only the present example of the autonomous women's movement, but also ethnographic examples of women acting as a solidarity group in opposing men. The women of the Ba-Ila in southern Africa may collectively refuse to work if one has a grievance against a man (Smith and Dale, 1920). A more likely theory of bonding seems to be that it is not biologically based but learned through the organization of productive and reproductive work.

## Historical Materialist
## Explanations of Sex Roles

Even if we reject the natural complement theory's claims that sex roles are either inevitable or desirable, we still have to explain the persistence, through most known societies, of a sexual division of labor and related sexual stereotypes of masculine and feminine behavior. This is due, I shall maintain, to patriarchal power relations between men and women based initially on men's biological advantages in two areas: that women are the biological reproducers of children, and that men as a biological caste are, by and large, physically stronger than women.[4] As Shulamith Firestone argues in *The Dialectic of Sex* (1970) and Simone de Beauvoir suggests in *The Second Sex* (1952), the fact that women bear children from their bodies subjects them to the physical weaknesses and constraints that pregnancy and childbirth involve. Being incapacitated for periods of time makes them dependent on men (or at least the community) for physical survival in a way not reciprocated by men. Breastfeeding children, which in early societies continued until the children were five or six years old, meant that women could not hunt or engage in war. Men have both physical and social advantages over women because of their biological reproductive role and the fact that allocating childrearing to women is the most socially efficient division of reproductive labor in societies with scarce material resources. Thus, in social situations in which men come to perceive their interests to lie in making women subservient to them, men have the edge in a power struggle based on sexual caste.

It is important to note at this point, however, that these biological differences between men and women are only *conditions* which may be *used* against women by men in certain economic and political organizations of society and in social roles. They are like *tools* rather than mandates. A tool is only justified if you agree with both the tool's efficiency and the worth of the task that it is being used for, given other available options in achieving the task. In a society with few material resources and no available means of birth control, the most efficient way of ensuring the reproduction of the next generation may be the sexual division of labor in which women, constantly subject to pregnancies, do the reproductive work of breastfeeding and raising the children, while the men engage in hunting, trading, and defense. In a society like ours, on the other hand, where we have the technology and means to control births, feed babies on formula food, and combat physical strength with weapons, the continuation of the sexual division of labor can no longer be justified as the most efficient mode for organizing reproductive work.

It seems that we should look for a social explanation for the continued underdevelopment and unavailability of the material resources for easing women's reproductive burden. This lack is due, I maintain, to a social organization of the forces of reproduction that perpetuates the sexual division of labor at home and in the job market, and thus benefits the perceived interests of men, not women.

The two biological disadvantages of women, relative male strength and the female role in biological reproduction, explain the persistence of the sexual division of labor and the sexual stereotypes based on this. Variations in the stereotypes seem to relate fairly directly to the power women have relative to men in the particular society. This, in turn, depends on the mode of production of the society and whether or not women's reproductive work of raising children is in conflict with their gaining any power in the social relations of production.

There are disagreements between anthropological theorists as to whether early human history contained matriarchal societies, in which bloodlines and property were traced through the maternal side and in which women had the edge over men in political and economic power. Early theorists like Engels (1972) and Morgan (1963) argue that the social organization of the family and women's power in society is directly related to women's role in production. In primitive hunting-and-gathering and agricultural societies, organization of production is communal and tribal. Women have a central role in production and reproduction, there is no separation of productive work from home and reproductive work, and bloodlines are matrilineal. Moreover, Engels uses examples like the Iroquois Indians, and Bachofen (1967), myths of powerful goddesses, to argue that these societies were not just matrilineal but also matriarchal. According to Engels's theory, the "world-historical defeat of the female sex" came when the mode of production changed to an animal-herding economy, and the sexual division of labor thus gave men control over production and over any surplus. Men thus gained political and economic power over women, whose productive and reproductive work was concentrated on production for use in the home rather than for exchange.

Engels's theory is somewhat too simple. It doesn't sufficiently account for the fact that in *any* noncommunal mode of production, the ability to control biological reproduction (progeny, future labor power) is a material power to be struggled for, and that there will be a dialectical struggle to control both production and reproduction in all but the most simple tribal societies.[5] It also doesn't take into account the possibility that even in communal modes of production there may be patriarchal power relations between men and women caused by male fear of women's biological ability to reproduce. This may result in "womb envy," and in male attempts to compensate for women's reproductive power by setting up male-dominated areas in economic, political, and religious relations.[6]

Whatever the origin of the power struggle between men and women to control reproduction, the fact seems to be that the degree of a woman's oppression in a society is related to the amount of power she has at any particular historical period in the relations of reproduction in the family as well as the relations of production in society. Her oppression is thus relative to her class position as well as to her power in relation to men in her family.

There is no easy formula by which to determine the amount of power women have by simply looking at how much productive work and childcare they do relative to men in a certain historical period. What is important is not the *amount* of work done but the control a woman has over her work and the kind of independence this control offers her in the case of actual or potential conflicts with men over how the work should be done. Thus, although American slave women did as much productive work as slave men, and were almost totally responsible for the childcare not only for their own children but for those of the plantation owner as well, slave women had no control over this work. Their children could be sold away from them, and they could be brutally punished if they refused to do the work assigned them by their masters. The lady of the plantation, on the other hand, did little productive work. She was more in a managerial position, usually responsible for managing the health care, clothing, and food of the slaves. She usually had little say in economic decisions about the plantation, since she was not considered a joint owner. On the other hand, the Victorian sexual division of labor and the cult of true womanhood gave the wealthy white woman almost total control over her children in decisions about childrearing. Relative to her husband, all in all, she had less power; relative to her female slave she had more; and her female slave in turn had more power than the male slave because of her central role in childrearing and the great likelihood that fathers rather than mothers would be sold away from children.

## The Social Articulation of the Natural Complement Theory

If we look at the beliefs of different societies about the proper roles for men and women, we note that these beliefs vary widely. We also see that societies always tend to appeal to the natural complement theory to back up their socially relative allocations of sex roles. The question arises, then, why, in the light of this obvious social variation, do people *persist* in clinging to the belief that there are inherent natural roles for men and women?

It would be simplistic to maintain that the ideology of sex roles directly reflects the degree of women's power in relation to men at a given historical period in a society. The medieval religious view of women was extremely low,[7] yet there is evidence that women had more power than the simple reflective view of ideology would lead us to believe. In fact, there were women who were sheriffs, innkeepers, and managers of large households. The elevation of the Virgin Mary as the ideal woman on a pedestal seems to contradict the other elements in the medieval religious view of women, and indeed, it should make us wary of assuming a one-to-one correlation between ideology and reality. So, for example, nineteenth-century Americans placed women on a pedestal where they were considered morally superior to men; but this, ironically, was in an economic, legal, and political context where they had less power than their Puritan ancestors.[8] Middle-class women had no role in commodity production, which had become the dominant mode of production in the nineteenth century. Women could not own property if they were married nor receive an education nor hold political office nor vote. Their husbands had complete legal control over children in case of divorce.

There is a more plausible way to understand how the ideology of sex roles is connected to the actual social and historical roles of men and women. Sex-role ideologies mystify the existing power relations between men and women and economic classes. This mystification justifies the social and economic roles of two dominant groups: men as a caste, on the one hand, and the dominant economic class on the other.

If we look at nineteenth-century America, we see the prevailing ideology, which held that women are too frail, "moral," and emotional to take part in commodity production (the amoral, competitive world of business). This ideology ignored the reality of black slave women, treated the same as male slaves and forced to do field work under brutal conditions. It ignored immigrant women, who worked long hours in crowded factories under conditions that caused many sicknesses and deaths. And it ignored farm women, who continued production for use on the farm. These working women made up the majority of the female population, yet the reality of the productive role was overlooked.

Why? A number of factors seem to be at work here. All end by supporting the interests and maintaining the status quo power relations of the white male bourgeoisie. The first factor was the need to pacify bourgeois wives, whose role in production had evaporated but who were crucial to maintaining the system by lending emotional support and being subservient to their husbands, and by training their children, the future owners and controllers of capital. There was also a need for the bourgeois male to justify his position of dominance over his wife in legal, political, and financial matters. Second, the hierarchical control that the bourgeois male enjoyed over men of the lower classes was seen as inevitable (after all, it is masculine nature to be competitive and avaricious, and may the best man win!). Third, lower-class working women were thought to be fallen women, degraded and unnatural because of their role in production, and this conveniently made them free targets for bourgeois men (with their "natural" sexual appetites) to lure into prostitution. Finally, as production became more alienating, hierarchical, and competitive, working-class men as well needed the haven of women's emotional support and also the male dominance that being the breadwinner allowed them. As a result, both the men and the women of the working class struggled to achieve the ideal complementary sex-role relationships, of woman-at-home/man-as-bread-winner that the cult of true womanhood assumed.

## Conclusions About the
## Natural Complement Theory

We have discussed several different views of the "natural" sex differences between men and women prevalent in different historical periods. When we observe the shift in ideology as to what constitutes "true" female and male nature, we note that the shift has nothing to do with the further scientific discovery of biological differences between men and women. It seems rather to correlate to changes in the relation between men's and women's roles in production and reproduction, and to what serves the interests of the dominant male economic class. Given this fact of its ideological role, the natural complement theory, and any other static universal theory of what the "natural relationship" of man to woman should be, loses credibility.

Instead, it seems more plausible to assume that human nature is plastic and moldable, and that women and men develop their sexual identities, their sense of self, and their motivations through responding to the social expectations placed upon them. They develop the skills and personality traits necessary to carry out the productive and reproductive roles available to them in their sociohistorical context, given their sex, race, ethnic identity, and class background.

If we wish to develop a realistic ideal for human development, then we cannot take the existing traits that differentiate men from women in this society as norms for behavior. Neither can we expect to find an ideal in some biological male and female substratum, after we strip away all the socialization processes we go through to develop our egos. Rather, with the present-day women's movement, we should ask: What traits are desirable and possible to teach people in order for them to reach their full individual human potential? And how would our society have to restructure its productive and reproductive relations in order to allow people to develop in this way?

## An Ideal Love Relationship

One argument for the development of androgynous personalities (and the accompanying destruction of the sexual division of labor in production and reproduction) is that without such a radical change in male and female roles an ideal love relationship between the sexes is not possible. The argument goes like this. An ideal love between two mature people would be love between equals. I assume that such an ideal is the only concept of love that is historically compatible with our other developed ideals of political and social equality. But as

Shulamith Firestone (1970) argues, an equal love relationship requires the vulnerability of each partner to the other. There is today, however, an unequal balance of power in male-female relationships. Contrary to the claims of the natural complement theory, it is not possible for men and women to be equal while playing the complementary sex roles taught in our society. The feminine role makes a woman less equal, less powerful, and less free than the masculine role makes men. In fact, it is the emotional understanding of this lack of equality in love relations between men and women which increasingly influences feminists to choose lesbian love relationships.

Let us consider the vulnerabilities of women in a heterosexual love relationship under the four classifications Juliet Mitchell (1973) gives for women's roles: production, reproduction, socialization of children, and sexuality.

1. *Women's Role in Production.* In the United States today, 42 percent of women work, and about 33 percent of married women work in the wage-labor force. This is much higher than the 6 percent of women in the wage-labor force around the turn of the century, and higher than in other industrialized countries. Nonetheless, sex-role socialization affects women's power in two important ways. First, because of job segregation by sex into part-time and low-paying jobs, women, whether single or married, are at an economic disadvantage in comparison with men when it comes to supporting themselves. If they leave their husbands or lovers, they drop to a lower economic class, and many have to go on welfare. Second, women who have children and who also work in the wage-labor force have two jobs, not one: the responsibility for the major part of childraising and housework, as well as the outside job. This keeps many housewives from seeking outside jobs and makes them economicially dependent on their husbands. Those who do work outside the home expend twice as much energy as the man and are less secure. Many women who try to combine career and motherhood find that the demands of both undermine their egos because they don't feel they can do both jobs adequately.[9]

2. *Women's Role in Reproduction.* Although women currently monopolize the means of biological reproduction, they are at a disadvantage because of the absence of free contraceptives, adequate health care, and free legal abortions. A man can enjoy sex without having to worry about the consequences the way a woman does if a mistake occurs and she becomes pregnant. Women have some compensation in the fact that in the United States today they are favored legally over the father in their right to have control of the children in case of separation or divorce. But this legal advantage (a victory won by women in the early twentieth century in the ongoing power struggle between the sexes

for control of children, i.e., control over social reproduction) does not adequately compensate for the disadvantages to which motherhood subjects one in this society.

3. *Women's Role in Socialization: As Wife and Mother.* The social status of women, and hence their self-esteem, is measured primarily in terms of how successful they are in their relationships as lovers, wives, and mothers. Unlike men, who learn that their major social definition is success in work, women are taught from childhood that their ultimate goal is love and marriage. Women thus have more invested in a love relationship than men, and more to lose if it fails. The "old maid" or the "divorcee" is still an inferior status to be pitied, while the "swinging bachelor" is rather envied.

The fact that men achieve self- and social definition from their work means that they can feel a lesser commitment to working out problems in a relationship. Furthermore, men have more options for new relationships than do women. The double standard in sexuality allows a man to have affairs more readily than his wife. Ageism is a further limitation on women: An older man is considered a possible lover by both younger and older women, but an older woman, because she is no longer the "ideal" sex object, is not usually considered a desirable lover by either male peers or younger men.

A woman's role as mother places her in a more vulnerable position than the man. Taking care of children and being attentive to their emotional needs is very demanding work. Many times it involves conflicts between the woman's own needs and the needs of the child. Often it involves conflict and jealousy between husband and children for her attention and emotional energy. It is the woman's role to harmonize this conflict, which she often does at the expense of herself, sacrificing her private time and interests in order to provide support for the projects of her husband and children.

No matter how devoted a parent a father is, he tends to see his time with the children as play time, not as work time. His job interests and hobbies take precedence over directing his energy to children. Thus he is more independent than the woman, who sees her job as making husband and children happy. This is the sort of job that is never completed, for there are always more ways to make people happy. Because a woman sees her job to be supporting her husband and mothering her children, the woman sees the family as her main "product." This makes her dependent on their activities, lives, and successes for her own success, and she lives vicariously through their activities. But as her "product" is human beings, when the children leave, as they must, to live independent lives, middle age brings an end to her main social function. The woman who has a career has other problems, for she has had to support her husband's career over hers wherever there was a conflict, because she knows male egos are tied up with success and "making it" in this competitive society. Women's egos, on the other hand, are primed for failure. Successful women, especially successful women with unsuccessful husbands, are considered not "true" women, but rather as deviants, "castrating bitches," "ball-busters," and "masculine women." For all these reasons, a woman in a love relationship with a man is geared by the natural complement view of herself as a woman to put her interests last, to define herself in terms of husband and children, and therefore to be more dependent on them than they are on her.

A woman is also vulnerable in her role as mother because there are limited alternatives if, for example, she wishes to break off her relationship with the father of her children. As a mother, her social role in bringing up children is defined as more important, more essential for the well-being of the children than the man's. Therefore, she is expected to take the children to live with her, or else she is considered a failure as a mother. But the life of a divorced or single mother with children in a nuclear-family-oriented society is lonely and hard: She must now either do two jobs without the companionship of another adult, in a society where jobs for women are inadequate, or she must survive on welfare or alimony with a reduced standard of living. When this is the alternative, is it any wonder that mothers are more dependent on maintaining a relationship—even when it is not satisfying—than the man is?

4. *Women's Role in Sexuality.* A woman's sexual role is one in which she is both elevated by erotic romanticism and deflated to being a mere "cunt"—good for release of male sexual passions but inter-changeable with other women. Because women play a subordinate role in society and are not seen as equal agents or as equally productive, men must justify a relationship with a particular woman by making her something special, mystifying her, making her better than other women. In fact, this idealization doesn't deal with her as a real *individual;* it treats her as either a beautiful object or as a mothering, supportive figure.

This idealization of women which occurs in the first stages of infatuation wears off as the couple settles into a relationship of some duration. What is left is the idea of woman as passive sex object whom one possesses and whose job as wife is to give the husband pleasure in bed. Since the woman is not seen as (and doesn't usually see herself as) active in sex, she tends to see sex as a duty rather than as a pleasure. She is not socially expected to take the active kind of initiative (even to the extent of asking for a certain kind of sex play) that would give her a sense of control over her sex life. The idea of herself as a body to be dressed and clothed in the latest media-advertised fashions "to please men" keeps her a slave to fashion and forces her to change her ego-ideal with every change in fashion. She can't see herself as an individual.

## Androgyny as a Progressive Ideal

It is the sexual division of labor in the home and at work that perpetuates complementary sex roles for men and women. In under-developed societies with scarce material resources such an arrangement may indeed be the most rational way to allow for the most efficient raising of children and production of goods. But this is no longer true for developed societies. In this age of advanced technology, men's relative strength compared to women's is no longer important, either in war or in the production of goods. The gun and the spinning jenny have equalized the potential role of men and women in both repression and production. And the diaphragm, the pill, and other advances in the technology of reproduction have equalized the potential power of women and men to control their bodies and to reproduce themselves.[10] (The development of cloning would mean that men and women could reproduce without the participation of the opposite sex.)

We have seen how complementary sex roles and their extension to job segregation in wage labor make an ideal love relationship between equals impossible for men and women in our society. The questions that remain are: Would the development of androgynous human beings through androgynous sex-role training be possible? If possible, would it allow for the development of equal love relationships? What other human potentials would androgyny allow to develop? And how would society have to be restructured in order to allow for androgynous human beings and equal love relationships?

There is good evidence that human babies are bisexual and only *learn* a specific male or female identity by imitating and identifying with adult models. This evidence comes from the discovery that all human beings possess both male and female hormones (androgen and estrogen, respectively), and also from concepts first developed at length by Freud. Freud argued that heterosexual identity is not achieved until the third stage of the child's sexual development. Sex identity is developed through the resolution of the Oedipus complex, in which the child has to give up a primary attachment to the mother and learn either to identify with, or love, the father. But Shulamith Firestone suggests that this process is not an inevitable one, as Freud presents it to be. Rather, it is due to the power dynamics of the patriarchal nuclear family.[11] Note that, in this analysis, if the sexual division of labor were destroyed, the mechanism that trains boys and girls to develop heterosexual sexual identities would also be destroyed. If fathers and mothers played equal nurturant roles in childrearing and had equal social, economic, and political power outside the home, there would be no reason for the boy to have to reject his emotional side in order to gain the power associated with the male role. Neither would the girl have to assume a female role in rejecting her assertive, independent side in order to attain power indirectly through manipulation of males. As a sexual identity, bisexuality would then be the norm rather than the exception.

If bisexuality were the norm rather than the exception for the sexual identities that children develop,[12] androgynous sex roles would certainly be a consequence. For, as discussed above, the primary mechanism whereby complementary rather than androgynous sex roles are maintained is through heterosexual training, and through the socialization of needs for love and sexual gratification to the search for a love partner of the opposite sex. Such a partner is sought to complement one in the traits that one has repressed or not developed because in one's own sex such traits were not socially accepted.

## The Androgynous Model

I believe that only androgynous people can attain the full human potential possible given our present level of material and social resources (and this only if society is radically restructured). Only such people can have ideal love relationships; and without such relationships, I maintain that none can develop to the fullest potential. Since human beings are social animals and develop through interaction and productive activity with others, such relationships are necessary.

Furthermore, recent studies have shown that the human brain has two distinct functions: one associated with analytic, logical, sequential thinking (the left brain), and the other associated with holistic, metaphorical, intuitive thought (the right brain). Only a person capable of tapping both these sides of him/herself will have developed to full potential. We might call this characteristic of the human brain "psychic bisexuality" (Painter, 1973), since it has been shown that women in fact have developed skills which allow them to tap the abilities of the right side of the brain more than men, who on the contrary excel in the analytic, logical thought characteristic of the left side. The point is that men and women have the potential for using both these functions, and yet our socialization at present tends to cut us off from one or the other of these parts of ourselves.[13]

What would an androgynous personality be like? My model for the ideal androgynous person comes from the concept of human potential developed by Marx in *Economic and Philosophical Manuscripts.* Marx's idea is that human beings have a need (or a potential) for free, creative, productive activity which allows them to control their lives in a situation of cooperation with others. Both men and women need to be equally active and independent; with an equal sense of control over their lives; equal opportunity for creative, productive activity; and a sense of meaningful involvement in the community.

Androgynous women would be just as assertive as men about their own needs in a love relationship: productive activity outside the home, the right to private time, and the freedom to form other intimate personal and sexual relationships. I maintain that being active and assertive—traits now associated with being "masculine"—are positive traits that all people need to develop. Many feminists are suspicious of the idea of self-assertion because it is associated with the traits of aggression and competitiveness. However, there is no inevitability to this connection: It results from the structural features of competitive, hierarchical economic systems, of which our own (monopoly capitalism) is one example. In principle, given the appropriate social structure, there is no reason why a self-assertive person cannot also be nurturant and cooperative.

Androgynous men would be more sensitive and aware of emotions than sex-role stereotyped "masculine" men are today. They would be more concerned with the feelings of all people, including women and children, and aware of conflicts of interests. Being sensitive to human emotions is necessary to an effective care and concern for others. Such sensitivity is now thought of as a "motherly," "feminine," or "maternal" instinct, but in fact it is a role and skill learned by women, and it can equally well be learned by men. Men need to get in touch with their own feelings in order to empathize with others, and, indeed, to understand themselves better so as to be more in control of their actions.

We have already discussed the fact that women are more vulnerable in a love relationship than men because many men consider a concern with feelings and emotions to be part of the woman's role. Women, then, are required to be more aware of everyone's feelings (if children and third parties are involved) than men, and they are under more pressure to harmonize the conflicts by sacrificing their own interests.

Another important problem with a nonandrogynous love relationship is that it limits the development of mutual understanding. In general, it seems true that the more levels people can relate on, the deeper and more intimate their relationship is. The more experiences and activities they share, the greater their companionship and meaning to each other. And this is true for emotional experiences. Without mutual understanding of the complex of emotions involved in an ongoing love relationship, communication and growth on that level are blocked for both people. This means that, for both people, self-development of the sort that could come from the shared activity of understanding and struggling to deal with conflicts will not be possible.

In our society as presently structured, there are few possibilities for men and women to develop themselves through shared activities. Men and women share more activities with members of their own sex than with each other. Most women can't get jobs in our sexist, job-segregated society which allow them to share productive work with men. Most men just don't have the skills (or the time, given the demands of their wage-labor jobs) to understand the emotional needs of children and to share the activity of childrearing equally with their wives.

How must our society be restructured to allow for the development of androgynous personalities? How can it be made to provide for self-development through the shared activities of productive and reproductive work? I maintain that this will not be possible (except for a small, privileged elite) without the development of a democratic socialist society. In such a society no one would benefit from cheap labor (presently provided to the capitalist class by a part-time reserve army of women). Nor would anyone benefit from hierarchical power relationships (which encourage competition among the working class and reinforce male sex-role stereotypes as necessary to "making it" in society).

As society is presently constituted, the patriarchal nuclear family and women's reproductive work therein serve several crucial roles in maintaining the capitalist system. In the family, women do the unpaid work of social reproduction of the labor force (childrearing). They also pacify and support the male breadwinner in an alienating society where men who are not in the capitalist class have little control of their product or work conditions. Men even come to envy their wives' relatively nonalienated labor in childrearing rather than dealing with those with the real privilege, the capitalist class. Since those in power relations never give them up without a struggle, it is utopian to think that the capitalist class will allow for the elimination of the sexual division of labor without a socialist revolution with feminist priorities. Furthermore, men in the professional and working classes must be challenged by women with both a class and feminist consciousness to begin the process of change.

In order to eliminate the subordination of women in the patriarchal nuclear family and the perpetuation of sex-role stereotypes therein, there will need to be a radical reorganization of childrearing. Father and mother must have an equal commitment to raising children. More of the reproductive work must be socialized—for example, by community childcare, perhaps with parent cooperatives. Communal living is one obvious alternative which would deemphasize biological parenthood and allow homosexuals and bisexuals the opportunity to have an equal part in relating to children. The increased socialization of childcare would allow parents who are incompatible the freedom to dissolve their relationships without denying their children the secure, permanent, loving relationships they need with both men and women. A community responsibility for childrearing would provide children with male and female models other than their biological parent—models that they would be able to see and relate to emotionally.

Not only would men and women feel an equal responsibility to do reproductive work, they would also expect to do rewarding, productive work in a situation where they had equal opportunity. Such a situation would of course require reduced workweeks for parents, maternity and paternity leaves, and the development of a technology of reproduction which would allow women complete control over their bodies.

As for love relationships, with the elimination of sex roles and the disappearance, in an overpopulated world, of any biological need for sex to be associated with procreation, there would be no reason why such a society could not transcend sexual gender. It would no longer matter what biological sex individuals had. Love relationships, and the sexual relationships developing out of them, would be based on the individual meshing together of androgynous human beings.

# Notes

I'd like to acknowledge the help and encouragement of the socialist and feminist intellectual communities at the University of Massachusetts in Amherst, particularly the help of Sam Bowles, Jean Elshtain, and Dennis Delap, who read and commented extensively on earlier drafts of this essay. John Brentlinger and Susan Cayleff also provided feedback and comments. Many students who read the essay were helpful and supportive. A first version of this paper was read in the fall of 1974 at Bentley College, Boston, Massachusetts.

This chapter is a revised version of an essay previously published in Mary Vetterling-Braggin, Frederick Elliston, and Jane English, eds., *Feminism and Philosophy*. Totowa, N.J., Rowman and Allanheld, 1977. Copyright © Littlefield, Adams & Co. Reprinted with permission of Rowman and Allanheld.

1. I owe these thoughts to Jean Elshtain and members of the Valley Women's Union in Northampton, Massachusetts, from discussions on androgyny.

2. Contrast the Stone Age tribe recently discovered in the Philippines, where competition is unknown, with the competitive male and female Dobus from Melanesia. See Ruth Benedict (1934).

3. Rousseau says, in a typical passage from *Emile*, "When once it is proved that men and women are and ought to be unlike in constitution and in temperament, it follows that their education should be different." And on a succeeding page he concludes, "A woman's education must therefore be planned in relation to man. To be pleasing in his sight, to win his respect and love, to train him in childhood, to tend him in manhood, to counsel and console, to make his life pleasant and happy, these are the duties of woman for all time, and this is what she should be taught while she is young. The further we depart from this principle, the further we shall be from our own good, and all our precepts will fail to secure her happiness or our own" (Rousseau, 1911, pp. 326, 328).

Gilder's conclusion is as follows: "But at a profounder level the women are tragically wrong. For they fail to understand their own sexual power; and they fail to perceive the sexual constitution of our society, or if they see it, they underestimate its importance to our civilization and to their own interest in order and stability. In general across the whole range of the society, marriage and careers—and thus social order—will be best served if most men have a position of economic superiority over the relevant women in his [sic] community and if in most jobs in which colleagues must work together, the sexes tend to be segregated either by level or function" (Gilder, 1973, p. 108).

4. It is not simply the fact that men are physically stronger than women which gives them the edge in sexual power relations. It is also women's lesser psychological capacity for violence and aggressiveness. However, this has as much to do with socialization into passive roles from early childhood as it does with any inequality in the amount of the male hormone androgen, which is correlated to aggressive behavior in higher primates. As Simone de Beauvoir points out in *The Second Sex* (1952), male children develop training in aggressive behavior from an early age, while female children are kept from the psychological hardening process involved in physical fights. Feeling that one is by nature submissive will cause one to be submissive; so even women who are equal in strength to men will appear to themselves and to men not to be so.

5. Perhaps part of the reason for the solidarity in these societies is due to the meager resources to be struggled for.

6. Karen Horney develops this theory in her book *Feminine Psychology* (1967), as does Eva Figes in *Patriarchal Attitudes* (1970). Note the striking difference between Horney's and Tiger's (1969) explanations of the phenomenon of male bonding.

7. Catholic Church doctrine maintains a dualism between soul and body. The soul is thought to be rational and spiritual, the valuable part of the self that loves God; while the body is sinful, animal, given to sexual lusts and passions. Women are identified with the body because of their childbearing function, hence with sexuality, evil, and the devil. (The story of Eve in Genesis is used to support this view.) It is women who lead men away from the pure

spiritual life and into the evils of sexuality: They are thus inferior beings whose only positive function is the reproduction of children. Even in this role they are merely receptacles, for the theory of reproduction is that woman is the lowly, unclean vessel into which man puts the seed of life.

8. In the cult of true womanhood prevalent in America and England in the nineteenth century, women are thought to be passive and emotional but *not* sexual or tied to the body. Rather, the woman is the moral and spiritual guardian of the male, who is thought to be more naturally sinful than she—avaricious, competitive, self-interested, and imbued with sexual passions. The one sphere, then, in which woman is thought to be naturally skilled is the home and the spiritual education of children and husband.

9. Socialization into complementary sex roles is responsible not only for job segregation practices' keeping women in low-paid service jobs which are extensions of the supportive work women do in the home as mothers, but also for making it difficult for women to feel confident in their ability to excel at competitive "male-defined" jobs.

10. Thanks to Sam Bowles for this point.

11. Firestone (1970). The boy and girl both realize that the father has power in the relationship between him and the mother, and that his role, and not the mother's, represents the possibility of achieving economic and social power in the world and over one's life. The mother, in contrast, represents nurturing and emotionality. Both boy and girl, then, in order to get power for themselves, have to reject the mother as a love object—the boy, because he is afraid of the father as rival and potential castrator; and the girl, because the only way as a girl she can attain power is through manipulating the father. So she becomes a rival to her mother for her father's love. The girl comes to identify with her mother and to choose her father and, later, other men for love objects; while the boy identifies with his father, sublimates his sexual attraction to his mother into superego (will power), and chooses mother substitutes, other women, for his love objects.

12. It should be understood here that no claim is being made that bisexuality is more desirable than homo- or heterosexuality. The point is that with the removal of the social mechanisms in the family that channel children into heterosexuality, there is no reason to suppose that most of them will develop in that direction. It would be more likely that humans with androgynous personalities would be bisexual, the assumption here being that there are no innate biological preferences in people for sexual objects of the same or opposite sex. Rather, this comes to be developed because of emotional connections of certain sorts of personality characteristics with the male and female body, characteristics which develop because of complementary sex-role training, and which would not be present without it.

The other mechanism which influences people to develop a heterosexual identity is the desire to reproduce. As long as the social institution for raising children is the heterosexual nuclear family, and as long as society continues to place social value on biological parenthood, most children will develop a heterosexual identity. Not, perhaps, in early childhood, but certainly after puberty, when the question of reproduction becomes viable. Radical socialization and collectivization of childrearing would thus have to characterize a society before bisexuality would be the norm not only in early childhood, but in adulthood as well. For the purposes of developing androgynous individuals, however, full social bisexuality of this sort is not necessary. All that is needed is the restructuring of the sex roles of father and mother in the nuclear family so as to eliminate the sexual division of labor there.

13. It is notable that writers, painters, and other intellectuals, who presumably would need skills of both sorts, have often been misfits in the prevalent complementary sex stereotyping. In fact, thinkers as diverse as Plato (in the *Symposium*) and Virginia Woolf (in *A Room of One's Own*) have suggested that writers and thinkers need to be androgynous to tap all the skills necessary for successful insight.

# ADDENDUM:
# WHY GYNANDRY IS A BETTER NAME

"Androgyny as an Ideal for Human Development," which just precedes this addendum, was written in 1977 as a critique of the natural complement theory of gender roles. The natural complement theory is the traditional conservative view, represented in most classical Western philosophies and religions. It presumes that women and men are incomplete halves of humanity who are naturally endowed with complementary but different personality traits, skills, and abilities. I argued that the natural complement theory is not only false but is the central ideology that has been used to legitimate the social construction of a stereotypical masculinity and femininity that perpetuate male dominance. In its place, I advocated androgyny as a feminist ideal for human development.

Since I wrote that paper, however, other feminists have extensively criticized the notion of androgyny as an ideal for human development. First, the psychoanalytic perspective, represented by Jean Elshtain (ca. 1977), questions whether androgyny is a possible ideal, as it seems to imply a state of genderlessness, which may be psychologically impossible. Elshtain is correct to challenge the possibility of a genderless androgyny. In any probable future human society, the sexual and reproductive differences between the male and female body are likely to generate socially different senses of gender. Even though postmodernist feminists emphasize that the concept of gender, and even biological sex, is a socially constructed category,[1] the functional difference that being the reproducer makes in sex/affective social relations will make sex a more important social distinction than skin color, hair, and other physical characteristics.

Nonetheless, it is possible to conceive of a society in which the female body and its social implications have been revalued in such a way that whatever traits are associated with the female body have equal value to those associated with the male body. In such a situation, the *symbolic* implications of gender-associated traits will be detachable from bodies altogether, and it will be possible for both women and men to strive for a human ideal that combines and reconstructs those traits historically associated with masculinity and with femininity into a new, unified human ideal. I would call this a gynandrous rather than an androgynous ideal because the revaluing of femininity required to achieve an autonomous yet caring person involves a "transvaluation" of values that goes beyond the traditional notion of androgyny in patriarchal societies.

In developing the notion of gynandry, I am responding to the radical feminist critique developed by Janice Raymond (1975, 1979). This view maintains that the concept of androgyny, based as it is on the root *andros* (or male) and the suffix *gynē* (or female), still privileges masculinity as the paradigmatic human nature and adds femininity as a complement. Furthermore the idea of combining masculinity and femininity in one person, and the attendant idea of developing both the masculine and feminine "sides" of oneself, still assumes the natural complement theory that masculinity and femininity are essentially different and complementary. This just perpetuates in a new guise the old myth of gender dualism.

Raymond argues that feminists need a new ideal for human development, which she calls *integrity* (Raymond, 1979). This assumes that there is a deep level of the personality, the authentic self, which has been repressed and distorted as a result of patriarchal socialization, and that the goal of individual and collective feminist struggle against patriarchy is to remove the alienating internal and external barriers to development of the authentic self.

I agree with the motivation behind Raymond's theory of integrity; we do need a new feminist ideal untainted by patriarchal hangovers. I disagree, however, with her suggestion of integrity as that ideal, for this assumes an essentialist core of the self that remains untouched by socialization. My alternative aspect theory of self implies that one's personal identity is always developed in social practices in relation to others. Thus resistance to oppressive social identities is based on conflicts in one's personal identity connected to conflicting roles in various social practices. For example, one of the underlying assumptions of all patriarchal ideologies of masculinity and femininity is that these qualities exclude each other. But those of us who work in formerly all-male occupations while at the same time engaged in woman-identified occupations, such as mothering, know that this assumption is false.

The aspect theory of self assumes that women's liberation requires a reorganization and redefinition of gendered practices so that they no longer involve inconsistent values. Because both male-identified and female-identified occupations and activities have been developed under patriarchal assumptions, we also will want to create this feminist harmonization by rejecting aspects of both masculinity and femininity as they are presently socially constructed. This reconstruction of a harmonious set of social and personal values, though, cannot be done ahistorically or intellectually. Raymond's concept of integrity seems to imply that one's present lack of self-integrity is simply a result of false consciousness, that by shedding those false ideas we return to our underlying true core. On the contrary, because identities are always based in a concrete history of social practices, we must find creative countercultural practices in which to embed ourselves to construct a different set of self-aspects. The model of a gynandrous self requires practices that create a set of traits, some of which are presently called masculine (autonomy, assertiveness, analytical clarity of thought) and some feminine (nurturance, responsiveness, intuition). It also requires practices allowing us to unlearn the negative historical aspects of these gender clusters (e.g., masculine ego-tripping, feminine passivity and manipulativeness). This is not going back or under to more authentic values; rather, it is transvaluing present values, calling forth new values by creating a historically unique combination of these values.

I call this process of developing new ideal feminist personalities *gynandry* to mark the concern with revaluing feminine strengths that have been submerged into subordinate practices in patriarchal societies.[2] Practices of nurturance, as they have focused on the so-called private sphere of women's family, kin, and friendship networks, have not influenced the sphere of public policy. Though both the first- and second-wave women's movements advocated the "feminization" of the public sphere of the economy and state politics—for example, the "social housekeeping" ideas of Jane Addams and other progressives in the first wave and the women's peace movement of the second wave—neither wave has been successful in achieving this. In both cases a key problem has been the predominance of liberal feminist reformism, that is, the idea that we can simply reform capitalist patriarchy and women will be able to be equal to men. But the revaluation of the feminine that is needed to build a truly gynandrous society will only be possible by reorganizing the public/private distinction that capitalism imposes, so as to guarantee a social, not merely a private, concern with meeting human needs, with providing human nurturance. This cannot occur in either a state capitalist society or hitherto existing patriarchal socialist societies. Instead, it requires a change to either a feminist market or council socialism of the sort I suggest in Chapter 10.

I hope I have made it clear how the ideal of gynandry answers the first and second criticisms leveled against the ideal of androgyny, namely, that it need not assume that gender identities will be dissolved in a genderless sense of self and it need not accept an ideal that is a mere pastiche of masculine and feminine traits as presently understood. A third criticism of androgyny is pointed out by radical lesbian feminists. This is that it is still a heterosexist ideal, for it assumes that the female principle lacks something by itself, as does the male principle. Love of the same, or woman for woman because of womanhood, is bypassed in favor of love of the different, both in oneself (one's masculine and feminine aspects) and in others. Thus it is implied that androgynous beings should love other androgynous beings and gender should not matter, making homosexual desire inferior to bisexual desire.

As I point out in Chapter 10, a gynandrous society does not imply the dissolution of the sexual identities of heterosexuality and homosexuality, though it might encourage more individuals to develop bisexual identities. This is partly because bodily differences will still create minimal gender differences in any social organization in the immediate future. Individuals may well prefer certain bodies over others because of symbolic sensual meanings not erased by a common cross-gender ideal of gynandry. Indeed, we cannot be sure to what extent a gynandrous society will completely reorganize erotic interests before the fact.

In any case, the development of a fully gynandrous society will involve a process that will take at least several generations, both for a democratic socialism to become fully operational and for old patterns and self-understandings to be restructured. We should thus expect that many feminists will continue to be lesbians in this transitional phase, and some men will continue to be gay. The defense of a long-run ideal of gynandry is consistent with the view that we must support a gay and lesbian identity politics in the short run.

A fourth problem with the concept of androgyny is that some have used it to argue against an autonomous women's movement politics on the grounds that gender dualism is an outmoded social construction. According to this view, feminist supporters, male or female, should work together to develop their androgynous potential. Because gender is alienating, men are as oppressed as women by patriarchy, for they are denied the development of their feminine possibilities. Thus feminism should eschew autonomous women's politics and advocate an integrationist organizing of both men and women against institutional sexism.

Though I accept coalitions of men and women in the fight against sexism, I think we also require an autonomous women's movement. Patriarchal gender construction is not as oppressive to men as it is to women because men's gendered social practices give them more social power and privileges than women. Just because our ideal society would downplay gender differences in the promotion of the ideal of gynandry, it does not follow that our transitional politics can afford to do this. After all, most men have been socialized in aspects of masculinity that help to perpetuate male dominance, and most women have been socialized to defer to men. We thus need a transitional politics that acknowledges the need for an autonomous women's movement at the same time that it encourages a gynandrous men's movement and a coalitionist socialist-feminist politics to work collectively to challenge white supremacist capitalist patriarchy.

Feminists should indeed unite against white supremacy. But how exactly does the goal of gynandry connect to the fight against racism? Audre Lorde has put one reason very eloquently in her essay "Scratching the Surface: Some Notes on Barriers to Women and Loving" (in Lorde, 1984). Racism, sexism, and heterosexism are all systems of belief and social practice that both exaggerate and denigrate differences of the supposed inferiors (of race, sex, sexual preference). Gynandry as an ideal is a challenge to gender dualism as a method of social organization that, if instituted, would at once reduce socially imposed differences among people and encourage the valuing of diversity. In that way, it would undermine imposed racial genders that distinguish between the good white woman or man and the bad or failed woman or man of color. The revision of the sexual symbolic codes necessary to institute gynandry would thus require a challenge to the double standards for gender because of racism and would remove one of the symbolic barriers to interracial solidarity.

Of course, people of color must develop their own feminist ideals and agendas. As a white woman I cannot presume that the particular historical revaluing of the feminine that people of color will pursue will yield exactly the same gynandrous mix of hitherto masculine and feminine traits as it will for white Anglos. On the other hand, the latest novel of Alice Walker, *The Temple of My Familiar* (1989), certainly seems to be moving in a similar direction as that of many white feminists and white male allies. We can only hope that a revitalized interracial Left in the United States in the 1990s will begin to set the stage for us to look together—in spite of cultural color and ethnic barriers and differences—toward a common vision for the new woman and man.

## Notes

1. Judith Butler argued this claim in an impressive lecture called "Sex/Gender and the Shape of Politics," March 14, 1989, at Amherst College. This view had been argued much earlier by Andrea Dworkin in *Womanhating* (1974). But Dworkin has been ambiguous of late as to whether she maintains her earlier views about the possible deconstruction of sex and gender, or whether she views the contemporary construction of masculinity and femininity as inescapable (cf. Dworkin, 1987).

2. An unclarity in understanding the ideal of gynandry is specifying what scope for diversity in personalities the ideal allows. In our ideal society would everyone have to be equally gynandrous, or could there be a variety of

personality types ranging from those that would be characterized by present categories as mostly feminine to those that are mostly masculine, as long as these types weren't imposed by gender? I accept Joyce Trebilcot's idea (1977) of a p-androgynous society, that is, one that values diversity in personality types, rather than an m-androgynous, or single personality, society.

It may well be that even when a gynandrous society is set up people will not find it easy to balance autonomy and nurturance, the core characteristics of presently constructed masculinity and femininity. All we can recommend is the removal of the social constraints against the attempt and a valorization of the struggle as valuable in itself, whether or not it can ever achieve the goal of a static harmonization.

# TEN

# A Feminist Democratic Socialism

A socialist-feminist vision of an ideal society is very much a product of the values of the particular society and historical period in which it is framed. The vision outlined here comes out of the context of contemporary U.S. history. It is a thought experiment that attempts to find ways to reconcile values articulated but not feasible in contemporary society, either because social and economic structures do not allow it or because they force one to sacrifice some of the values in order to gain others. For example, sexual pleasure and emotional commitment are often thought to be in conflict, as are democratic parenting practices and achieving to the highest of one's ability in the world of paid employment. The notion of equal opportunity for all is given lip service by most Americans yet is not attainable by women, racial minorities, or those from low-income families.

All of the values mentioned above *could* be jointly achieved, though, if we were to alter the economic and social structures—the capitalist economy, patriarchal families, impoverished single-parent families, racial and sexual divisions of labor and living—that sustain these conflicts and inequalities.

## General Goals and Ideas

A socialist-feminist model for a future U.S. society must develop a vision that both encourages a sense of community and group solidarity and respects individual autonomy. In this way, such a model would be in line with that of Marge Piercy in *Woman on the Edge of Time* (1974). Piercy envisages small, chosen communities based on the different subcultures already present in U.S. society—native American, black, Latino—but with the difference that one's biological origins would not determine into which community one was accepted as an adult, this being open to personal choice. There would be an egalitarian division of material resources to such communities based on numbers of people and their needs rather than the privileges of inherited family wealth.

Piercy raises a serious question, as had Firestone before (1970): Must the biological differences between the sexes in reproduction be altered, minimized, or both in order to create conditions for a gender reciprocal sex/affective energy exchange in parenting? Both of these authors think so. Piercy's model has nonbiological parents choosing to parent children. The fetus is brought to term in an artificial incubator to avoid privileging bonding between the biological mother and child. There are always three parents, not two, and these are of mixed genders, with the men having been hormonally treated so as to be able to take turns breastfeeding the baby.

Although this model is appealing in some ways, it generates concern about whether the means of achieving such a radical change could ever avoid undesirable social controls on individual autonomy. For example, mandatory hormone treatments for male parents raise the general problem of biological tampering and who is to control it. What guarantee is there that gender, racial, and ethnic discrimination would not influence the choice of the babies to be artificially incubated? Furthermore, how would the danger of creating a class of surrogate mothers in the process be avoided? This would be a cheaper solution than artificial incubators and could create a group of women subordinate to a male elite who would control female reproductive powers in their own interest. A dystopia of this sort is chillingly portrayed in Margaret Atwood's *Handmaid's Tale* (1987), in which a class of handmaidens is expected to reproduce babies who then become the property of the commander class.

Thus the dangers of trying to create a society that achieves reproductive equalization by artificial reproduction are too great to be worth the risk. It is also unlikely that many women would be willing to give up bodily birthing or many men would be willing to take estrogen to enlarge their breasts so as to be able to breastfeed babies, though we can imagine bottle feeding becoming the norm in the future. In any case, we must find another way to equalize men's and women's roles in parenting. This can only come from instituting a socialist political economy that provides the material structures to support a range of parenting options without penalizing anyone, particularly the women and children, who are involved in them. I further discuss this later in the chapter.

The general goals of community and autonomy have been a part of American values since the colonial period, yet they have also been in tension. The Puritans attempted to found a community based on conformity to a Calvinist reading of the Bible that emphasized the right of Protestant individual autonomy from Church of England doctrine. In the process, however, they generated nonconformists like Anne Hutchinson and Roger Williams who insisted on their autonomous right to disagree with the reading of the Bible approved of by the church fathers. The tendency toward individualism in a context where group solidarity was needed to survive continued as successive waves of immigrants from different cultures found themselves in competition in wage labor. Nonetheless, these historical tensions in American values can be resolved in a socialist-feminist model society. But first we need to clarify what is involved in these values.

Group solidarity is not merely an intellectual or moral commitment to give the needs of the group and individuals within it a higher priority than one's own interests. Rather, it implies a desire to see that the needs of the group and its individuals are met. One's incorporative identification with the group, then, involves an increase in sex/affective energy to oneself and others in the group when the needs of individual members or of the group as a whole are achieved.

Individual autonomy, on the other hand, may mean setting individual goals, values, or needs that are in conflict with those of the group. For example, an interest in solitary mountain climbing may sometimes be at odds with the collective work necessary for the good of any group in which such a person is a member. A woman's or couple's desire for an inordinate amount of children may also tax the material resources of the group to be called on to provide support services for parenting and for the children. Or a person's sexual desires may be defined as risky or forbidden by the majority.

In *Blood at the Root* (Ferguson, 1989a) I develop a feminist sexual morality that distinguishes between basic, risky, and forbidden sexual practices. Thus, practices that involve reciprocal exchanges of sex/affective energy are basic practices whereas those suspected of leading to inequalities of the partners (heterosexual marriage, consensual S/M sex, and prostitution) are risky. Those clearly either nonconsensual or unequal are forbidden (rape, parent-child incest, adult-child sex). The point of making this distinction is to mediate the contemporary feminist sex debate by allowing a personal space of disagreement between feminists (risky sex) where individuals have the right to make their own choices and feminists agree to disagree without writing each other out of the feminist community.[1]

Though I have maintained a line between areas of public responsibility and private freedoms that was initially questioned by radical feminism, this does not imply that the status quo public/private separation can be maintained intact. Radical feminists were correct to argue that issues we now think of as private are also political, that is, they involve power relations between individuals and thus are subject to moral inquiry and disagreement by others. Countercultural feminism of the 1970s was mistaken in assuming that from the edict that "the personal is the political" it followed that the correct feminist morality in the private or personal area can be decided by a democratic consensus of women! Rather than eliminate the distinction between the public and the private, we need to rethink the areas to which public decisionmaking should apply and those in which individuals should have the right to take their own risks and make their own values.

The above considerations suggest that we need to support a culture of individual autonomy in our socialist-feminist society. But we also need to create institutional structures that would meet material needs in a more egalitarian way than capitalist societies have done. This is a necessary precondition for encouraging a culture of solidarity or community.

The concept of sex/affective production developed in this book assumes that humans have material needs for sexuality, nurturance, and affection that are met when sex/affective energy is generated between persons. A society maximizing egalitarian and democratic values would tend to increase reciprocal sex/affective energy. Contrary to the assumption of class-divided, patriarchal societies, the social distribution of sexuality, nurturance, and affection need not operate on a scarcity or a zero-sum model. If we were to minimize the repressive aspects of such social hierarchies as husband/wife, parent/child, teacher/ student, and boss/worker, we would increase the total amount of sex/ affective energy to be distributed in a more egalitarian way. One strategy to achieve this would be peer group bonding in work groups, councils, and households for collective decisionmaking on issues both large and small that affect participants' lives. Those with expertise in various areas because of age or training would act more as advisers and less as top-down authorities in a society that would encourage participatory democracy, that is, workers' control and child, student, client, and patient input into educational, therapeutic, and medical structures. In the process of learning to cooperate and respect one another's input, people would give and receive much more nurturance than is presently possible.

The overall goal of the political economy of this ideal society would be democratic socialism. Besides addressing the question what type of political economy would create a feasible democratic socialism, I must also elaborate on six values that make this vision feminist: first, eliminating gender dualism; second, setting up a nonracist and non-ethnicist society; third, maximizing democratic parenting; fourth, promoting sex for pleasure; fifth, promoting committed sexual relationships; and, sixth, guaranteeing gay and lesbian rights.

## A Democratic Socialist Political Economy: Command, Market, and Council Socialist Models

We must spend some time discussing several different models, especially in the light of the recent shake-ups in the existing state socialist societies in the Soviet Union, Eastern Europe, and China. Two different models, market and council socialism, oppose the command economy model of most of these countries.

How are we to decide on a vision of democratic socialism appropriate to our historical circumstances in the United States? First, it is important to clarify what exactly we are looking for. Let's distinguish between a utopian vision, one that would work only if this were the best of all possible worlds, and a feasible vision, one that has a good likelihood of being plausible to a people with our historically constituted values and that is likely to achieve our goals with a reasonable level of success. A feasible socialism, according to Alec Nove (1983), is one that we can envisage being set in place so that our children could enjoy its fruits when they are adults.

Given the failures of the hitherto state socialist countries of the USSR, China, and Eastern Europe, we must question whether socialism could plausibly be adopted in the United States without changing the model envisaged. For example, much ink has been used to critique the command economy model of a socialist society (cf. Albert and Hahnel 1978, 1981; Nove, 1983, for general overviews of this literature), used until recently in the Soviet Union, Cuba, China, and most of Eastern Europe (with the notable exception of Yugoslavia). By this model, there is a central planning board that sets both production goals for five years based on their assessment of consumer needs and social goals of economic development. Prices and wages are set independently of supply and demand, as the concern is to subsidize the basic goods for consumers regardless of demand, at a fair ratio with respect to wages.

Many writers, socialist and nonsocialist alike, have argued that having an economy entirely based on central planning is inefficient. There is simply no rational way independent of consumer demand to calculate a fair or reasonable price for every one of the million items that must be produced in an industrial society based on production for exchange. Furthermore, allowing such decisionmaking power to be centralized in a small group of planners inevitably produces a hierarchical bureaucracy that is incompatible with economic democracy, that is, with workers' control over production decisions. There is, of course, fierce debate about whether the failures of existing socialisms are inevitable or simply a result of their having been peasant societies forced to industrialize under socialist central planning before they had even developed the concept of bourgeois political democracy, that is, the notion of civil rights against state power and formal rights to multiparty systems and representative democracy. Would a command economy, if set in place in the United States, have vastly different results because of our strong heritage of formal democracy?

I tend to agree with the critics of the command economy model that there is a functional connection between the lack of political democracy and the presence of a command economy. Czechoslovakia, for example, is an industrialized country that had experience of bourgeois political democracy before it voted in the Communist party. When it set up a command economy and allowed the party the power to control production decisions through central planning, however, the Communist party was able to establish near total political control as well and thus, until very recently, eliminate its organized political opposition.

What about market socialism? Nove defends a mixed-economy market socialist model (Nove, 1983). He points to the experience of Hungary, which in 1968 introduced some elements of the market into its economy, thereby allowing some prices and wages to fluctuate with supply and demand. The expanded autonomy this has allowed production units has been particularly successful with farms, which are freer to decide what to produce and where to purchase their inputs; prices for their goods are negotiated without resorting to compulsory delivery quotas from central planners. The ability of peasants to raise their income from both private and collective endeavors, and the availability of consumer goods on which to spend such income, has in turn increased productivity. Hungary's economy stood in contrast to the dismal situations that existed in Poland and the Soviet Union, where consumer goods were not available and productivity sagged because of the lack of material incentives.

Yugoslavia is another example of a market socialist economy that contains a feature not present in Hungary: workers' self-management— that is, workers rather than central planners make investment, wage, and price decisions. Although there is a state sector of government, health, and education workers on salary, most of the economy is a decentralized market sector. Market considerations are allowed largely to influence workers' decisions on wages and prices and how to distribute profits.

One of the problems in deciding which model is feasible for the United States is knowing how to separate the accidental failures of the Yugoslavian political economy from those functional to its market socialism. Nove argues that a high unemployment rate is one bad functional consequence, as workers have an incentive not to hire extra workers in order to increase their individual shares of the firm's profits. Furthermore, there is the problem of who is to be held responsible if a firm fails, for example, if managers make bad investment decisions that cause the company to lose money. Especially if there is a high turnover of labor in the firm, the present workers cannot be held responsible for a decision that was the consequence of previous workers' decisions. Furthermore, the absence of central planning means that the regional differences in resources continue to allow workers in one area to achieve higher profits than in others, which seems unfair.

Nove's solution is a socialist mixed economy, which differs from a capitalist mixed economy like our welfare state capitalism in that there is no private ownership of large corporations; these and the banks are nationalized. On the other hand, there are two other sectors, a socialized sector of workers' cooperatives and a private sector of small businesses owned by working entrepreneurs. In the nationalized sector there would have to be agreement on a wage policy between the unions and the government that would allow for some central planning to offset the possibility of inflation, so as to avoid the incessant driving up of wages and prices by unions. In the socialized sector there would have to be fixed wages with some bonuses related to profit to avoid the unemployment problem. Nove also suggests that a feature of the workers' cooperatives in Mondragon, Spain, could be adopted to increase workers' identification with the profitability of the firm: Limited shares could be owned by workers such that dividends would accrue to the workers on retirement or transfer to another company. He also suggests that there would need to be limited deductions from workers' paychecks in the case of losses by the company, which would incline the workers to support economically and socially efficient decisions.

Besides versions of the command and market socialist models, there is also the council socialist model propounded by Michael Albert and Robin Hahnel (1981). Rejecting both of the other two models for their inegalitarian and undemocratic tendencies, they argue for a planned yet decentralized economy that emphasizes participatory democracy as well as representative democracy in the regulating of the economy. The economy would aim to develop more regional and local self-sufficiency in terms of the planning and development of local industry and would make economic blueprints for development based on an "iterative" process of consultation and consensus between workers' and consumers' councils at the local, regional, and national levels.

The key dispute between a mixed-market socialist model and a council socialist model is whether the latter is viable in both aspects of that notion. That is, could Americans, used to the existence of markets and individual autonomy to try (even if only to fail) at private small business endeavors, really be persuaded that only workers' cooperative businesses should be allowed? Would they be convinced that such a tedious negotiating process as envisaged by council socialism is feasible? And wouldn't there have to be a lot of old-fashioned "big" government, including a bureaucracy of experts, to set up such a model (the transition problem)? Second, even if we were persuaded to adopt this model, would it work? Note that the iterative process of consultation and consensus between workers' and consumers' councils at all levels involves an incredible amount of information in terms of consumer and producer needs and preferences in all parts of the country, even the world, assuming the right to international trade. It also involves an interminable number of meetings while local, regional, and national councils and representatives haggle back and forth about a fair plan that does not privilege California over New York State or Mexico, or the workers and consumers in Amherst, Massachusetts, over those in Springfield, Massachusetts. Would it not be likely that all but a small, cantankerous elite of workers and consumers would simply get tired of the process and opt out to let the others represent them, with all the problems of the "tyranny of structurelessness" noted by critics of 1970s New Left feminist attempts to create nonhierarchical structures that operated by consensus?[2]

In short, though in my recent book *Blood at the Root* I advocated council socialism as a feasible socialist-feminist vision for the United States, I am now less sanguine about this model and am leaning toward Nove's mixed-market socialism. As I understand his model, there is no independent market in capital; that is, banks are nationalized. There would be workers' cooperative businesses operating in a market of consumer goods and services. Participatory democracy would operate with respect to wages, sharing of profits, and so on. Workers' councils would be required in every work site, whether worker-, state-, or privately owned, and these would have control over the process of production. Unlike a totally decentralized council socialism, however, it would delegate more decisions to elected representatives in state and federal government legislatures. These bodies would make up state and federal budgets, much as is done today, with the difference that they would do so after revising and voting on recommendations by planning boards of economic experts elected at the local, regional, and national levels. These plans would suggest economic priorities for the year (e.g., affirmative action quotas, comparable worth wage guidelines, production goals, and investment priorities in various sectors). Except in the areas of childcare, essential service work, health care, education, public transportation, utilities, and housing, which would be provided, as a social right, free or at low cost by a mix of state and federal programs, consumer goods would be produced on the market, subject to competitive prices. Thus even in the nationalized sector, firms would be subject to competition on the market, both with public and private firms and with foreign firms.

Whether or not one's ideal model of a socialist economy eliminates all markets as well as large-scale private property in the means of production, some general national goals of a socialist-feminist vision would act as touchstones to the success of any model. A basic goal would be material security for all, including state-provided free health care and schooling; job training; free, quality public childcare services; and a minimum income for all whether or not they are old enough or too old to do paid labor. Another would be ending racial and gender divisions of wage labor through job-training programs and affirmative action guidelines for jobs and competitive higher education programs. Finally, adequate resources for public education would have to replace inadequate ghetto schools and inferior education programs for racial and ethnic minorities.

## The Elimination of Gender Dualism

As feminists we must seek collective ways to revalue the feminine in a viable socialist-feminist society. This means that many of the historical skills of most women's sex/affective labor—nurturance, emotional sensitivity, receptivity to the desires of others, skills in the healing arts—must be revalued and taught to men as well as women. This will require not only a breakdown in the gender division of labor in the household and in wage labor but also the acknowledgment that this type of work, as skilled work, should be given comparable worth to male-defined professional work. Childcare workers, elementary school teachers, nurses, and social workers all deserve pay and fringe benefits comparable to those given university professors, physicians, and psychiatrists. Ending gender dualism in wage labor calls for programs that recalibrate the standard wages for men's and women's work requiring comparable though not identical skills. It would also take public, worker-controlled childcare at places of work, flex-time jobs that would allow both male and female parents to work part time to care for small children, and extended maternity and paternity leaves.

In seeking to revalue the feminine in our advanced industrial capitalist society, we are not creating a universal model of an ideal human nature. Rather, we are creating a historically specific model of a gynandrous person that is likely to be quite different from that which would develop in a society with a different history and a different mode of economic production. For example, some societies lack our concept of individual autonomy, developed out of the Protestant revolt against Catholic and Episcopalian state churches, as well as the bourgeois concept of individual rights against the state. We have also experienced the nineteenth-century public/private split in dominant white bourgeois culture between men's competitive production for exchange in wage labor and women's cooperative production for use in the household, which came to be symbolic of "men's work" and "women's work" in general (Benston, 1969). Although in our society the conflict in values between individual autonomy and social solidarity or community can be symbolically identified as a conflict between male-identified selfish interests and female-identified altruism, such an opposition makes no sense in a society where individual autonomy as such is not valued, or where the sexual division of labor does not divide public and private in the way ours historically did. Thus feminists in our society have a gynandrous ideal for human development that is likely quite different from the ideal in a society lacking the concepts of public/private, individual freedom, or democratic process.

Assuming our historical context, a gynandrous person would be someone with a democratic rather than an authoritarian personality, that is, one who desires as much as possible reciprocal rather than hierarchical sex/affective energy exchanges with others, including sexual, love, friendship, parenting, and wage-work interactions.

When we speak of the elimination of gender dualism, we are not speaking of the elimination of gender per se, as I argued in the Addendum to Chapter 9. Rather, reference is to the elimination of institutional constraints, such as the sexual division of labor, and ideological assumptions, such as the natural complement theory, which force individuals to see genders as having a fixed social content or as excluding each other (Dworkin, 1974). Though most individuals in our model socialist-feminist society would probably think of themselves as having a core gender of either male or female, it would be easier for them to think of this as not excluding the other gender; and some individuals might not experience themselves as having any primary gender at all.

The elimination of gender dualism, however, would not thereby preclude the choice of complementary emotional roles by individuals, in sexual, love, parenting, or household relationships. Because such roles would no longer be tied to gender or even to all aspects of individuals' interactions (Newton and Walton, 1984), they would not support such hierarchical relationships between individuals as male dominance or compulsory heterosexuality. Symbolic aspects of gender would probably continue to be tied to the female or male body in spite of the breakdown of the sexual division of labor; it is likely, then, that gay, lesbian, and heterosexual sexual preferences would continue to exist, though there would probably be many more practicing bisexuals than there are today.[3]

What are the social conditions necessary for the emergence of this new gynandric human? We will require not only a democratic socialist economy but also revised institutions of parenthood and childhood. These reforms are not possible in capitalism for two reasons. First, they require a radical elimination of the sexual division of labor, a move that would be highly unprofitable for large private corporations. Second, they would mean challenging the notion supported by capitalism that individuals have no right to interfere with the "private" sphere of the family and the household. Only a socialist culture could redraw the line between public and private in the manner I suggest in the next two sections so as better to promote gender equality and racial social solidarity.

## Ending Racism and Classism

Ending the gender division of labor can be seen as part of a wider project of breaking down the rigid divisions that currently exist between mental and manual labor. A society that values allowing individuals their full potential development of skills cannot be satisfied with creating individuals who are forced to develop mental skills to the exclusion of manual skills or, conversely, to develop manual skills at the sacrifice of the development of critical mental skills. Our goal should be to organize the economy and schooling so as to promote as far as possible the rotation of jobs, both those that are rewarding, such as decision-making and supervising, and those that are costly, such as hazardous, boring, or physically tiring jobs.

Thus our model society must find ways to break down the class construction of our present society that is due to the mental/manual split. Our present advanced capitalist society includes, besides a capitalist class of owners, a professional class that specializes in mental skills, including greater training in critical thinking and decisionmaking, and a working class composed of two parts: the skilled manual workers who develop skills but for the most part are given little decisionmaking over what, how much, and when things are produced, and an unskilled or "de-skilled" working class that learns some boring, repetitive skill or service in order to fit into a mostly automated assembly line or service industry (Walker, 1979). And cutting across these classes, of course, is the sex class division between men who don't and women who do unpaid or unremunerated housework, health care for elder relatives, and childcare at home, often in addition to sex-segmented wage labor.

An economic organization that would move toward breaking down both this class mental/manual labor split and the sex class paid/unpaid sex/affective labor split would have to break down the current public/private division of the economy. One plan that might accomplish these goals is the following. All workers would have a workweek totaling thirty hours, divided into two fifteen-hour sections. One section would be in what we can call standard sector work: construction, factories, doctoring, teaching, skilled clerical, and white-collar work. The other section would be service work. Service work would be rotating. It would consist of all the manual, unskilled, and generally low-status service work, whether this low status were due to objective considerations, such as that the work is boring, repetitive, or unpleasant, or social considerations, such as that it is thought of as women's work or work for servants. These types of jobs would include garbage collection, recycling wastes, janitorial work, paraprofessional health care, and aiding in schools. Some of these jobs would be work now generally done by low-status men such as racial minorities or immigrants. Others are women's sex/affective labor, including physical care of the elderly, sick, and disabled in hospitals and retirement homes, and educational support work with infants, children, and young adults in childcare centers and schools.

With economic priorities in this ideal society tending toward production to meet human needs rather than profit, the turn away from defense spending, and the reappropriation of the social surplus of the society away from the capitalist class, there could be a large upsurge in demand for unskilled construction work in the building of new clinics and daycare centers and the dismantling of old inhumane housing structures. These might be jobs that many teenage boys and girls might want to do as part of their work/study program in the schools or part of their year or two in the national or international youth service to be explained below.

Individuals would have their choice of service work for half their workweek. They could join a work brigade to do the above-mentioned construction work renovating their communities, work that would be guided by skilled workers and professional contractors working their standard-sector jobs. Or they could do the other types of jobs mentioned above. A typical service job center would have skilled coordinators doing their standard-sector jobs (e.g., childcare coordinators) and service-sector volunteers who would receive job training from the coordinators and would contract to put in a minimum number of months in doing this kind of work. Those performing unsatisfactorily at these jobs could be asked to transfer to other work after a process of evaluation by the workers' council.

A very important component of the service work requirement would be a minimum commitment (say, three hours a week) for all workers to participate in work in a childcare center for children ranging in age from infants to kindergarten. This would involve working regularly in a community or work center of one's own choice doing childcare, and would be mandatory for both men and women, whether they are parents or single, and regardless of their sexual preference.

Socializing and communalizing childcare in this way would break down the parental roles of nurturant versus macho parent that most kids get in this society, and would give them a secure way to get ongoing nurturance from other adults besides their biological parents. Single people would have the opportunity and part of the responsibility for the care of the coming generation, thus acknowledging everyone's social responsibility for children. The issues of social parenting and children's rights will be discussed further in the next section.

Jobs in the standard sector could initially have quotas for women and minorities, disabled and older people, and so on. This expansion of our present affirmative action programs would serve to break down race and sex stereotypes and other oppressive social inequalities. Racism, ethnicism, and sexism could be further broken down by a massive assault on white Anglo-Saxon Protestant culture control. The schools, mass media, and government-subsidized cultural groups (music, theater, etc.) would reeducate all Americans to the richness of American and Third World ethnic and racial cultures. This would mean emphasizing in particular Afro-American, native American, Asian, Latin American, and Jewish music, languages, food, and values. It would mean revitalizing the remnants of non-Anglo-Saxon white immigrant cultures (Slavic, Irish, Polish, Mediterranean, etc.). As in Cuba, cultural workers' self-definition as artists would be reoriented. No longer would they think of themselves as talented, special individuals out to express their own inner meanings with no clear responsibility to an audience or social group. Rather, they would think of themselves as teachers of the people, sharing their skills with them as part of their service work (e.g., doing after-work courses and workshops in factories and schools).

Classism and family class privilege could be attacked by free education through the university level and free adult education in the community and at people's workplaces. Education for self-development could be seen as a right that continues for a person's lifetime, not simply as a means to narrow job training as in our present system. Free health, maternity, and birth control services would eliminate some of the material burdens of our present society that disproportionately fall on poor women. Unemployment would be eliminated by the vast increase of jobs like teaching and medical care and the material rebuilding of society with non–environmentally "harmful" sources of energy (e.g., solar-heated buildings, low-rent quality housing for all who need it, new schools and daycare centers, etc.). To handle some of the past damage that our country and other First World countries have wrought on Third World countries through imperialism, there could be youth and adult brigades of workers sent to help in technical, economic, and social development of the sort requested by the beneficiary countries themselves. Indeed, a mandatory one or two years of work in a national or international youth service corps could take the place of time spent in the armed services, and could involve various forms of service work, including, if necessary, militia training for defense purposes (I assume the professional armed services would be replaced by civilian militias).

## Parenting and Childhood

Feminist parenting, like our socialist economy, ought to promote the goals of collective solidarity and individual autonomy, as well as suitable conditions for the development of gynandrous individuals. Because in my feminist vision the economy and public school system will be structured so as to allow both men and women to engage in infant and early child care and teaching, it does not require that one model of the ideal family, such as the heterosexual co-parenting family, be adopted in order to further the possibility of gynandrous children. Though heterosexual couples who raise children together would be expected to co-parent, people would also have the option to raise children in other households as well. As many have pointed out (cf. Joseph, 1983; Raymond, 1986), single-mother families, lesbian families, extended families, and communal households can also be nonsexist environments if supported by the appropriate external collective nurturance context (whether extended kin network, nonsexist schools and childcare, community networks, etc.) that will provide children with a range of male and female role models, personalities, and life-styles. The important principle to keep in mind is that in this new society, no one would be socially or materially penalized, either as a child or adult, for living in a particular type of household (cf. Helmbold and Hollibaugh, 1983).

An important way the revolutionary government could facilitate the breakdown of patriarchal sex roles would be to pass a law similar to the Domestic Family Code in Cuba. The Cuban law makes both men and women equally responsible for housework and for the maintenance of minor children by wage work. Our adaptation of this code could place parental obligations equally on all adults of the same or opposite sex who cohabit with children. Both biological and chosen social family living would be acceptable. Any unrelated people and couples could live together, in any numbers, contrary to the local housing codes in many communities today.

Our model society would have to have a way to regulate the social responsibility for children of those who live in communal households in a way comparable, but superior, to that of patriarchal marriage arrangements. That is, there has to be some way to ensure that unrelated adults provide security to children who become incorporated with them by not just choosing to drop out of the child's life whenever they wish. Also, some rights to see former children housemates should be allowed to such social parents. And, on the other hand, children should have some choice as to which of possibly many adults who cohabit with them they want to continue to spend time with.

The notion of rights for children requires a change in our stultifying division between adulthood and childhood. We need to challenge the assumption of classical liberalism that there is a natural division between learners—those who are too immature or lack the rationality to be choosers—and choosers—those who have full political and civil rights (cf. Bowles and Gintis, 1986). Such a dictum was used for centuries to deny women, slaves, immigrants, and children any democratic input into social decisionmaking that affected their lives. As Howard Cohen points out, it is based on the erroneous assumption that individuals can only have rights if they are believed to have certain competencies (Cohen, 1980). But much as wealthy people in this society are assumed to have the right to hire agents (lawyers, etc.) to compensate for their lack of ability in certain areas, so a socialist-feminist society should assume that all human beings should have rights to participate (with the help of others if necessary) in the decisionmaking that affects their lives. Only in this way can we break the last vestiges of authoritarianism and encourage the development of the kind of democratic parenting practices that will create the most prepared citizens for a democratic life, namely, those who have learned from an early age how to think critically and choose for themselves.

This would mean that children should be allowed to be members of workers' and consumers' councils as well as family/household councils to participate in political decisionmaking. Children over seven should have the right to vote in national elections, with schools supplying full political debates on the issues and candidates to inform them of the issues in a manner they can understand.

In terms of the issue of children's and adults' rights to live in or leave a household, one way to provide for some security yet allow individuals freedom is to substitute a new concept of a "household contract" for the present marriage contract. This would be a voluntary arrangement that children over seven, couples, and single people would enter into to live together for a minimum period of two years and to commit themselves to sex/affective and economic support and household sharing of tasks. Anyone who had lived with a child for a minimum of two years would have child visitation rights, assuming the child consented. All children would have personal counselors, perhaps connected to the school or community center, who would help them think through psychological problems with their household, and would mediate between biological and social parents and a prospective new household if the child expressed a desire to live elsewhere.

The division between productive adult members of society and unproductive "learners" subject to authoritarian learning processes is especially noticeable in the present social division between school and wage labor. Teenagers in particular are oppressed by this social organization that keeps them in school with no sense that their education is connected to productive work benefiting the community. As economic dependents, they have no independent material base from which to challenge willful and arbitrary school and parental power. In our new society all children would receive an economic stipend that they could have control over (in consultation with their counselors). Work/study programs in the schools would be organized along similar lines to those of adult production. Students could study for twenty hours a week and do service work for ten hours a week. Included in this service work could be apprentice work for future jobs in the standard sector (as Cuba presently organizes its work/study programs). Children over the age of ten would also be expected to do regular work in childcare collectives as a part of their service work.

## Pleasure Sex and Reproductive Rights

A feminist egalitarian society should acknowledge the right of those who meet the minimum conditions for personal autonomy and maturity to consensual sex for pleasure. We have already indicated that the problem of adult-child sexuality remains a thorny issue that cannot be settled by a general principle but would depend on the depth of democratic participatory structures in the society as well as economic and social living options for children. If every household had a minimally democratic decisionmaking structure, including house meetings in which children had a say, if children were expected to do socially productive work in school work/study programs, if children had some options to leave households of origin that they found unsatisfactory and economic stipends from the state that would provide them with a minimum economic independence, then we could expect the issue of adult-child sex to be much more open for experimentation than it is today. But only when social conditions are egalitarian enough so that children themselves organize a sex-for-youth movement will the conditions be right for such a change.

In terms of heterosexual relations between men and women, the key material change that will have to occur to allow sex for pleasure to be a nonsexist goal is the guarantee of full reproductive rights for women: not only contraceptive and birth control information available in the schools together with nonsexist and nonheterosexist sex education, but also community-funded abortion services and living situations for pregnant women and single mothers. Full reproductive rights also have to include the right to homosexual sex with no social penalties, and the development of full rights to artificial reproduction techniques for gays and lesbians and noncoupled heterosexuals.

Pleasure sex as a valid goal has been given a large setback in our society by the development of AIDS and the fear this has created about casual, promiscuous sex. The New Right has taken advantage of this situation to whip up homophobic attitudes against gay male cruising life-styles. We cannot allow such developments to detract from the right to seek consensual sex for pleasure, whether it be casual sex or the prelude to more committed relationships. Of course, promoting sex for pleasure will also require a commitment to public education about safe sex, as well as the availability of condoms and other contraceptives.

Many feminists find distasteful the idea of promoting sex for pleasure. They would argue that casual sex life-styles, such as "cruising," are male-identified, as they promote a focus on sex for physical pleasure rather than sex as a means to deepen emotional intimacy and affectionate connection. As such, they would argue that seeking sex only for physical pleasure is dehumanizing, for it uses oneself and the other person as merely a sexual object and thus doesn't tap the deeper potential for sex that is to be used as a reciprocal deepening of an intimate knowledge of, connection, and commitment to another human.

My view, on the contrary, is that we should defend a diversity strategy on the question of the uses of sex. Valuing sex for pleasure does not have to mean eschewing the value of sex for emotional intimacy and commitment. To the contrary, I would argue that a model society ought to promote committed sex and ought to set up material and social supports that make committed couple relationships possible. It is only in a patriarchal context where the male sex has been given the right to seek its own physical pleasure and to use the female sex as an object to this end that casual sex for pleasure has demeaning implications.

In a nonsexist context where sexual pleasure was given the social meaning that, say, skiing for pleasure now has, there would be nothing demeaning in heterosexuals and homosexuals seeking casual sex for pleasure. It is only where the promotion of sex for pleasure tends to undermine the search for committed sex that feminists need to worry about sexual objectification. The pre-AIDS gay cruising life-style may perhaps be criticized fairly for having encouraged this outlook in many men, with the deleterious consequences of setting up a competitive premium on youth and physique that mitigated against age and committed relationships (cf. Bryant, 1986).

A note on pornography and prostitution: Would such practices exist in a feminist ideal society? With regard to the first, part of the problem lies in definitions. In an advanced industrial society that has gone through a consumerist phase, sexually explicit images and writing designed to promote "prurient" desires will be likely to continue to exist in some guise (Soble, 1986). It is also true that all images and descriptions will be objectifying to some degree, for they all abstract from the uniqueness of the individual imaged or described and in that sense make all "objects" of fantasy for one or more of their physical characteristics. I don't agree with those feminists who suppose that the interest in all such objectifications will dissipate when individuals are able to be in touch with their tender, emotional sexual sides. (This is implied if not actually stated by Griffin, 1981.)

On the other hand, if violent and sexist pornography is due to male dominance and sexual repression, we would expect that these images would no longer be desirable, as the material conditions creating fear and struggle between the sexes (mother-dominated parenting, compulsory heterosexuality, the sexual division of labor in gender) are eliminated. Our society could monitor such images as well as those involved in the mass media in general by elected community media boards, who would carry out public hearings on controversial publications, films, and other media programs and images.

Prostitution is another debatable issue. Many socialists have supposed that prostitution would die away in a gender egalitarian society where women have equal economic and social power with men. Others suppose that there may always be individuals who cannot find consensual sex for pleasure without hiring other individuals to provide this service for them.

My view is that prostitution should be decriminalized and that legal penalties should be properly enforced against pimps and organized crime's coercion of women into sex work, including pornography. Only then will we be able to see whether individuals will continue to choose to work as, and to hire, prostitutes. In such a different sex/affective setting, we would imagine either that prostitution would die out, or it would become gender neutral, that is, there would be as many male as female prostitutes. In either case, just the removal of the stigma of prostitution would also remove the stigma against equal social options for the validation of female sexuality in comparison to male sexuality.

## Committed Sex and Friendship

A couple relationship that is sexual, committed to deep emotional intimacy, trust, and sharing is a value that until recently has been normatively restricted to those who are heterosexual and married in our society. Such couple relationships meet human needs for security and sex/affective connection and, as such, are of intrinsic value. When there are a number of such couples who are monogamous and who have community connections together (work, religious, place of residence, political identity, etc.), they tend to stabilize the community bonds as well. Thus, such coupling is valuable for intrinsic and extrinsic reasons.

Traditional marriage was a way of guaranteeing stable couples who would stabilize community bonds. Traditional marriage also regulated and minimized sexual rivalries so that sexual jealousies and conflicts over the rights and obligations to children would not interfere with productive life (cf. Freud, 1961). But traditional marriage was also patriarchal. Furthermore, the prioritizing of couple relationships, particularly heterosexual relationships, tends to make women's friendships secondary. And as I and others have argued, prioritizing women's friendships is a necessity if feminists are to alter the patriarchal sex/affective bonding system that keeps men's ties with each other strong while women's ties with each other are either weak or reactionary (e.g., in patriarchal kin networks).

What structures and practices would our model society have to substitute for marriage in order to encourage committed sexual coupling and yet also to support friendship networks? Ceremonies of commitment, which would be open to those of any sex, could supplant marriage ceremonies, and be based on a more limited time commitment (e.g., five years rather than life). Friendship networks could be encouraged by similar ceremonies honoring friends, or even community networks of friends. These later could be structurally supported by regular get-togethers that might involve consciousness-raising sharing of emotions and discussions. And of course, women's caucuses, gay caucuses, and lesbian caucuses would be a regular feature of political life at the community, school, and work site.

## Heterosexuality/Homosexuality

Proponents of androgyny often assume that the elimination of gender dualism with the elimination of the idea of the genders as "natural complements" supposes the development of bisexuality (Ferguson, 1977). This does not necessarily follow, particularly in the near future, where the notion of the heterosexual couple raising at least one child together will probably continue to hold sway as a social value. As we have discussed above, sex can be used for pleasure or for committed couple relationships. However, heterosexual intercourse can also be used to produce children. Where a committed couple relationship and raising children are valued, then, heterosexuality will probably continue to be the preferred sexual identity of the majority of individuals, even where artificial reproductive techniques are available on demand, regardless of sexual preference.

Thus, though the breakdown of compulsory heterosexuality and gender dualism will be likely to create a situation where many more people develop bisexual identities, it is not likely that everyone will do so. Lesbian and gay caucuses will still be required to validate and politically defend the choice of same-sex relationships both for pleasure sex and for committed sex.

## Conclusion

I have sketched above a feasible socialist-feminist vision as a goal to defend, develop, and articulate in organizing for radical social change in the United States today. The model attempts to harmonize the goals of individual autonomy, community, democracy, and the social and material equality of people. Though any human society aiming for such ambitious goals is bound to achieve them only imperfectly, I hope I have persuaded the reader that such values could be attained far better in the sort of social order I have outlined than in our present order. But *is* such a radical change in the economy, the state, families, and personal life achievable? And if so, what are the strategies we need to achieve it? This topic is considered in the final chapter.

# Notes

This chapter is an expanded version of "A Socialist-Feminist Vision and Strategy for the Future," in Ann Ferguson, *Blood at the Root: Motherhood, Sexuality and Male Dominance*. London: Pandora/Unwin & Hyman, 1989. Copyright © 1989 by Ann Ferguson. Reprinted by permission of the copyright holder and publisher.

1. Obviously, what is included in forbidden versus risky versus basic practices will be dependent in part on the changing historical reality in which such a feminist morality is used. For example, a society that guaranteed children over twelve economic independence and job security and that involved democratic parenting to give young people experience in making their own decisions might justify very different lines between acceptable, risky, and forbidden adult-child sexuality than we have in our present society.

2. Albert and Hahnel have answers to these criticisms of council socialism. See their article in Shalom, 1983. I agree, however, with Siriani's criticisms, also in that volume. It remains doubtful how direct democracy can handle all the issues involved in consumer distribution without interminable meetings or something that evolves in practice into a representative command economy model.

3. One question not discussed here is whether it would be proper to characterize a society as gynandrous where individuals might exhibit a variety of personalities ranging from more masculine to more feminine in our contemporary understandings. Clearly, nothing in my model excludes the possibility of different sorts of gynandrous societies, some of which would tend to create homogeneous non-gender-specific personalities and some of which would allow for more heterogeneity—including our contemporary masculine and feminine types, though not in the extreme versions of authoritarianism and self-denigration featured in patriarchal gender dualisms. Trebilcot (1977) distinguishes between monoandrogynism, an ideal society with homogeneous individuals combining desirable aspects of masculinity and femininity in uniform ways, and polyandrogynism, a society that would exhibit a range of personality types, some of which would approach our contemporary masculine and some our contemporary feminine personalities. My view of gynandry would advocate a version of polyandrogynism.

ELEVEN

# Socialist-Feminist and Antiracist Politics: Toward Sexual Democracy

## Strategies for a Better Progressive Coalition Politics in the United States

Since the New Deal of the 1930s, there had not really been an effective coalition politics in the United States that has managed to challenge simultaneously our three primary systems of social domination: racism, sexism, and capitalism. From the popular-front anti-Nazi politics of the 1930s and 1940s to the civil rights, Black Power, student, and anti-Vietnam New Left politics of the 1960s and the women's and gay liberation movements of the 1970s and 1980s, there have been two conflicting tendencies in popular social movements: cultural separatism and vanguardism on the one hand and coalitionist assimilationism on the other. Cultural separatism, whether it be the hippie, Black Power, student "free university," or lesbian separatist movements, involves rejecting the hegemony of the dominant culture by creating a culture of resistance that defines its values, visions, and priorities independently of the dominant culture. Usually those involved in such cultural movements have also developed a sense of themselves as a vanguard of change for those fellow victims of oppression still locked in the false consciousness of the dominant culture. Marxist sectarian socialist parties have also been vanguardist, though their concern has been less with building an oppositional culture than with party formation.

The other pole of popular social movements, assimilationism, attempts to find a niche for oppressed groups by extending to them the values and opportunities open to dominants in the status quo. This has often involved a coalitionist and integrationist strategy. For example, while black nationalism tried to set up Black Power community schools outside of the public school system to reinforce the idea that "black is beautiful," liberal antiracists like the Southern Christian Leadership Conference, the National Urban League, and the National Association for the Advancement of Colored People (NAACP) worked to integrate the public schools. Similarly, while radical feminists set up autonomous women's community schools that would empower women to challenge male domination, liberal feminists' organizations like the National Organization of Women and the National Women's Political Caucus (NWPC) supported abortion rights, the Equal Rights Amendment, and affirmative action initiatives to guarantee women equal access to higher education and jobs.

Although separatist and assimilationist tendencies are both necessary tools to organize certain popular sectors, neither alone can prove an effective avenue for radical social change of the sort needed to eliminate racism, sexism, and economic class inequalities in this country. Separatist politics tends to focus on building a counterculture of pride and resistance. But such countercultures, though necessary, are not sufficient for change: They can be repressed by the coercive state apparatus, as were the Black Panthers, or co-opted by consumerist capitalism, as have some women's businesses. Or else they are rendered ineffective by the structural forces of the dominant system, for example, black unemployment, inferior schools in the ghettos, and the sexual division of wage labor in which women's work is paid less than men's. Because the majority of people tend to be influenced more by status quo economic, political, and social structures than by countercultures, there is also the danger that the separatists lose contact with the "troops" they are trying to empower and become static, self-enclosed subcultures that persuade only a small minority to join them.

Mainstream liberal labor unions, black organizations, and women's groups, though they, too, are necessary institutions, cannot by themselves lead to real change because of their tendency to become co-opted. The legalization of collective bargaining in the Wagner Act has meant that national trade union leaderships end up enforcing the agreements made with management over more radical local unions and caucuses. Manning Marable (1985) documents how President Lyndon Johnson's Great Society reforms have benefited only a small segment of blacks, those in the professional and business class, while a huge underclass of people of color has developed (cf. Wilson, 1987). NOW and NWPC have spent much energy pushing for the passage of the Equal Rights Amendment, which, even if it were enacted, would not guarantee equal work for women: Only comparable worth legislation that guarantees that work of comparable skill in different job categories will be paid equally would be likely to do this. Furthermore, liberal feminist pro-choice groups like the National Abortion Rights Action League (NARAL) have defined the fight for reproductive rights too narrowly to deal with issues of forced sterilization, medicaid payments for abortion, available and affordable quality childcare, or even gay and lesbian rights—all issues that have greater impact on working-class and poor people of color than on middle- and upper-class white feminists.

In the 1970s the socialist-feminist women's unions attempted to deal with the dilemma of separatism versus assimilationism by distinguishing a third option: autonomy. The idea is that there is a dual need, both for a separate political space for members of an oppressed group (for example, women) to work out their strategy and for coalitions and alliances with allies of the dominant group (for example, men) in order to challenge the multifaceted nature of social domination in our society. We used to joke that autonomy meant that you had to go to twice as many meetings—for example, women's caucus or group meetings as well as mixed male and female leftist organization meetings. Another 1970s group, the Black Liberation Army, left its membership open to whites but explicitly involved anticapitalist and black nationalist politics. Autonomy, in other words, could be the mean between the two extremes of separatism and assimilationism, but only if social conditions provide enough ferment to allow for a principled coalition-building between groups also involved in organizing multilayered movements of resistance.

Unfortunately, the New Left social movements that socialist-feminists relied on to make plausible the autonomy option have dissipated in most areas of the country, leaving only pockets of activism, usually around solidarity with Central American anti-imperialist struggles, some progressive union struggles, and some local community-building projects of peoples of color. What remains is the initially hopeful but now mainstreamed presidential electoral campaign efforts of Jesse Jackson and the Rainbow Coalition, some student activism around divestiture of stocks in apartheid South Africa, and small socialist and feminist organizations and projects like the secretaries' organization (Nine to Five), the Democratic Socialists of America, Solidarity, and the Reproductive Rights National Network. There are also radical gay and lesbian groups and networks (for example, the AIDS Coalition to Unleash Power, or ACT-UP), which because of their work in the AIDS issue have come to target the connections among capitalism, antiracism, and homophobia for the failure of the U.S. medical research and health care systems to deal adequately with the problem.

Though the situation for the Left in general, and for socialist-feminism and antiracist activists in particular, looks grim today, I think we should take heart from the recent radical upheavals in the state socialist societies of Eastern Europe, the Soviet Union, and China. After all, only a few years ago right-wing ideologues like Jeane Kirkpatrick were arguing that such totalitarian countries could never change from within, suggesting no hope for a democratization of those countries. If those countries can transform so radically and unexpectedly, what does this suggest about the possibility for radical change in this country? Though the Jackson coalition has lost its early promise because of its co-optive turn toward a centralized, hierarchical decisionmaking structure with the single goal of getting Jackson elected president, the Rainbow Coalition's initial success in connecting local activists around issues of gender, race, class, and heterosexist domination does show that such a populist movement is possible in this country and is just waiting to be organized.

Principled coalitions between dominants and subordinates are only plausible in historical periods of crisis when the systems of social domination in place in a social formation (in our case, capitalist, patriarchal welfare state racism) are increasingly unable to meet the material and social expectations the dominant ideology promises, even for those in prominent positions. Luckily for advocates of radical social change, the United States today is in such a crisis. Though whites' material and status interests have been constructed in opposition to those of people of color, and men's material and sex/affective interests have been pitted against women's, the contradictory values and realities of our society today, together with its growing economic crisis, set the stage for a massive historical redefinition and reconstruction of both our values and understanding of our material interests. We need to organize around a vision, such as the one I developed in the previous chapter, which would resolve the current racial, class, and sex/affective contradictions of our society and begin to cure our class, racial, and sexual alienation.

We need a new coalitionist strategy that can develop a radical politics of the majority that nonetheless supports a radical pluralism. That is, we must understand the need for separatist cultures of empowerment for oppressed people as well as the need for a counterhegemonic culture with a general world view of a social alternative with which to replace the dominant order. We must develop a radical vision of an alternative United States that takes into account the demands of all oppressed groups and minorities and yet has a viable analysis of how such demands can simultaneously be realized. In my opinion the only feasible approach to this, given our historical values and present resources, is some form of decentralized democratic socialist society.

A progressive coalition should have as its basic operating procedure a commitment to participatory democracy. It would encourage an anarcho-socialist-feminist process in which self-defining caucuses of those with particular interests would separate from the whole to develop their demands and ideas, yet come back together in a coalition group or network. The coalition would have a common platform or set of demands developed out of the special interest groups.

Unlike the classical Marxist-Leninist strategy of vanguard party-building, our strategy of participatory democracy in leftist coalitions should not deny autonomous subgroups within such coalitions. It would differ from a liberal pluralist strategy both in its understanding that simple reforms to the existing state structure are not sufficient and in its inclusive rather than competitive process of defining the common interest of the coalition—not by the least common denominator but by the most common divisions! Less paradoxically, we can say that such coalitions would be looking to add rather than subtract differences from the group's agenda. For example, such coalitions should support the right to a gay or lesbian life-style even though only 10 percent of the coalition is lesbian and gay, and the right of single mothers to adequate child support payments even though single mothers are a minority of the coalition. The coalition should be proud of its diversity—in fact should think of itself as representing the majority of people by protecting a number of special interest groups (workers, lesbians and gays, women, racial minorities, single mothers, the homeless, the poor) that together make up a majority of the population of the United States.

Is it plausible to maintain that men and women, on the one hand, and blacks and whites, on the other, can work together politically to challenge sexism, racism, and capitalism? After all, the theory of racial genders discussed in Chapter 6 implies that these overlapping social domination systems give rise to differences rather than similarities in personal identities. Marxism, liberal pluralism, and separatist identity politics, such as radical feminism and black nationalism, tend to assume unified theories of self, thus supposing that interest groups that are in conflict with one another cannot be involved in coalition politics. The feminist aspect theory of self that I maintain, however, holds that there is no unified theory of self. This connects to the view that there is no unified gender, racial, or class identity that automatically cuts across lines of the other two categories. Rather, whether one sees oneself as unified or divided by gender, race, or class differences is relative to particular social practices.

Thus, even though men are opposed to women, blacks and other racial minorities are opposed to whites, gays to straights, and different economic classes are opposed in some key social practices in the state, family, economy, and community, in other practices we may be allied.

That is, our interests may be adversarial in some ways and blend in others. The structure of left-wing organizations and coalitions must acknowledge the need to struggle about the oppositional aspects and interests of gender, race, sexual preference, and class. We must also build countercultural practices that do not reproduce privilege and that support an incorporative sense of the merging of individual with common interests in the group. In effect our coalitions must forge a new counterhegemonic collective identity for their members to redefine our interests as intertwined through the egalitarian and participatory political practices of our coalitions. At the same time it must acknowledge the right, for members whose social identities in the larger hegemonic culture subject them to oppression, to meet separately in order to articulate their ongoing concerns for the coalition based on their experiences of oppression. Indeed, it is likely that single-issue organizing around particular constituencies (e.g., labor union issues, reproductive rights, violence against women, racist incidents, etc.) will continue, with effective multi-issue coalitions forming occasionally for national demonstrations or around certain candidates for local and national elections.

## The Meaning of Eastern Europe: Is Socialism Dead? Or, Why Keep Socialist-Feminism?

An important question concerns our self-definitions as leftist and feminist activists. Socialist countries have fallen far short of their ideals, to the point that socialism has now become a dirty word, not merely among the traditionally anticommunist U.S. population but also among the rebelling populations of Eastern Europe. Second, socialists involved in grassroots activism in the twentieth-century United States have tended to be vanguardists who instrumentally attempt to use struggles around single issues and all oppressed groups to recruit people for the more important priority of fighting capitalism.

These are two good reasons to question whether we should continue to defend a version of socialism as our vision in speaking of ourselves as socialist-feminists. Isn't this vision now outmoded as it has been shown to be unachievable? Therefore, to avoid the negative connotations of "socialism," shouldn't we construct a brand new model and political identity, perhaps the idea of radical democratic feminism?

Two hitherto socialist-feminist writers, Zillah Eisenstein (1979, 1990) and Chantal Mouffe (Laclau and Mouffe, 1985; Mouffe, 1990) make this claim in separate articles in a recent issue of *Socialist Review* (90/ 2, vol. 20, no. 2 [April–June 1990]) entitled "Now What? Responses to Socialism's Crisis of Meaning." Eisenstein argues that socialist-feminism no longer adequately characterizes the new feminist theoretical position of those of us who have modified Marxism in a feminist direction and have been engaged with the question of the differences between women (race, ethnicity, class, and sexual orientation). Rather, we have moved through early socialist-feminist positions and hence have changed the meaning of feminism itself, whereas U.S. socialists and Marxists have changed their position little if at all. Thus not only are we no longer defining ourselves as opposed to them, but the paucity of good ideas in the socialist tradition to deal with the failures of democracy of the existing state socialist societies suggests that we should cut our political losses and define ourselves as radical democrats rather than socialists. Mouffe argues in a related manner, but her emphasis is more on the importance of the failure of socialist visions to understand the importance of defending yet extending liberal democracy's vision of a pluralist society. She urges us to define ourselves as radical pluralists (cf. also Weeks, 1985) and to defend a concept of radical democracy that could point out the structural problems of capitalism with respect to allowing full citizen rights to all individuals but would not have a substantive vision of socialism.

Though I agree with the premises of Eisenstein's and Mouffe's arguments, those criticizing the practice, vision, and viability of existing socialisms and socialist groups in the United States, I do not think their conclusion, that we ought to eschew developing our own democratic socialist model, follows. Because all political movements have some implicit goals for activism, not spelling out a goal other than that of cultural pluralism will tend to reinforce the idea that we can achieve the elimination of all the "isms" simply by pushing for the right to be different within capitalism. But the ways that capitalism, patriarchy, and racism interpenetrate in our society today will make it impossible to eliminate one without the other. Rather than fall into a minimalism to avoid being tarred by the unpopular socialist brush, we need to paint ourselves clearly as holding a new democratic socialist model that has its basis in existing U.S. values of equality and individual freedom that cannot be realized as our society is structured today. Every successful social movement must have a set of full goals and a vision of a transformed society to give its followers hope. We cannot afford to abandon the task of creating an alternative vision, even if socialism is unpopular at the moment, or we will only end up strengthening New Right and conservative forces who are just waiting for their opportunity to quash the idea of real alternatives to capitalism, patriarchy, and racism as usual. This is why it is important to establish different models of a decentralized socialist society and to insist that these are viable alternatives. If the problem is that a U.S. socialist movement does not exist as a movement for feminism to define itself against, then U.S. feminism needs to help re-create such a movement, as is, for example, Barbara Ehrenreich, co-chair of the Democratic Socialists of America (DSA), and as are single-issue socialist-feminist networks like R2N2. Only in this way can we do more than pay lip service to the difference problem in feminist theory, that feminists need to broaden the definition of feminism and feminist goals so they refer to concrete issues seen as central by women of color and working-class and poor women.

## A Transitional Morality for a Leftist Feminist Counterculture

One of the strengths of the U.S. women's movement of the 1960s and 1970s was its emphasis on examining the personal as a site of political power relations, thus resisting the neat dichotomy between public and private that is usually invoked to cut off discussion of sexism, racism, or homophobia. In the 1980s the feminist sex debate between those opposing pornography, S/M practices, and man-boy love and those supporting a pluralist right to choose has problematized the easy slogan "The personal is the political." After all, shouldn't we be able to make alliances with those whose adult consensual sexual choices don't agree with ours? And if so, don't we need to resurrect some distinction between those aspects of the personal that legitimately should be politicized (advocated or forbidden) and those that should be left to private preference?

Although it seems an obvious move to minimize our political disagreements over sexual differences by redrawing the line between the personal and the political, the question remains where and how to draw the line. In *Blood at the Root* (1989a) I suggested doing this by distinguishing between basic, risky, and forbidden practices from a feminist point of view, which assumes that it is a personal decision to engage in basic and risky practices but that forbidden practices should be politically challenged.

Just as we need to redraw the line between the personal and the political, I maintain that we need to redraw the line between the moral and the political. As a New Left coalition has to develop a counter-hegemonic culture of participatory democracy to oppose the elitist values of our existing system, we need to engage the hope and imagination of masses of people by a new vision of an ideal society to strive for as well as a transitional morality of appropriate ways to live our lives in the process of struggling for a democratic socialism.

In the previous chapter I sketched a model of an ideal society based on democratic socialism and sexual democracy. In so doing, I am outlining a visionary morality, a set of goals and the social structures that would make the realization of those values possible. In this chapter I am concerned instead with a transitional morality appropriate for the revolutionary process necessary to reach these goals. A set of such understood values as bottom-line ways of treating allies is central to the building of a populist antiracist, antisexist politics. Opportunistic strategies such as those commonly practiced in electoral politics are simply insufficient to galvanize individuals to the kind of self- and collective sacrifices needed for a total reconstruction of the values of dominant culture.

The transitional morality I advocate supports a cultural pluralism in sexual life-styles and personal life choices, as long as these life-styles don't substantially infringe on others' rights to respect and self-determination. *Respect, self-determination,* and *pluralism* are the three key values of a transitional morality for a coalition aiming at an overthrow of the existing capitalist, racist, and patriarchal structures.[1] Justice for various oppressed groups requires that each be able to develop its own voice, sense of self, and political agenda. The model for political interaction between dominants and (former) subordinates in the coalition should be a process in which the arbitrary one-way imposition of authority, the perpetuation of stereotypes, and the refusal of respect for diverse cultures are all constantly questioned (cf. Terry, 1972). Whites, men, and middle- and upper-class people must learn to see themselves as collaborators rather than bosses in this process. We must learn how to cede some of our structural and personal power in the service of a more egalitarian communication process.

The adoption of these general moral values and the use of more pluralist decisionmaking procedures (e.g., caucuses, rotating steering committees, etc.) does not mean that there will not be disagreements about the limits of cultural pluralism or the extent to which identity politics may be allowed to subvert the common agenda of the coalition. For example, the coalition may decide to defend the rights of consensual S/M practitioners but refuse to associate with public displays of S/M regalia (whips and chains, etc.) on the grounds that these symbols may be misunderstood by the general public. The coalition may agree on the right to self-determination in sexuality by teenagers but not on the rights of adults to consensual sex with youth where there is a wide age gap. The coalition may agree to give its support to a public "take back the night" march against violence against women but disagree whether men should also be allowed to march and whether the coalition should support the march if the issue of racist violence is not addressed as well.

The limits of identity politics are indicated in these political disagreements (cf. also Weeks, 1985). Radical pluralism as a politics for organizing the dispossessed into a populist coalition has three limits. First is the problem of priorities. All of the identities politicized in recent social movements, including women, blacks and other racial minorities, lesbians and gays, and people with AIDS, involve different contents and political priorities depending on the other contexts of domination in which they are engendered. Thus we may disagree about what issues to prioritize.

Second, identity politics spawns a pluralism of identities, not all of which are compatible with a leftist coalition politics. The obvious reactionary identity political tendencies, such as neo-Nazism based on a racist Aryan identity, and the New Right "total woman," clearly have no place in the coalition. But pedophiles and sex workers present an issue, as do those advocating polygamy in the black community to handle the problem of a shortage of black males for marriage partners. A transitional morality cannot give us the answers to all the particular questions that come up about which identity politics to support, which to relegate to the "private" (risky) sphere, and which to reject. At most, it suggests a process of making these decisions by a dialogue honoring respect, self-determination, and participatory democracy in the decisionmaking process in which such difficult questions are raised.

The third problematic aspect of identity politics is that it is easily co-optable in the United States, with its ideology of civil rights and autonomy for minority groups. Passage of a gay rights bill, for example, may suggest that gay liberation has been won, even though legislation doesn't deal with other institutional ways that compulsory heterosexuality persists. Furthermore, capitalist commodity fetishism, by encouraging the production of women's music, race records, sex toys, gay pornography, and so on can persuade members of identity countercultural communities that they can succeed in validating their identities by separatist tactics.

Only a determined and sophisticated radical coalitionism can mitigate these negative tendencies of identity politics. We can't simply reject such politics out of hand, for racism, ethnicism, sexism, heterosexism, and sexual repression will continue to create personal identities that are liable to be either co-opted or radicalized, depending on the political context available to individuals. Separatist identity politics, then, will continue to exist and will often act as a necessary eye-opener to the repressive aspects of our society for those who may go on to become radical coalitionists later. A radical coalitionism must create a political context that respects the autonomy of groups organizing around identity politics and at the same time offers an alternative structure that allows a countercultural space to act as a corrective for the co-optive aspects of identity politics and a negotiating space for creating solidarity between different groups.

## A New Left Agenda for the 1990s

Our capitalist, patriarchal, racist state is in crisis. The transition that it represents, from family-based patriarchy to public patriarchy, has focused public consciousness on those formerly controlled by the patriarchal family structure (women, youth, homosexuals) and on families that do not have a patriarchal structure, particularly families headed by black, single mothers. In the 1960s, to rebel against their marginalization in state decisionmaking, these groups formed student, women's, gay liberation, and welfare rights movements. We need to revitalize these movements. The demands of the civil rights and women's movements have forced some institutional concessions for women and minorities (affirmative action and entitlement programs). This disequilibrium in the status quo has spurred the New Right to try to institutionalize its own reactionary program, for example, to dismantle affirmative action programs, to reverse *Roe* v. *Wade* as a constitutional protection of the right to abortion, to pass the Hyde Amendment to deny federal funding for abortion, and to cut welfare and social services. Although the Right has won some victories, notably the recent Supreme Court rollbacks on abortion rights and affirmative action, there will continue to be a social crisis around these issues, for women and racial minorities are not likely to have rights taken away without ongoing resistance (cf. Winant, 1990).

The United States is also in continued crisis with respect to its foreign policy. We can no longer afford the costly defense and imperialist interventional foreign policy favored by our political elites as well as even the minimal services we have come to expect in the welfare state. Precisely because the established equilibrium of domination relations at home and abroad seems less steady now, there is a real possibility for the development of strong New Left, feminist, and antiracist coalitions.

In Chapters 4 and 6 I argued that our present social formation is based on a political economy of racism and a symbolic code of sexual racism as well as a sexist political economy and a corresponding sex/affective symbolic code. Strategies for challenging the hegemony of both of these features must be developed. And of course the persistent class of hierarchies of U.S. capitalism, based on income, status, and degree of control over work, must be confronted by a democratic socialist vision and agenda that rejects inegalitarianism and the false meritocracy on which it rests. As all three of these "isms" are increasingly interconnected, agendas to challenge one will ameliorate one or more of the others.

## CHALLENGING RACISM

The perpetuation of a black underclass must be halted by federally funded community action programs such as job training and job creation in black, Asian, Latino, and native American communities that give members some democratic input into program decisionmaking. For example, are houses for the homeless being built? If so, are those who are given jobs to build them as much as possible those who will live in them? Are they given input into their design? Are job-training programs for unemployed minority youth set up? If so, do the programs allow the recruits themselves some say in the sort of jobs they want training for? Or do they simply funnel youth into dead-end, alienating jobs? Is new money being supplied to inner-city ghetto schools? If so, who controls how this money is spent? Is there a real possibility of minority community input into the educational content and priorities of their children's schooling?

Racism is a cross-class phenomenon. Thus it must continue to be challenged by effective affirmative action programs and strong initiatives in public education that regularly examine and critique racism, that supplement the regular teaching of U.S. history by attention to the contributions of Afro-Americans and minority Asian, Latino, and native American communities of color. Courses on popular culture should highlight the contributions of all racial minorities to music and dance.

## CHALLENGING THE CLASS HIERARCHIES OF CAPITALISM

The fact that women and children will constitute half of all poor families by the year 2000 shows the overlap of capitalism and patriarchy and the need of feminists to take democratic socialism seriously as a solution to the poverty of many women. In the short run, the feminization of poverty must be stopped by legislating better economic supports: federally funded childcare, health care, and reproductive options (abortion on demand, no forced sterilization), job training, and available jobs to allow single mothers to escape from poverty. Further, the stigma of undeserving single-mother welfare recipients must be overcome by a system of general family allowances for those in lower-income groups. There should be a guaranteed minimum family income, regardless of the family structure or wage-earning status of the parents. In this way, the line between deserving and undeserving poor could be bypassed.

Classism and sexism could be creatively challenged by the same means: a comprehensive program of comparable worth to revalue work of comparable skill and importance that is now paid less because it is considered manual as opposed to mental, black as opposed to white, or women's as opposed to men's work. Revaluing job categories will help to dismantle the sexual, racial, and class divisions of labor that unfairly limit status, social opportunities, and income to those in work socially defined as "inferior."

## CHALLENGING SEXISM AND HETEROSEXISM

Socialist-feminists know that challenging public patriarchy means much more than passing the ERA and affirmative action legislation. It must also involve a whole revamping of the social structures and mores of sexuality and the family. Three central trends in our society that we must find symbolic ways to validate are:

1. The separation of sexuality from reproduction
2. The redefinition of kinship, which involves a reconceptualization of the family or household
3. The redefinition of the public versus private, individual versus social distinctions

All progressive groups should adopt a political agenda that highlights the defense of sexual freedoms in the broadest sense—reproductive rights for women, defense of lesbian/gay rights, defense of consensual sex for minors.[2] At the same time we must define a New Left family politics based on the somewhat contradictory implications of the family as the site not only of sexism and heterosexism but also of resistance to racism and classism. How can we dislodge the New Right from its symbolic position as the defender of good old American values while also avoiding the liberal tendency to validate the paternalistic role of the welfare state in reproducing public patriarchy?

With respect to family public policy, a key ingredient must be to refuse traditional definitions of the family that may reinstitute patriarchal, nuclear households. This means that extended- and single-family households must not be seen as "the problem" the state is trying to resolve by increasing job-training programs for black youths (Joseph, 1983). We should demand that the state create opportunities for couple co-parenting—mandatory flex-time jobs, a minimum family income to replace AFDC, maternity and paternity leaves, comparable worth, community-controlled childcare—but we also want to respect the right of noncouples—single parents, lesbian/gay parents, and communal households—to raise children. In short, we need to redefine the notion of "family" so that these alternative households and others, for example, two-household joint-custody parents, are socially acceptable.

Two public policy initiatives would be to legitimize gay and lesbian families and communal households. Moves like those of former Governor Michael Dukakis of Massachusetts to prevent foster parenting by gay parents must be strongly opposed. Another policy initiative would be to grant tax breaks for communal parenting: Anyone living in a communal household with children, whether biologically related or not, would be given tax incentives designed to recognize their input into household childcare and finances. Such a system could replace the punitive AFDC system, which penalizes single mothers who live with men assumed to be the fathers of their children. Finally, domestic partnership legislation is needed that allows nonmarried cohabitors of the same or opposite sex familial rights, for example, in health insurance coverage, income tax status, and joint property rights to eliminate the economic privileges of legal heterosexual marriage.

A feminist sexual and family political agenda is incomplete without economic measures to equalize gender, racial, and class inputs into housework and childcare. The feminization of poverty is a strong historical trend creating commonalities between white and black single mothers, increasingly subordinated to a public patriarchal system. Reversing this trend will require a turnaround in Republican cuts in social service programs and an economic conversion of military funds to peaceful uses. As I indicated in Chapter 10, there will have to be massive government spending programs, such as in job training for young people of color, improvements in public schools, and affordable quality childcare and health care. But there will also have to be a radicalization of the welfare programs and the tax structure of this country. Instead of welfare benefits, there should be a guaranteed minimal family income for all, subsidized by federal tax credits to families, whether or not they are working in wage labor.

The negative sex/affective patterns and symbolic codes of single motherhood—isolated mothers caring for children with little help from fathers or other community members—must be altered. This should not be attempted by hierarchical sex education programs in which adults berate teenagers about the negative aspects of single mothering. Instead, a feminist safe-sex and parenting educational movement should organize separate as well as mixed peer support groups for teenage boys and girls. Those for girls should include both teenage mothers and others and could be facilitated by adult educators who emphasize the self-determination of the groups in discussions.

Sex and parenting support groups could explore the meaning of fatherhood; problems of single motherhood; contraception and safe sex; co-parenting; lesbian, gay, and bisexual sexuality; lesbian, gay, and communal family households; and domestic violence, rape, and incest, as well as traditional sex education. Alternatives to nuclear families for single parents, such as single-mother support groups and childcare swaps, single parents sharing a household, and so forth, could be discussed. Demystifying venereal diseases and AIDS and encouraging the overcoming of romantic and patriarchal barriers to the use of safe-sex techniques should be the job of the adult educators.

An important part of opposing the New Right and questioning the patriarchal racist symbolization of welfare as handouts to the undeserving, sexually promiscuous poor is the battle to fund AIDS research and to educate the public so as to encourage safe-sex practices. AIDS is presented in patriarchal and racist ideologies as a punishment for carnal sins, a symbolism doubly effective because its initial target populations have been gay men, HIV drug users, and nonwhite populations. The connection to HIV drug users has caused a higher incidence of AIDS in nonwhite than in white communities in the United States (Patton, 1985, 1990; Watney, 1987). Though initial homophobia, racism, and classism have made it difficult for these high-risk groups to develop effective coalition politics, there are increasing efforts to build such coalitions that now also include feminists.

A counterhegemonic popular culture to defy racism, classism, and sexism must have a social life based on an interracial and cross-class community. This is not to say that minority communities will not continue to require their own autonomous networks, just as trade unionists need autonomous groups to organize the working class and feminists need both autonomous networks and the right to separatist lesbian feminist communities. But the necessary trust to develop the kind of anti-oppression coalitions described here calls for the rejection of vanguardist politics. Thus, though "Black is beautiful" and "Lesbians are woman-loving women" should be accepted as necessary self-affirmations of Afro-American cultural nationalist and lesbian-feminist elements, respectively, coalitions must attack uses of separatist culture that condemn interracial liaisons and claim that straight women aren't true feminists. In other words, effective democratic socialist coalitions can support only nondivisive identity politics, which upholds the need for autonomous identity-group organizing but rejects the strategy of total separatism.

## Conclusion

Feminists and leftists with a class and race consciousness must realize that challenging the present social order involves both effective coalition strategies for uniting women and men across race and class boundaries and an explicitly socialist-feminist agenda for reconstructing the welfare state. This will involve creating populist programs, that is, federal- and state-funded self-help programs for lower-income communities with democratic participation by their members. Because such programs threaten white male elites and destabilize capitalist markets that resist democratic input where profitability is not the bottom line, such an agenda will constantly be subject to reaction and backlash by right-wing forces. Only if and when a full democratic socialist economy is achieved, perhaps initially with market socialism and then with the council socialist model suggested in Chapter 10, could we expect to institutionalize an antisexist and antiracist state. And even then we should expect that remnants of the former white male elite will be working to undermine such a state. Nonetheless, feminists and progressives must find ways to make political and friendship bonds across gender, racial, and economic-class lines to unite in the long, complex struggle for such a socialist, feminist, and antiracist program.

This book has charted the personal, political, and intellectual odyssey of a middle-class, academic white woman brought up in middle America in the conservative 1950s. Little did I dream of the changes that the United States would witness from the 1960s to the 1980s: civil rights struggles, anti–Vietnam War demonstrations, a students' rights and hippie countercultural movement, the women's movement, the gay and lesbian liberation movement, the environmental movement, and the world peace movement to freeze the nuclear arms race, to name a few. Nor did I envision the changes I would undergo in response to the crises in U.S. society: In my life the theoretical and political have become the personal.

Younger generations and those from other races and class backgrounds have histories different from mine and thus may see the past and future possibilities otherwise. In spite of diversity, however, momentous changes in the recent past show that equally historic changes are possible in the future. Only if we empower ourselves by a political process of questioning given authorities who have a vested interest in misrepresenting reality (the government, mass media, corporations, schools, churches, the wealthy elite) will we be able to understand the actual workings of the social systems that shape our world. We must find a way to build a popular democracy, one that shakes us out of our passivity, complacency, and despair. In grassroots community organizing we can begin to build a base for trust that will allow us to debate and to fight for visions of a better future.

Popular liberation struggles all around the world, from Nicaragua and El Salvador to Eastern Europe, China, and South Africa, show both the promise and the difficulty of challenging a given power structure. There are bound to be disagreements and internecine battles. Nonetheless, to attempt nothing is to gain nothing. We have made important steps in human rights and social justice since the 1960s. We cannot afford to stand by and watch this progress be erased by the New Right, nor can we rest on our laurels and assume that the job is completed until there is full racial and gender equality and economic democracy. History has shown that this cannot occur in a capitalist system.

History is less clear about the solution to current social inequalities. But we have no alternative: Either we attempt to transform history or history will bury us. We cannot retire from the odyssey for democracy and social equality. For our children and future generations, we must continue to develop a practical vision of a socially egalitarian United States. I have argued that this will take a democratic socialism committed to fighting racism and sexism. May my daughter, my stepsons and foster son, my students, and all children, white and of color, straight or gay, rich or poor, experience a more just, more egalitarian, and less hypocritical United States. Long live the new American Revolution!

## Notes

1. Robert Terry develops the ethic of respect, self-determination, and pluralism as an ethic of justice for "new whites" to adopt against conservative and liberal values that further dominate blacks or blame the victim by suggesting that black culture is to blame for racism (cf. Terry, 1972).

2. It is a hopeful sign of a coalescence of hitherto separate identity politics into more of a coalitionist approach that gay male rights advocates highlighted the importance of supporting the April 9, 1989, National Organization of Women's march on Washington to support the passage of the Equal Rights Amendment and to defend the constitutional right to abortion being challenged in the Supreme Court.

# Bibliography

Adam, Barry D. (1978). *The Survival of Domination: Inferiorization and Everyday Life*, New York, Elsevier.

―――― (1987). *The Rise of a Gay and Lesbian Movement*, Boston, Twayne/G. K. Hall.

―――― (1989). "Pasivos y Activos en Nicaragua: Homosexuality Without a Gay World," *Outlook* 1, no. 4 (Winter 1989): 74–82.

Albert, Michael, and Robin Hahnel (1978). *Unorthodox Marxism: An Essay on Capitalism, Socialism and Revolution*, Boston, South End Press.

―――― (1981). *Socialism Today and Tomorrow*, Boston, South End Press.

Alexander, David (1987). "Gendered Job Traits and Women's Occupations," Ph.D. thesis, Department of Economics, Amherst, University of Massachusetts.

Allan, S., L. Sanders, and J. Wallis, eds. (1974). *Conditions of Illusion: Papers for the Women's Movement*, Leeds, Feminist Books.

Allen, Ernest, Jr. (1985–1986). "Afro-American Identity: Reflections on the Pre–Civil War Era," *Contributions in Black Studies: A Journal of African and Afro-American Studies* 7 (1985–1986): 45–93.

Allen, Jeffner (1984). "Motherhood: The Annihilation of Women," in Joyce Trebilcot, ed., 1984, pp. 315–330.

―――― (1986). *Lesbian Philosophy: Explorations*, Palo Alto, Calif., Institute of Lesbian Studies.

―――― , ed. (1990). *Lesbian Philosophies and Culture*, Binghamton, State University of New York Press.

Allen, Ted (1975). " 'They Would Have Destroyed Me': Slavery and the Origins of Racism," *Radical America* 9, no. 3 (May–June 1975): 41–64; reprinted as "Class Struggle and the Origin of Racial Slavery: The Invention of the White Race," Boston, New England Free Press.

Allison, Dorothy (1980). "Weaving the Web of Community," *Quest* 5, no. 1: 75–92.

Altman, Dennis (1974). *Homosexual, Oppression and Liberation*, London, Allen Lane.

―――― (1983). *The Homosexualization of America*, Boston, Beacon.

Amott, Teresa (1985). "Race, Class and the Feminization of Poverty," *Socialist Politics* 3 (April 1985).

Aptheker, Bettina (1983). *Woman's Legacy: Essays on Race, Class and Gender,* Amherst, University of Massachusetts Press.

Arcana, Judith (1976). *Our Mothers' Daughters,* London, Women's Press.

Ariès, Philippe (1962). *Centuries of Childhood: A Social History of Family Life,* New York, Random House.

Atwood, Margaret (1987). *The Handmaid's Tale,* New York, Ballantine/Random.

Bachofen, J. J. (1967). *Myth, Religion and Mother Right,* tr. Ralph Manheim, Princeton, N.J., Princeton University Press.

Bahro, Rudolf (1978). *The Alternative in Eastern Europe,* London, New Left Books.

Balbus, Isaac (1982). *Marxism and Domination,* Princeton, N.J., Princeton University Press.

Barker-Benfield, G. J. (1976). *The Horrors of the Half Known Life: Male Attitudes Toward Women and Sexuality in Nineteenth Century America,* New York, Harper.

Barrett, Michelle (1980). *Women's Oppression Today,* London, Verso.

Barrett, Michelle, and Mary McIntosh (1982). *The Anti-social Family,* London, Verso.

Barry, Kathleen (1979). *Female Sexual Slavery,* Englewood Cliffs, N.J., Prentice-Hall.

Bart, Pauline (1970). "Mother Portnoy's Complaint," *Transaction* 8, nos. 1 and 2.

———— (1981). "Review of Chodorow's *The Reproduction of Mothering,*" *Off Our Backs* 11, no. 1 (January 1981); reprinted in Joyce Trebilcot, ed., 1984, pp. 147–152.

de Beauvoir, Simone (1952). *The Second Sex,* New York, Knopf.

Bebel, August (1971). *Women Under Socialism,* New York, Schocken.

Begus, Sarah (1987). "The Social Relations of Sexuality: Ideology, Consciousness, Sexual Practice and Domination," M.A. thesis, Baltimore, Johns Hopkins University.

Benedict, Ruth (1934). *Patterns of Culture,* Boston, Houghton Mifflin.

Benjamin, Jessica (1980). "The Bonds of Love: Rational Violence and Erotic Domination," *Feminist Studies* 6, no. 1: 144–174; reprinted in Ann Snitow et al., eds., 1983, pp. 280–299.

Benston, Margaret (1969). "The Political Economy of Women's Liberation," *Monthly Review* 21, no. 4 (September 1969).

Bernikow, Louise (1980). *Among Women,* New York, Harmony Books.

*Black Scholar* (1978). "The Sexual Revolution" 9, no. 7 (April 1978).

Blauner, Robert (1972). *Racial Oppression in America,* New York, Harper.

Bookman, Ann, and Sandra Morgan, eds. (1988). *Women and the Politics of Empowerment,* Philadelphia, Temple University Press.

Boswell, John (1980). *Christianity, Social Tolerance and Homosexuality,* Chicago, University of Chicago Press.

Bourdieu, Pierre (1977). *Outline of a Theory of Practice,* Cambridge, Cambridge University Press.

Bowles, Samuel, and Herbert Gintis (1977). "Heterogeneous Labor and the Labor Theory of Value," *Cambridge Journal of Economics* 1, no. 2, 1977.

———— (1986). *Democracy and Capitalism: Property, Community and the Contradictions of Modern Social Thought,* New York, Basic.

Brown, Carol (1981). "Mothers, Fathers and Children: From Private to Public Patriarchy," in Lydia Sargent, ed., 1981, pp. 239–268.

Brownmiller, Susan (1976). *Against Our Will: Men, Women and Rape,* New York, Bantam.

Bryant, Dorothy (1986). *A Day in San Francisco,* New York, Moon Books.

Buckley, Mary (1989). "The 'Woman Question' in the Contemporary Soviet Union," Sonya Kruks et al., eds., 1989, pp. 251–281.

Bulkin, Elly, Minnie Bruce Pratt, and Barbara Smith (1984). *Yours in Struggle: Feminist Perspectives on Anti-semitism and Racism,* Brooklyn, N.Y., Long Haul Press.

Bunch, Charlotte (1975). "Not for Lesbians Only," in *Quest,* eds., 1981, pp. 67–73.

———— (1976). "Beyond Either/Or: Feminist Options," *Quest* 3, no. 1; reprinted in *Quest,* eds., 1981, pp. 44–56.

Bureau of the Census (1977). "Marital Status and Living Arrangements: March 1976," *Current Population Reports,* ser. P-20, no. 306 (January).

Burris, Barbara (1973). "The Fourth World Manifesto," in Anne Koedt et al., eds., 1973, pp. 322–352.

Burstyn, Varda, ed. (1985). *Women Against Censorship,* Vancouver, Toronto, Douglas & McIntyre.

Butler, Judy (1987). "Variations on Sex and Gender: Beauvoir, Wittig and Foucault," in Seyla Benhabib and Drucilla Cornell, eds., *Feminism as Critique,* Minneapolis, University of Minnesota Press, pp. 128–142.

———— (1990). *Gender Trouble: Feminism and the Subversion of Identity,* New York, Routledge.

Campbell, Beatrix (1980). "A Feminist Sexual Politics," *Feminist Review* 5.

Cannon, Terry, and Johnetta Cole (1978). *Free and Equal: The End of Racial Discrimination in Cuba,* New York, Venceremos Brigade.

Caplan, Pat, ed. (1987). *The Cultural Construction of Sexuality,* London, Tavistock.

Carby, Hazel V. (1985). "On the Threshold of Woman's Era: Lynching, Empire and Sexuality in Black Feminist Theory," *Critical Inquiry* (Autumn 1985): 262–277.

———— (1986). "It Just Be's Dat Way Sometime: The Sexual Politics of Women's Blues," *Radical America* 20, no. 4 (June–July 1985): 9–24.

Carmichael, Stokeley, and Charles Hamilton (1967). *Black Power,* New York, Random House.

Caulfield, Mina Davis (1975). "Imperialism, the Family and Cultures of Resistance," *Socialist Revolution* 20, vol. 4, no. 2 (October 1975): 67–86.

Cavin, Susan (1985). *Lesbian Origins,* San Francisco, Ism Press.

Chesler, Phyllis (1979). *With Child: A Diary of Motherhood,* New York, Crowell.

Chicago Women's Liberation Union (1973). *Socialist Feminism,* Chicago, mimeo.

Chodorow, Nancy (1974). "Family Structure and Feminine Personality," in Michelle Rosaldo and Louise Lamphere, eds., 1974, pp. 43–66.

———— (1978a). "Mothering, Object Relations and the Female Oedipal Configuration," *Feminist Studies* 4, no. 1 (February 1978): 137–158.

_____ (1978b). *The Reproduction of Mothering*, Berkeley, University of California Press.

_____ (1979). "Mothering, Male Dominance and Capitalism," in Zillah Eisenstein, ed., 1979, pp. 83–106.

Cleaver, Eldridge (1968). *Soul on Ice*, New York, Delta.

Cliff, Michelle (1980). *Claiming an Identity They Taught Me to Despise*, Watertown, Mass., Persephone Press.

Cohen, Howard (1980). *Equal Rights for Children*, Totowa, N.J., Littlefield, Adams.

Combahee River Collective (1979). "A Black Feminist Statement," in Zillah Eisenstein, ed., 1979, pp. 362–372; also in Cherrie Moraga et al., eds., 1981, pp. 210–218.

Cook, Blanche (1977). "Female Support Networks and Political Activism," *Chrysalis*, no. 3: 43–61.

Copeland, Lewis (1939). "The Negro as a Contrast Conception," in Edgar T. Thompson, ed., 1939.

Coward, Rosalind (1983). *Patriarchal Precedents: Sexuality and Social Relations*, London, Routledge.

Cox, Oliver Cromwell (1948). *Caste, Class and Race: A Study in Social Dynamics*, New York, Monthly Review.

Croll, Elizabeth (1978). *Feminism and Socialism in China*, New York, Schocken.

Daly, Mary (1978). *Gyn/Ecology: The Meta-ethics of Radical Feminism*, Boston, Beacon.

_____ (1982). *Pure Lust: Elemental Feminist Philosophy*, Boston, Beacon.

_____ (1988). *The Wickedary*, Boston, Beacon.

Davies, Margery (1979). "Woman's Place Is at the Typewriter: The Feminization of the Clerical Labor Force," in Zillah Eisenstein, ed., 1981, pp. 248–271.

Davin, Delia (1989). "Of Dogma, Dicta and Washing Machines: Women in the People's Republic of China," in Sonya Kruks et al., eds., 1989, pp. 354–358.

Davis, Angela (1971). "The Black Woman's Role in the Community of Slaves," *Black Scholar*, no. 2.

_____ (1977). "Rape, Racism and the Capitalist Setting," *Black Scholar* 9, no. 7.

_____ (1981). *Women, Race and Class*, New York, Random House.

Davis, Madeline, and Elizabeth Laporsky Kennedy (1986). "Oral History and the Study of Sexuality in the Lesbian Community: Buffalo, New York 1940–1960," *Feminist Studies* 12, no. 1 (Spring 1986): 7–26.

Degler, Carl (1980). *At Odds: Women and the Family in America from the Revolution to the Present*, New York, Oxford University Press.

Deleuze, Giles, and Felix Guattari (1977). *Anti-Oedipus*, New York, Viking.

Delphy, Christine (1984). *Close to Home: A Materialist Analysis of Women's Oppression*, Amherst, University of Massachusetts Press.

d'Emilio, John (1983). "Capitalism and Gay Identity," in Ann Snitow et al., eds., 1983, pp. 100–116.

d'Emilio, John, and Estelle Freedman (1988). *Intimate Matters: A History of Sexuality in America*, New York, Harper.

Deming, Barbara (1973). "Love Has Been Exploited Labor," *Liberation* (May 1973).

Demos, John (1970). *A Little Commonwealth: Family Life in Plymouth Colony*, New York, Oxford University Press.

Dill, Bonnie Thornton (1975). "The Dialectics of Black Womanhood," in Sandra Harding, ed., 1987, pp. 97–108.

—— (1983). "Race, Class and Gender: Prospects for an All-inclusive Sisterhood," *Feminist Studies* 9, no. 1 (Spring 1983): 131–150.

Dimen, Muriel (1982). "Seven Notes for the Reconstruction of Sexuality," *Social Test*, no. 6: 22–30.

Dinnerstein, Dorothy (1976). *The Mermaid and the Minotaur: Sexual Arrangements and Human Malaise*, New York, Harper.

Donovan, Josephine (1985). *Feminist Theory: The Intellectual Traditions of American Feminism*, New York, Frederick Ungar.

Donzelot, Jacques (1979). *The Policing of Families*, New York, Pantheon.

Douglas, Ann (1977). *The Lady and the Minister: The "Feminization" of American Culture*, New York, Knopf.

Du Bois, W.E.B. (1961). *The Souls of Black Folk*, New York, Dodd, Mead.

Dworkin, Andrea (1974). *Womanhating*, New York, Dutton.

—— (1978). "Biological Superiority: The World's Most Dangerous Idea," *Heresies*, issue on "Women and Violence," no. 6 (Summer 1978).

—— (1981). *Pornography: Men Possessing Women*, New York, Perigee/Putnam Sons.

—— (1987). *Intercourse*, New York, Free Press.

Dworkin, Andrea, and Catharine MacKinnon (1985). *The Reasons Why*, Cambridge, Harvard Law School.

Dyson, Michael (1989). "The Plight of Black Men," *Zeta Magazine* 2, no. 2 (February 1989): 51–56.

Easton, Barbara (1978). "Feminism and the Contemporary Family," *Socialist Review* 39, vol. 8, no. 3 (May–June 1978): 11–36.

Ehrenreich, Barbara (1983). *The Hearts of Men*, Garden City, N.Y., Anchor/Doubleday.

Ehrenreich, Barbara, and John Ehrenreich (1979). "The Professional-Managerial Class," in Pat Walker, ed., 1979, pp. 5–48.

Ehrenreich, Barbara, and Deirdre English (1973a). *Complaints and Disorders: The Sexual Politics of Sickness*, Old Westbury, N.Y., Feminist Press.

—— (1973b). *Witches, Midwives and Nurses: A History of Women Healers*, Old Westbury, N.Y., Feminist Press.

—— (1975). "The Manufacture of Housework," *Socialist Revolution* 26, vol. 5, no. 4 (October–December 1975): 5–40.

—— (1978). *For Her Own Good: One Hundred Fifty Years of the Experts' Advice to Women*, Garden City, N.Y., Anchor/Doubleday.

Ehrenreich, Barbara, and Annette Fuentes (1984). "Life on the Global Assembly Line," in Alison Jaggar and Paula Rothenberg, eds., 1984, pp. 279–291.

Ehrenreich, Barbara, Elizabeth Hess, and Gloria Jacobs (1986). *Remaking Love: The Feminization of Sex*, New York, Doubleday.

Ehrenreich, Barbara, Karin Stallard, and Holly Sklar (1983). *Poverty in the American Dream: Women and Children First,* Boston, South End Press.

Ehrensaft, Diane (1980). "When Men and Women Mother," *Socialist Review* 49, vol. 10, no. 1 (January–February 1980); reprinted in Joyce Trebilcot, ed., 1984, pp. 41–61.

Einhorn, Barbara (1989). "The Women's Movement in the German Democratic Republic," Sonya Kruks et al., eds., 1989, pp. 282–305.

Eisenstein, Zillah, ed. (1979). *Capitalist Patriarchy and the Case for Socialist-Feminism,* New York, Monthly Review.

———— (1984). *Feminism and Sexual Equality,* New York, Monthly Review.

———— (1989). "Reflections on a Politics of Difference," in Sonya Kruks et al., eds., 1989, pp. 333–337.

———— (1990). "Specifying U.S. Feminisms in the Nineties: The Problem of Naming," *Socialist Review* 90/2, vol. 20, no. 2 (April–June 1990): 45–56.

Ellis, Havelock (1936). *Studies in the Psychology of Sex,* New York, Random House.

Elshtain, Jean (ca. 1977). "Against Androgyny," unpublished manuscript.

Engels, Friedrich (1972). *The Origin of the Family, Private Property and the State,* ed. Eleanor Leacock, New York, International Publishers.

———— (1978). "Socialism, Utopian and Scientific," in Robert C. Tucker, ed., 1978, pp. 683–717.

Epstein, Steve (1987). "Gay Politics, Ethnic Identity: The Limits of Social Constructionism," *Socialist Review* 93/94, vol. 17, no. 3: 9–56.

Erikson, Kai T. (1966). *The Wayward Puritans: A Study in the Sociology of Deviance,* New York, Wiley.

Escoffier, Jeffrey (1985). "Sexual Revolution and the Politics of Gay Identity," *Socialist Review* 82/83, vol. 15, nos. 4 and 5 (July–October 1985): 119–154.

Evans, Sara (1980). *Personal Politics,* New York, Random House.

Ewen, Stuart (1976). *Captains of Consciousness: Advertising and the Social Roots of Consumer Culture,* New York, Harper.

Faderman, Lillian (1981). *Surpassing the Love of Men,* London, Junction.

Fanon, Frantz (1967). *Black Skins, White Masks,* tr. Charles Markmann, New York, Grove.

———— (1968). *The Wretched of the Earth,* New York, Grove.

Faraday, Annabel (1981). "Liberating Lesbian Research," in Kenneth Plummer, ed., 1981, pp. 112–129.

Ferguson, Ann (1977). "Androgyny as an Ideal for Human Development," in Mary Vetterling-Braggin et al., eds., 1977, pp. 45–69.

———— (1979). "Women as a New Revolutionary Class in the United States," in Pat Walker, ed., 1979, pp. 279–309.

———— (1981a). "The Che-Lumumba School: Creating a Revolutionary Family-Community," *Quest* 5, no. 3: 13–26.

———— (1981b). "Patriarchy, Sexual Identity and the Sexual Revolution," *Signs* 7, no. 1: 158–172.

———— (1983). "The Sex Debate in the Women's Movement: A Socialist-Feminist View," *Against the Current* (September–October, 1987): 10–17.

_____ (1984a). "On Conceiving Motherhood and Sexuality: A Feminist Materialist Approach," in Joyce Trebilcot, ed., 1984, pp. 153–184.

_____ (1984b). "Sex War: The Debate Between Radical and Libertarian Feminists," *Signs* 10, no. 1 (Fall 1984): 106–112.

_____ (1985). "Public Patriarchy and How to Fight It: A Tri-systems View," unpublished manuscript.

_____ (1986a). "Pleasure, Power and the Porn Wars," *Women's Review of Books* 3, no. 8 (May 1986): 9–13.

_____ (1986b). "Motherhood and Sexuality: Some Feminist Questions," *Hypatia* 1, no. 2 (Fall 1986): 3–22.

_____ (1987). "A Feminist Aspect Theory of the Self," supplementary vol. 13 of *Canadian Journal of Philosophy*, eds. Marsha Hanen and Kai Nielsen, *Science, Feminism and Morality*, Alberta, Canada, University of Calgary Press, pp. 339–356.

_____ (1989a). *Blood at the Root: Motherhood, Sexuality and Male Dominance*, London, Pandora/Unwin & Hyman.

_____ (1989b). "Sex and Work: Women as a New Revolutionary Class in the U.S.," in Roger Gottlieb, ed., *An Anthology of Western Marxism from Lukacs and Gramsci to Socialist-Feminism*, New York, Oxford University Press.

_____ (1990). "Is There a Lesbian Culture?" in Jeffner Allen, ed., 1990, pp. 63–88.

_____, ed. (1986). "Motherhood and Sexuality Issue," *Hypatia*, vol. 1, no. 2 (Fall 1986).

Ferguson, Ann, and Nancy Folbre, (1981). "The Unhappy Marriage of Capitalism and Patriarchy," in Lydia Sargent, ed., 1981, pp. 313–338.

Figes, Eva (1970). *Patriarchal Attitudes*, New York, Stein and Day.

Firestone, Shulamith (1970). *The Dialectic of Sex*, New York, Bantam.

Fisher-Manick, Beverly (1977). "Race and Class: Beyond Personal Politics," *Quest* 3, no. 4 (Spring 1977): 2–15; reprinted in *Quest*, eds., 1981, pp. 149–160.

Flax, Jane (1976). "Do Feminists Need Marxism?" *Quest* 3, no. 1 (Summer 1976); reprinted in *Quest*, eds., 1981, pp. 174–186.

_____ (1984). "A Look at the Cuban Family Code," in Alison Jaggar and Paula Rothenberg, eds., 1984, pp. 340–341.

Flexner, Eleanor (1972). *Centuries of Struggle: The History of the Women's Rights Movement in the United States*, New York, Atheneum.

Folbre, Nancy (1979). *Patriarchy and Capitalism in New England, 1620–1900*, Ph.D. thesis, Department of Economics, Amherst, University of Massachusetts.

_____ (1980). "Patriarchy in Colonial New England," *Review of Radical Political Economics* 12, no. 2 (Summer 1980): 4–13.

_____ (1982). "Exploitation Comes Home: A Critique of the Marxian Theory of Family Labour," *Cambridge Journal of Economics*, no. 6: 317–329.

_____ (1983). "Of Patriarchy Born: The Political Economy of Fertility Decisions," *Feminist Studies* 9, no. 2 (Summer 1983): 261–284.

_____ (1985). "The Pauperization of Motherhood: Patriarchy and Public Policy in the United States," *Review of Radical Political Economics* 16, no. 4 (Winter, 1985): 72–88.

—— (1987a). "Intergenerational Transfers and the Origins of Social Security," presented at the Population Association of America meetings, Chicago, April 29–May 2, 1987.

—— (1987b). "Patriarchy as a Mode of Production," in Randy Albelda, Christopher Gunn, and William Walker, eds., *Alternatives to Economic Orthodoxy,* New York, M. E. Sharpe, pp. 323–338.

—— (1988). "Whither Families? Toward a Socialist Feminist Family Policy," *Socialist Review* 18, no. 4 (October–December 1988): 57–75.

Folbre, Nancy, and Heidi Hartmann (1986). "The Rhetoric of Self Interest and the Ideology of Gender," in Arjo Klamer, Donald McClosky, and Robert Solow, eds., *The Consequences of Economic Rhetoric,* New York, Cambridge University Press.

Foucault, Michel (1977). *Discipline and Punish: The Birth of the Prison,* tr. Alan Sheridan, New York, Pantheon.

—— (1978). *The History of Sexuality.* Vol. 1, *An Introduction: The Will to Know,* New York, Pantheon.

—— (1985). *The History of Sexuality.* Vol. 2, *The Use of Pleasure,* New York, Pantheon.

—— (1986). *The History of Sexuality.* Vol. 3, *The Care of the Self,* New York, Pantheon.

Frazier, E. Franklin (1948). *The Negro Family in the U.S.,* Chicago, University of Chicago Press.

Fredrickson, George M. (1986). *White Supremacy: A Comparative Study in American and South African History,* New York, Oxford University Press.

Freud, Sigmund (1961). *Civilization and Its Discontents,* New York, Norton.

—— (1963a). *Sexuality and the Psychology of Love,* New York, Colliers.

—— (1963b). *Three Essays on the Theory of Sexuality,* New York, Basic.

—— (1964). "Femininity," in *Collected Papers,* vol. 22, *New Introductory Lectures in Psychoanalysis,* London, Hogarth.

Friedan, Betty (1963). *The Feminine Mystique,* New York, Norton.

Frye, Marilyn (1983). *The Politics of Reality,* Trumansburg, N.Y., Crossing Press.

Gardner, Jean (1979). "Women's Domestic Labor," in Zillah Eisenstein, ed., 1979, pp. 173–189.

Geertz, Clifford (1973). *The Interpretation of Cultures,* New York, Basic.

Giddings, Paula (1984). *When and Where I Enter: The Impact of Black Women on Race and Sex in America,* New York, Bantam.

Gilder, George (1973). *Sexual Suicide,* New York, Bantam.

Gilligan, Carol (1982). *In a Different Voice: Psychological Theory and Women's Development,* Cambridge, Harvard University Press.

Gilman, Charlotte Perkins (1966). *Women and Economics,* New York, Harper.

Gilmartin, Christina (1989). "Gender, Politics and Patriarchy in China: The Experiences of Early Women Communists, 1920–27," in Sonya Kruks et al., eds., pp. 82–108.

Girard, Alain (1968). "The Time Budget of Married Women in Urban Centers," *Population.*

Glazer, Nathan, and Daniel P. Moynihan (1970). *Beyond the Melting Pot,* Cambridge, MIT Press.

Goldman, Wendy Zeva (1989). "Women, the Family and the New Revolutionary Order in the Soviet Union," in Sonya Kruks et al., eds., 1989, pp. 59–81.

Gordon, Linda (1976). *Woman's Body, Woman's Right: A Social History of Birth Control in America,* New York, Penguin.

Gordon, Linda, and Allen Hunter (1977). "Sexuality, the Family and the New Right," *Radical America* 11, no. 6 (November 1977–February 1978): 9–26.

Gorz, André (1967). *Strategy for Labor,* Boston, Beacon.

Gough, Kathleen (1975). "The Origin of the Family," in Rayna Reiter, ed., 1975, pp. 51–76.

Grahn, Judy (1984). *Another Mother Tongue: Gay Words, Gay Worlds,* Boston, Beacon.

Gramsci, Antonio (1971). *Selections from the Prison Notebooks,* eds. Quinton Hoare and Geoffrey Newell, New York, International Publishers.

Griffin, Susan (1979). *Rape: The Power of Consciousness,* New York, Harper.

––––––– (1981). *Pornography and Silence,* New York, Harper.

Grimshaw, Jean (1986). *Philosophy and Feminist Thinking,* Minneapolis, University of Minnesota Press.

Gutman, Herbert (1977). *The Black Family in Slavery and Freedom, 1750–1925,* New York, Random House.

Habermas, Jürgen (1979). *Communication and the Evolution of Society,* tr. Thomas McCarthy, Boston, Beacon.

Haller, John S. (1971). *Outcasts from Evolution: Scientific Attitudes of Racial Inferiority, 1859–1900,* Chicago, University of Illinois Press.

Harding, Sandra (1981). "What is the Real Material Base of Patriarchy and Capital?" in Lydia Sargent, ed., 1981, pp. 135–164.

––––––– (1986). *The Science Question in Feminism,* Ithaca, N.Y., Cornell University Press.

–––––––, ed. (1987). *Feminism and Methodology,* Bloomington, Indiana University Press.

Harding, Sandra, and Merrill Hintikka, eds. (1983). *Discovering Reality: Feminist Perspectives on Epistemology, Metaphysics, Methodology and Philosophy of Science,* Dordrecht, Reidel.

Harris, Marvin (1964). *Patterns of Race in the Americas,* New York, Norton.

––––––– (1979). *Cultural Materialism: The Struggle for a Science of Culture,* New York, Random.

Hartmann, Heidi (1975). "Capitalism and Women's Work in the Home," Ph.D. thesis, Department of Economics, New Haven, Yale University.

––––––– (1979). "Capitalism, Patriarchy and Job Segregation by Sex," in Zillah Eisenstein, ed., 1979, pp. 206–247.

––––––– (1981a). "The Family as the Locus of Gender, Class and Political Struggle: The Example of Housework," *Signs* 6, no. 3 (Spring 1981): 366–394.

––––––– (1981b). "The Unhappy Marriage of Marxism and Feminism," in Lydia Sargent, ed., 1981, pp. 1–42.

Hartmann, Mary, and Lois Banner, eds. (1974). *Clio's Consciousness Raised,* New York, Harper.

Hartsock, Nancy (1983). *Sex, Money and Power,* New York, Longman.

Hartz, Louis (1964). *The Founding of New Societies*, New York, Harcourt Brace Jovanovich.

Hatem, Mervat (1986). "The Politics of Sexuality and Gender in Segregated Patriarchal Systems: The Case of Eighteenth and Nineteenth Century Egypt," *Feminist Studies* 12, no. 2: 251–274.

Heilbrun, Carolyn (1973). *Toward a Recognition of Androgyny*, New York, Harper.

Helmbold, Lois, and Amber Hollibaugh (1983). "The Family: What Holds Us, What Hurts Us, The Family in Socialist America," in Stephen Rosskamm Shalom, ed., 1983, pp. 191–222.

Herman, Judith (1982). *Father-Daughter Incest*, Cambridge, Harvard University Press.

Hite, Shere (1977). *The Hite Report*, New York, Dell.

—— (1987). *The Hite Report II: Women and Love*, New York, Knopf.

Hoagland, Sarah Lucia (1988). *Lesbian Ethics: Toward New Value*, Palo Alto, Calif., Institute of Lesbian Studies.

Hoch, Paul (1979). *White Hero, Black Beast: Racism, Sexism and the Myth of Masculinity*, London, Pluto.

Hogan, Lloyd (1984). *Principles of Black Political Economy*, London, Routledge.

Holliday, Laurel (1978). *The Violent Sex: Male Psychobiology and the Evolution of Consciousness*, Guerneville, Calif., Bluestocking Press.

Hooks, Bell (1981). *Ain't I a Woman? Black Women and Feminism*, Boston, South End Press.

—— (1984). *Feminist Theory from Margin to Center*, Boston, South End Press.

Horney, Karen (1967). *Feminine Psychology*, New York, W. W. Norton.

Hull, Gloria, Patricia Scott, and Barbara Smith, eds. (1982). *All the Women Are White, All the Men Are Black, But Some of Us Are Brave*, Old Westbury, N.Y., Feminist Press.

Hurston, Zora Neale (1986). *Their Eyes Were Watching God*, London, Virago.

Hurtado, Alda (1989). "Relating to Privilege: Seduction and Repression in the Subordination of White Women and Women of Color," *Signs* 14, no. 4 (Summer 1989): 833–855.

Jacobs, Michael (1986). "The Contradictory Relationship of Gay Men to Feminism," unpublished manuscript, Economics Department, New School of Social Research, New York.

Jaggar, Alison (1983). *Feminist Politics and Human Nature*, Totowa, N.J., Rowman and Allanheld.

Jaggar, Alison, and Paula Rothenberg, eds. (1984). *Feminist Frameworks*, New York, Harper.

Jeffreys, Sheila (1985). *The Spinster and Her Enemies: Feminism and Sexuality, 1880–1930*, London, Routledge/Pandora.

Johnson, Fern (1987). "Women's Culture and Communication: An Analytical Perspective," in Cynthia M. Lout and Sheryl Friedley, eds., *Beyond Boundaries: Sex and Gender Diversity in Education*, in press.

Johnson, Fern, and Elizabeth Aries (1983). "The Talk of Women Friends," *Women's Studies International Forum*, no. 6: 353–361.

Jordan, Winthrop (1968). *White over Black*, Chapel Hill, University of North Carolina Press.

Joseph, Gloria (1981). "The Incompatible Ménage à Trois: Marxism, Feminism and Racism," Lydia Sargent, ed., 1981, pp. 91–108.

———— (1983). "Black Family Structures: Foundations for the Future," in Stephen Rosskamm Shalom, ed., 1983, pp. 231–239.

Joseph, Gloria, and Jill Lewis (1981). *Common Differences: Conflicts in Black and White Perspectives*, New York, Doubleday/Anchor.

Justus, Joyce Bennett (1981). "Women's Role in West Indian Society," in Filomena Steady, ed., 1981, pp. 431–450.

Katz, Jonathan (1978). *Gay American History: Lesbian and Gay Men in the U.S.A.*, New York, Avon.

Kenworthy, Lane (1990). "What Kind of Economic System? A Leftist's Guide," *Socialist Review* 90/2, vol. 20, no. 2 (April–June 1990): 102–124.

Kinsey, Alfred C., Wardell B. Pomeroy, and Clyde E. Martin (1948). *Sexual Behavior in the Human Male*, Philadelphia, Saunders.

———— (1953). *Sexual Behavior in the Human Female*, Philadelphia, Saunders.

Kittay, Eva, and Diana Meyers, eds. (1986). *Women and Morality*, Totowa, N.J., Rowman and Allanheld.

Kitzinger, Celia (1987). *The Social Construction of Lesbianism*, London, Sage.

Kochman, Thomas (1981). *Black and White: Styles in Conflict*, Chicago, University of Chicago Press.

Koedt, Anne (1970). "The Myth of the Vaginal Orgasm," in Anne Koedt et al., eds., 1973, pp. 198–207.

Koedt, Anne, Ellen Levine, and Anita Rapone, eds. (1973). *Radical Feminism*, New York, Quadrangle.

Kollias, Karen (1975). "Class Realities: Create a New Power Base," *Quest* 1, no. 3 (Winter 1975); reprinted in *Quest*, eds., 1981, pp. 125–138.

Kollontai, Alexandra (1975). *The Autobiography of a Sexually Emancipated Communist Woman*, New York, Schocken.

Konner, Melvin (1982). "She and He," *Science* (September 1982): 54–61.

Kraditor, Aileen S. (1965). *The Ideas of the Women's Suffrage Movement, 1890–1920*, New York, Columbia University Press.

Krafft-Ebing, Richard von (1892). *Psychopathia Sexualis*, London, F. A. Davis.

Krieger, Susan (1983). *The Mirror Dance: Identity in a Woman's Community*, Philadelphia, Temple University Press.

Kristeva, Julia (1977). *About Chinese Women*, London, Marvin Boyers.

Kruks, Sonya, Rayna Rapp, and Marilyn B. Young, eds. (1989). *Promissory Notes: Women in the Transition to Socialism*, New York, Monthly Review.

Kruks, Sonya, and Ben Wisner (1989). "Ambiguous Transformations: Women, Politics and Production in Mozambique," in Sonya Kruks et al., eds., 1989, pp. 148–171.

Kuhn, Annette, and Ann Marie Wolpe, eds. (1978). *Feminism and Materialism*, London, Routledge.

Laclau, Ernesto, and Chantal Mouffe (1985). *Hegemony and Socialist Strategy: Towards a Racial Democratic Politics*, London, Verso.

Ladner, Joyce (1972). *Tomorrow's Tomorrow: The Black Woman*, Garden City, N.Y., Doubleday.

Lakoff, Robin (1975). *Language and Women's Place*, London, Harper and Row.

Landes, Joan B. (1989). "Marxism and the 'Woman Question,' " in Sonya Kruks et al., eds., 1989, pp. 15–28.

Lampland, Martha (1989). "Biographies of Liberation: Testimonials to Labor in Socialist Hungary," in Sonya Kruks et al., eds., 1989, pp. 306–324.

Lederer, Laura (1980). *Take Back the Night: Women on Pornography*, New York, William Morrow.

Leeds Revolutionary Feminists (1981). *Love Your Enemy? The Debate Between Heterosexual Feminism and Political Lesbianism*, London, Onlywomen Press.

Leghorn, Lisa, and Katherine Parker (1981). *Women's Worth: Sexual Economics and the World of Women.* London, Routledge.

Leis, Nancy (1974). "Women in Groups: Ijaw Women's Associations," in Michelle Rosaldo and Louise Lamphere, eds., 1974, pp. 223–242.

Lenin, V. I. (1974). *State and Revolution,* New York, International Publishers.

———— (1975). *Imperialism, the Highest Stage of Capitalism,* Peking, Foreign Languages Press.

Lerner, Gerda (1986). *The Creation of Patriarchy,* New York, Oxford University Press.

Lévi-Strauss, Claude (1969). *The Elementary Structures of Kinship,* Boston, Beacon.

———— (1971). "The Family," in H. Shapiro, ed., *Man, Culture and Society,* London, Oxford University Press.

Lewis, Oscar (1970). *Anthropological Essays,* New York, Random.

Lindsey, Karen (1981). *Friends as Family,* Boston, Beacon.

Lippert, Jon (1977). "Sexuality as Consumption," in Jon Snodgrass, ed., 1977, pp. 207–212.

Lorde, Audre (1978). "Uses of the Erotic: The Erotic as Power," in Audre Lorde, 1984, pp. 53–59.

———— (1984). *Sister Outsider,* Trumansburg, N.Y., Crossing Press.

Lorraine, Tamsin (1990). *Gender, Identity, and the Production of Meaning,* Boulder, Colo., Westview Press.

Lugones, Maria C. (1986). "Playfulness, World Traveling and Loving Perception," *Hypatia* 2, no. 1 (Spring 1986), reprinted in Jeffner Allen, ed., 1990, pp. 159–180.

Lugones, Maria C., and Elizabeth V. Spelman (1983). "Have We Got a Theory for You! Feminist Theory, Cultural Imperialism and the Demand for 'The Woman's Voice,' " *Women's Studies International Forum* 6, no. 6: 573–581.

Lukács, Georg (1968). *History and Class Consciousness,* London, Merlin.

McCrate, Elaine (1985). "The Growth of Non-marriage Among U.S. Women, 1954–1983," Ph.D. thesis, Department of Economics, Amherst, University of Massachusetts.

McDonough, Roisin, and Rachel Harrison (1978). "Patriarchy and Relations of Production," in Annette Kuhn and A. M. Volpe, eds., 1978, pp. 11–41.

McIntosh, Mary (1968). "The Homosexual Role," *Social Problems* 16, no. 2 (Fall 1968): 182–192.

———— (1978). "The State and the Oppression of Women," in Annette Kuhn and A. M. Volpe, eds., 1978, pp. 254–289.

McKenny, Mary (1977). "Class Attitudes and Professionalism," *Quest* 3, no. 4; reprinted in *Quest*, eds., 1981, pp. 139–148.

MacKinnon, Catharine (1979). *Sexual Harassment of Working Women*, New Haven, Yale University Press.

———— (1982). "Feminism, Marxism, Method and the State: An Agenda for Theory," *Signs* 7, no. 3 (Spring 1982): 515–544.

———— (1983). "Feminism, Marxism, Method and the State: Toward Feminist Jurisprudence," *Signs* 8, no. 4 (Summer 1983): 635–658.

———— (1987). *Feminism Unmodified: Discourses on Life and the Law*, Cambridge, Harvard University Press.

Maccoby, Eleanor, E., ed. (1966). *The Development of Sex Differences*, Stanford, Stanford University Press.

Marable, Manning (1980). *From the Grassroots*, Boston, South End Press.

———— (1981). *Black Water: Historical Studies in Race, Class Consciousness and Revolution*, Dayton, Ohio, Black Praxis Press.

———— (1985). *How Capitalism Underdeveloped Black America*, Boston, South End Press.

Marcuse, Herbert (1964). *One-Dimensional Man*, Boston, Beacon.

———— (1969). *Essay on Liberation*, Boston, Beacon.

———— (1972). *Counter-revolution and Revolt*, Boston, Beacon.

Marx, Karl (1972). *The Eighteenth Brumaire of Louis Bonaparte*, New York, International Publishers.

———— (1977). *Karl Marx: Selected Writings*, ed. David McLellan, Oxford, Oxford University Press.

———— (1978). "Estranged Labor," in Robert C. Tucker, ed., 1978, pp. 70–81.

Marx, Karl, and Friedrich Engels (1850). *The German Ideology*, New York, International Publishers.

Mead, Margaret (1963). *Sex and Temperament*, New York, William Morrow.

Meillassoux, Claude (1981). *Maidens, Meal and Money: Capitalism and the Domestic Economy*, New York, Cambridge University Press.

Meulenbelt, Anja, Joyce Outshoorn, Selma Sevenhuijsen, and Petra de Vries, eds. (1984). *A Creative Tension: Key Issues of Socialist-Feminism*, Boston, South End Press.

Miller, Jean Baker (1976). *Toward a New Psychology of Women*, Boston, Beacon.

————, ed. (1973). *Psychoanalysis and Women*, Baltimore, Penguin.

Miller, Patricia Y., and Martha R. Fowkles (1980). "Social and Behavioral Constructions of Sexuality," *Signs* 5, no. 4 (Summer 1980): 783–800.

Millett, Kate (1970). *Sexual Politics*, Garden City, N.Y., Doubleday.

Mitchell, Juliet (1973). *Women's Estate*, New York, Random House.

———— (1974). *Psychoanalysis and Feminism*, New York, Pantheon.

Molyneux, Maxine (1985). "Mobilization Without Emancipation? Women's Interests, the State and Revolution in Nicaragua," *Feminist Studies* 11, no. 2 (Summer 1985): 227–254.

Moraga, Cherrie, and Gloria Anzaldua, eds. (1981). *This Bridge Called My Back: Writings by Radical Women of Color*, Watertown, Penn., Persephone.

Morgan, Lewis (1963). *Ancient Society*, ed., Eleanor Leacock, New York, World.

Mouffe, Chantal (1990). "Radical Democracy or Liberal Democracy?" *Socialist Review* 90/2, vol. 20, no. 2 (April–June 1990): 57–66.

Moynihan Report (1965). *The Negro Family: The Case for National Action*, Washington, D.C., U.S. Department of Labor, U.S. Government Printing Office.

Myers, Lena Wright (1980). *Black Women: Do They Cope Better?* Englewood Cliffs, N.J., Prentice-Hall.

Myron, Nancy, and Charlotte Bunch, eds. (1974a). *Class and Feminism*, Baltimore, Diana.

——, eds. (1974b). *Women Remembered: A Collection of Biographies*, Baltimore, Diana.

——, eds. (1975). *Lesbianism and the Women's Movement*, Baltimore, Diana.

Nazzari, Muriel (1989). "The 'Woman Question' in Cuba: An Analysis of Material Constraints on Its Resolution," in Sonya Kruks et al., eds., 1989, pp. 109–126.

Nestle, Joan (1987). *A Restricted Country*, Ithaca, N.Y., Firebrand Books.

Newton, Esther, and Shirley Walton (1984). "The Misunderstanding: Towards a More Precise Sexual Vocabulary," in Carole Vance, ed., 1984, pp. 242–250.

Nicholson, Linda (1986). *Gender and History*, New York, Columbia University Press.

Nove, Alec (1983). *The Economics of Feasible Socialism*, London, George Allen and Unwin.

O'Brien, Mary (1981). *The Politics of Reproduction*, London, Routledge.

Omi, Michael, and Howard Winant (1986). *Racial Formation in the United States*, New York, Routledge/Methuen.

Orobio de Castro, Ines (1987). "How Lesbian Is a Female Trans-sexual?" in *Proceedings, "Homosexuality, Which Homosexuality?" Conference, Social Sciences* 2, Amsterdam, Free University Press, pp. 110–115.

Ortner, Sherry B. (1974). "Is Female to Male as Nature Is to Culture?" in Michelle Rosaldo and Louise Lamphere, eds., 1974, pp. 67–88.

—— (1982). "Gender and Sexuality in Hierarchical Societies: The Case of Polynesia and Some Comparative Implications," in Sherry B. Ortner and Harriet Whitehead, eds., 1982, pp. 359–409.

Ortner, Sherry B., and Harriet Whitehead, eds. (1982). *Sexual Meanings: The Cultural Construction of Gender and Sexuality*, New York, Cambridge University Press.

Painter, Charlotte, and M. J. Moffet, eds. (1975). *Revelations: Diaries of Women*, New York, Random House.

Palmer, Phyllis (1983). "White Women/Black Women: The Dualism of Female Experience in the United States," *Feminist Studies* 9, no. 1 (Spring 1982): 151–170.

Patton, Cindy (1985). *Sex and Germs: The Politics of AIDS*, Boston, South End Press.

—— (1990). *Inventing AIDS*, New York, Routledge.

Penelope, Julia (1985). "The Mystery of Lesbians," parts 1–3, *Lesbian Ethics* 1, nos. 1–3.

Perlo, Victor (1980). *Economics of Racism USA: Roots of Black Inequality*, New York, International Publishers.

Person, Ethel (1980). "Sexuality as the Mainstay of Identity: Psychoanalytic Perspectives," *Signs* 5, no. 4 (Summer 1980): 605–630; reprinted in Catherine Stimpson and Ethel Spector Person, eds., 1980, pp. 36–61.

Phelps, Linda (1975). "Patriarchy and Capitalism," *Quest* 2, no. 2 (Fall 1975): 34–48.

Piercy, Marge (1974). *Woman on the Edge of Time*, New York, Fawcett.

Pietropinto, Anthony, and Jacqueline Simenauer (1977). *Beyond the Male Myth*, New York, Times Books.

Plummer, Kenneth (1975). *Sexual Stigma: An Interactionist Account*, London, Routledge.

———, ed. (1981). *The Making of the Modern Homosexual*, London, Hutchinson.

"Political Economy of Women" issue (1973). *Review of Radical Political Economics* (Summer 1973).

Pollack, Andy (1988). "A Critique of William Julius Wilson," *Against the Current* 3, no. 4 (September–October 1988): 7, 8, 44–51.

Ponse, Barbara (1978). *Identities in the Lesbian World: The Social Construction of Self*, Westport, Conn., Greenwood Press.

Poster, Mark (1978). *Critical Theory of the Family*, London, Pluto.

Poulantzas, Nicos (1975). *Classes in Contemporary Capitalism*, New York, Humanities Press.

*Quest*, eds. (1981). *Building Feminist Theory: Essays from Quest*, New York, Longmans.

Radicalesbians (1970). "The Woman-identified Woman," in Anne Koedt et al., eds., 1973, pp. 240–245.

Raymond, Janice (1975). "The Illusion of Androgyny," *Quest* 2, no. 1 (Summer 1975): 57–66.

——— (1979). *The Transsexual Empire: The Making of the She-male*, Boston, Beacon.

——— (1986). *A Passion for Friends*, Boston, Beacon.

Reed, Evelyn (1973). *Women's Revolution from Matriarchal Clan to Patriarchal Family*, New York, Pathfinder.

Reich, Michael (1981). *Racial Inequality*, Princeton, Princeton University Press.

Reich, Wilhelm (1949). *Character Analysis*, New York, Farrar, Straus & Giroux.

——— (1970). *Mass Psychology of Fascism*, New York, Farrar, Straus & Giroux.

——— (1973). *The Discovery of the Orgone: The Function of the Orgasm*, New York, Farrar, Straus & Giroux.

——— (1974). *The Sexual Revolution*, New York, Farrar, Straus & Giroux.

Reiter, Rayna, ed. (1975). *Toward a New Anthropology of Women*, New York, Monthly Review.

Rich, Adrienne (1976). *Of Woman Born: Motherhood as Experience and Institution*, New York, W. W. Norton.

——— (1978). *The Dream of a Common Language*, New York, W. W. Norton.

——— (1979). *On Lies, Secrets and Silence*, New York, W. W. Norton.

——— (1980). "Compulsory Heterosexuality and Lesbian Existence," *Signs* 5, no. 4 (Summer 1980): 631–660; reprinted in Catherine Stimpson and Ethel Spector Person, eds., 1980.

Root, Jane (1984). *Pictures of Women: Sexuality*, London, Routledge/Pandora.

Rosaldo, Michelle, and Louise Lamphere, eds. (1974). *Women, Culture and Society*, Stanford, Stanford University.

Roscoe, Will (1988). "The Zuni Man-Woman," *Outlook* 1, no. 2 (Summer 1988): 56–67.

Rousseau, Jean-Jacques (1911). *Emile*, New York, E. P. Dutton.

Rossi, Alice, ed. (1974a). *Feminist Papers*, New York, Bantam.

———— (1974b). "Social Roots of the Women's Movement in America," in Alice Rossi, ed., 1974.

———— (1977). "A Biosocial Perspective on Parenting," *Daedalus* 106, no. 2: 1–32.

Rowbotham, Sheila (1972). *Women, Resistance and Revolution*, New York, Random House.

———— (1973). *Women's Consciousness, Man's World*, Baltimore, Penguin.

Rowbotham, Sheila, Lynne Segal, and Hilary Wainwright (1979). *Beyond the Fragments: Feminism and the Making of Socialism*, London, Merlin Press.

Rubin, Gayle (1975). "The Traffic in Women," in Rayna Reiter, ed., 1975, pp. 157–210.

———— (1984). "Thinking Sex: Notes for a Radical Theory of the Politics of Sexuality," in Carole Vance, ed., 1984, pp. 267–319.

Rubin, Lillian (1976). *Worlds of Pain*, New York, Basic.

Ruddick, Sara (1980). "Maternal Thinking," *Feminist Studies* 6, no. 2 (Summer 1980): 342–367; reprinted in Joyce Trebilcot, ed., 1984, pp. 213–230.

———— (1984). "Preservative Love and Military Destruction: Some Reflections on Mothering and Peace," in Joyce Trebilcot, ed., 1984, pp. 231–262.

Runte, Annette (1987). "Male Identity as a Phantasm: The Difficult Borderline Between Lesbianism and Female Trans-sexualism in Autobiographical Literature," in *Proceedings, "Homosexuality, Which Homosexuality?" Conference, Social Sciences* 2, Amsterdam, Free University Press, pp. 216–229.

Ryan, Mary (1975). *Womanhood in America*, New York, Watts.

Sahli, Nancy (1979). "Smashing: Women's Relationships Before the Fall," *Chrysalis*, no. 8: 17–28.

Said, Edward W. (1978). *Orientalism*, New York, Pantheon.

Sanday, Peggy Reeves (1981). *Female Power and Male Dominance: On the Origins of Sexual Inequality*, New York, Cambridge University Press.

Sargent, Lydia, ed. (1981). *Women and Revolution*, Boston, South End Press.

Sartre, Jean-Paul (1960). *Anti-Semite and Jew*, New York, Grove.

———— (1969). "Black Orpheus," in Jules Chametzky and Sidney Kaplan, eds., *Black and White in American Culture*, Amherst, University of Massachusetts Press, pp. 415–450.

Sawicki, Jana (1986). "Foucault and Feminism: Toward a Politics of Difference," *Hypatia* 1, no. 2 (Fall 1986): 23–36.

Saxton, Alexander (1970). "Race and the House of Labor," in Gary B. Nash and Richard Weiss, eds., *The Great Fear: Race in the Mind of America*, New York, Vintage.

Sayers, Janet (1982). *Biological Politics: Feminist and Anti-feminist Politics*, London, Tavistock.

Sayres, Sohnya, Anders Stephanson, Stanley Aronowitz, and Fredric Jameson, eds. (1984). *The Sixties Without Apology*, Minneapolis, University of Minnesota Press.

Schwartz, Judith (1979). "Questionnaire on Issues in Lesbian History," *Frontiers* 4, no. 3 (Fall 1979): 1–12.

Scott, Hilda (1974). *Does Socialism Liberate Women?* Boston, Beacon.

Shalom, Stephen Rosskamm, ed. (1983). *Socialist Visions*, Boston, South End Press.

Shepherd, Gill (1987). "Rank, Gender and Homosexuality: Mombasa as a Key to Understanding Sexual Options," in Pat Caplan, ed., 1987, pp. 240–270.

Shorter, Edward (1975). *The Making of the Modern Family*, New York, Basic.

Sidel, Ruth (1986). *Women and Children Last: The Plight of Poor Women in Affluent America*, New York, Viking/Penguin.

Silveira, Jeanette (1984). "Why Men Oppress Women," *Lesbian Ethics* 1, no. 1: 34–56.

Simons, Christina (1979). "Companionate Marriage and the Lesbian Threat," *Signs* 7, no. 1 (Autumn 1981): 172–187.

Simons, Margaret A. (1979). "Racism and Feminism: A Schism in the Sisterhood," *Feminist Studies* 5, no. 2 (Summer 1979): 384–390.

Simson, Rennie (1983). "The Afro-American Female: The Historical Context of the Construction of Sexual Identity," in Ann Snitow et al., eds., 1983, pp. 229–235.

Small, Margaret (1975). "Lesbians and the Class Position of Women," in Nancy Myron and Charlotte Bunch, eds., 1975, pp. 49–62.

Smith, Barbara, ed. (1983). "Introduction," in *Home Girls: A Black Feminist Anthology*, New York, Kitchen Table Press.

Smith, Daniel Scott (1974). "Family Limitation, Sexual Control and Domestic Feminism in Victorian America," in Mary Hartmann and Lois Banner, eds., 1974.

Smith, Edwin W., and Andrew M. Dale (1920). *The Ila-speaking Peoples of Northern Rhodesia*, London, Macmillan.

Smith-Rosenberg, Carroll (1975). "The Female World of Love and Ritual: Relations Between Women in Nineteenth-Century America," *Signs* 1, no. 1 (Autumn 1975): 1–29.

Snitow, Ann, Christine Stansell, and Sharon Thompson, eds. (1983). *Powers of Desire: The Politics of Sexuality*, New York, Monthly Review.

Snodgrass, Jon, ed. (1977). *For Men Against Sexism*, New York, Times Change Press.

Soble, Alan (1986). *Pornography*, New Haven, Yale University Press.

Sokoloff, Natalie (1980). *Between Money and Love: The Dialectics of Women's Home and Market Work*, New York, Praeger.

Spelman, Elizabeth V. (1982). "Theories of Race and Gender: The Erasure of Black Women," *Quest* 5, no. 4: 36–62.

———— (1988). *The Inessential Woman*, Boston, Beacon.

Spillers, Hortense (1984). "Interstices: A Small Drama of Words," in Carole Vance, ed., 1984, pp. 73–100.

Stacey, Judith (1983). *Patriarchy and Socialist Revolution in China*, Berkeley, University of California Press.

———— (1987). "Sexism by a Subtler Name: Postindustrial Conditions and Postfeminist Consciousness," *Socialist Review* 96, vol. 17, no. 6 (November–December 1987): 7–30.

Stack, Carol (1974). *All Our Kin*, New York, Harper and Row.

———— (1981). "Sex Roles and Survival Strategies in the Urban Black Community," in Filomena Steady, ed., 1981, pp. 349–368.

Stalin, Joseph (1951). *The Woman Question: Selections from the Writings of Karl Marx, Friedrich Engels, V. I. Lenin, Joseph Stalin*, New York, International Publishers.

Steady, Filomena Chioma, ed. (1981). *The Black Woman Cross-culturally*, Boston, Schenkman.

Stember, Charles Herbert (1976). *Sexual Racism*, New York, Harper.

Stewart, Katie (1981). "The Marriage of Capitalist and Patriarchal Ideologies: Meanings of Male Bonding and Male Ranking in U.S. Culture," in Lydia Sargent, ed., 1981, pp. 269–312.

Stimpson, Catherine, and Ethel Spector Person, eds. (1980). *Women, Sex, and Sexuality*, Chicago, University of Chicago Press.

Stone, Elizabeth, ed. (1981). *Women and the Cuban Revolution*, New York, Pathfinder.

Strickland, William (1989). "Sleaze: How Bipartisan Racism Defiled the 1988 Presidential Campaign," *Zeta Magazine* 2, no. 1 (January 1989): 8–19.

Tax, Meredith (1970). "Woman and Her Mind: The Story of Everyday Life," Boston, New England Free Press.

Taylor, Barbara (1983). *Eve and the New Jerusalem: Socialism and Feminism in the Nineteenth Century*, New York, Pantheon.

Terry, Robert W. (1972). *For Whites Only*, Grand Rapids, Mich., William B. Eerdmans.

Thompson, E. P. (1966). *The Making of the English Working Class*, New York, Vintage/Random.

Thompson, Edgar, ed. (1939). *Race Relations and the Race Problem*, Durham, N.C., Duke University Press.

Tiger, Lionel (1969). *Men in Groups*, New York, Random House.

Tong, Rosemarie (1984). *Women, Sex and the Law*, Totowa, N.J., Rowman and Allanheld.

Trebilcot, Joyce (1977). "Two Forms of Androgynism," in Mary Vetterling-Braggin, Frederick Elliston, and Jane English, eds., 1977, pp. 70–78.

———— (1979). "Conceiving Women," *Sinister Wisdom* 11 (Fall 1979): 43–50.

———— (1983). *Taking Responsibility for Sexuality*, Berkeley, Acacia Books.

————, ed. (1984). *Mothering: Essays in Feminist Theory*, Totowa, N.J., Rowman and Allanheld.

Tucker, Robert C., ed. (1978). *The Marx-Engels Reader*, New York, W. W. Norton.

Valverde, Marianna (1987). *Sex, Power and Pleasure*, Philadelphia, New Society.

Vance, Carole, ed. (1984). *Pleasure and Danger: Exploring Female Sexuality*, London, Routledge.

Van Staveren, Mariette (1987). "Bars and Butches: The Respectability Pursued by Daughters of Bilitis," in *Proceedings, "Homosexuality, Which Homosexuality?" Conference, Social Sciences* 2, Amsterdam, Free University Press, pp. 46–58.

Vetterling-Braggin, Mary, ed. (1982). *"Femininity," "Masculinity" and "Androgyny,"* Totowa, N.J., Littlefield, Adams.

Vetterling-Braggin, Mary, Frederick Elliston, and Jane English, eds. (1977). *Feminism and Philosophy*, Totowa, N.J., Rowman and Allanheld.

Vogel, Lise (1983). *Marxism and the Oppression of Women: Toward a Unitary Theory*, New Brunswick, N.J., Rutgers University Press.

Walker, Alice (1982). *The Color Purple*, New York, Harcourt Brace Jovanovich.

———— (1989). *The Temple of My Familiar*, New York, Simon and Schuster.

Walker, Pat, ed. (1979). *Between Labor and Capital*, Boston, South End Press.

Wallace, Michelle (1979). *Black Macho and the Myth of the Super Woman*, New York, Dial/Warner.

———— (1988). "Reading 1968 and the Great American Whitewash," *Zeta Magazine* 1, no. 12 (December 1988): 43–48.

Wandor, Michelene (1974). "The Conditions of Illusion," in S. Allan, L. Sanders, and J. Wallis, eds., 1974.

Wasserstrom, Richard (1979). "On Racism and Sexism," in Richard Wasserstrom, ed., 1979, *Today's Moral Problems*, New York, Macmillan.

Watney, Simon (1987). *Policing Desire: Pornography, AIDS and the Media*, Minneapolis, University of Minnesota Press.

Weedon, Chris (1987). *Feminist Practice and Poststructuralist Theory*, London, Basil Blackwell.

Weeks, Jeffrey (1979). *Coming Out: A History of Homosexuality from the Nineteenth Century to the Present*, London, Quartet Books.

———— (1981). *Sex, Politics and Society*, New York, Longman.

———— (1985). *Sexuality and Its Discontents: Meanings, Myths and Modern Sexualities*, London, Routledge.

———— (1986). *Sexuality*, Chichester, England, Ellis Horwood.

Weinbaum, Batya (1976). "Women in Transition to Socialism: Perspectives on the Chinese Case," *Review of Radical Political Economics* 8, no. 1: 34–58.

———— (1978). *The Curious Courtship of Women's Liberation and Socialism*, Boston, South End Press.

———— (1983). *Pictures of Patriarchy*, Boston, South End Press.

Weinbaum, Batya, and Amy Bridges (1979). "The Other Side of the Paycheck: Monopoly Capital and the Structure of Consumption," in Zillah Eisenstein, ed., 1979, pp. 190–205.

Weir, Lorna, and Leo Casey (1984). "Subverting Power in Sexuality," *Socialist Review* 75/76, vol. 14, no. 3–4 (May–August 1984): 139–155.

Weisskopf, Susan Contratto (1980). "Maternal Sexuality and Asexual Motherhood," *Signs* 5, no. 4 (Summer 1980): 766–782.

Weitzman, Lenore (1985). *The Divorce Revolution: The Unexpected Social and Economic Consequences for Women and Children*, New York, Free Press.

West, Cornel (1986). *Prophesy/Deliverance*, esp. ch. 2, "The Genealogy of Modern Racism," Philadelphia, Westminster.

White, Frances (1984). "Listening to the Voices of Black Feminism," *Radical America* 18, no. 2–3: 7–26.

Whitehead, Harriet (1982). "The Bow and the Burdenstrap: A New Look at Institutionalized Homosexuality in Native North America," in Sherry Ortner and Harriet Whitehead, eds., 1982, pp. 80–115.

Willis, Ellen (1982). "Toward a Feminist Sexual Revolution," *Social Text*, no. 6 (Fall 1982): 3–21.

———— (1983). "Feminism, Moralism and Pornography," in Ann Snitow et al., eds., 1982, pp. 460–467.

———— (1984). "Radical Feminism and Feminist Radicalism," in Sohnya Sayres et al., eds., 1984, pp. 91–117.

Wilson, William J. (1978). *The Declining Significance of Race*, Chicago, University of Chicago Press.

———— (1987). *The Truly Disadvantaged: The Inner City, the Under Class and Public Policy*, Chicago, University of Chicago Press.

Winant, Howard (1990). "Postmodern Racial Politics: Difference and Inequality," *Socialist Review* 90/1, vol. 20, no. 1 (January–March 1990): 121–150.

Wittig, Monique (1971). *Les guerrillères*, tr. Peter Owen, New York, Viking.

———— (1981). "One Is Not Born a Woman," *Feminist Issues* 1, no. 2 (Winter 1981): 47–54.

———— (1986). *The Lesbian Body*, Boston, Beacon.

Wolf, Christa (1978). "Berührung: Maxie Wanders 'Guten Morgen, Du Schöne,' " *Neue Deutsche Literatur* 2: 53–63.

Wolff, Richard, and Steven Resnick (1987). *Economics: Marxian vs. Neo-classical*, Baltimore, Johns Hopkins University Press.

Women's Agenda (1976a). "Women and Childcare," *Women's Agenda* (March–April 1976).

———— (1976b). "Women and Poverty," *Women's Agenda* (June 1976).

Women's Studies Group CCCS, eds. (1978). *Women Take Issue*, London, Hutchinson.

Wright, Erik Olin (1978). *Class, Crisis and the State*, London, New Left Books.

Yarborough, Susan (1979). "Lesbian Celibacy," *Sinister Wisdom* 11 (Fall 1979): 24–29.

Young, Iris (1980). "Socialist Feminism and the Limits of Dual Systems Theory," *Socialist Review* 10, no. 50/51 (March–June 1980): 169–188.

———— (1981). "Beyond the Unhappy Marriage: A Critique of the Dual Systems Theory," in Lydia Sargent, ed., 1981, pp. 43–70.

———— (1984). "Is Male Gender Identity the Cause of Male Domination?" in Joyce Trebilcot, ed., 1984, pp. 129–146.

Young, Marilyn (1989). "Chicken Little in China: Women After the Cultural Revolution," in Sonya Kruks et al., eds., 1989, pp. 233–250.

Zaretsky, Eli (1976). *Capitalism, the Family and Personal Life*, New York, Harper.

Zinn, Maxine Baca (1989). "Family, Race and Poverty in the 80s," *Signs* 14, no. 4 (Summer 1989): 856–874.

Zita, Jacquelyn (1981). "Historical Amnesia and the Lesbian Continuum," *Signs* 7, no. 1 (Autumn 1981): 172–187.

# About the Book and Author

In a book that is both a critical analysis of contemporary society and the record of a feminist intellectual odyssey, Ann Ferguson, one of the most influential socialist-feminist theorists, develops a new theory of social domination. Tracing the development of socialist-feminist theory from its roots in the politics of the New Left to its present post-Marxist forms, Ferguson defends a multisystems approach encompassing not just sex, race, and class but their overlapping interactions as well. The result is a richer and ultimately more fruitful account of oppression in contemporary society.

Of special interest are Ferguson's analysis of racism, her account of androgyny and gynandry, a new feminist model of democratic socialism in the United States, and the issues raised by a feminist sisterhood divided by race, class, and sexual preference. Both generous and critical, committed both to politics and to understanding, *Sexual Democracy* is an important book not just for feminist theorists but for any student of contemporary social thought.

Ann Ferguson is professor of philosophy and women's studies at the University of Massachusetts–Amherst. She is author of *Blood at the Root* and many articles on feminist political theory.

# Index